THE END OF AMERICAN
EXCEPTIONALISM

THE END OF
AMERICAN
EXCEPTIONALISM

Frontier Anxiety from
the Old West to the New Deal

David M. Wrobel

UNIVERSITY PRESS OF KANSAS

An abridged version of chapters one and two appeared as "The Closing Gates of Democracy: Frontier Anxiety before the Official End of the Frontier," *American Studies* 32, 1(Spring 1991): 49–66.

Published by the University Press of Kansas (Lawrence, Kansas 66049), which was organized by the Kansas Board of Regents and is operated and funded by Emporia State University, Fort Hays State University, Kansas State University, Pittsburg State University, the University of Kansas, and Wichita State University

Library of Congress Cataloging-in-Publication Data

Wrobel, David M.
  The end of American exceptionalism : frontier anxiety from the Old
West to the New Deal / David M. Wrobel.
    p. cm.
  Includes bibliographical references (p.   ) and index.
  ISBN 0-7006-0561-4 (alk. paper)
  1. Frontier thesis. 2. Frontier and pioneer life—United States.
3. National characteristics, American. 4. United States—
Civilization—1865-1918. 5. United States—
Civilization—1918-1945. I. Title.
  E179.5.W76 1992
  973.8—dc20   92-15682

British Library Cataloguing in Publication Data is available.

Printed in the United States of America
10 9 8 7 6 5 4 3 2 1

The paper used in this publication meets the minimum requirements of the American National Standard for Permanence of Paper for Printed Library Materials Z39.48-1984.

CONTENTS

PREFACE

It is now an exciting time to be writing western history, with Patricia Nelson Limerick, Richard White, Donald Worster, and a host of others calling into question the noble and heroic image of the American West.[1] Perhaps the most significant element in the approach of these "revisionists" is their critique of the Turnerian division of American western history into pre- and postfrontier epochs.[2] Frederick Jackson Turner, and generations of historians who adopted his model, emphasized a sharp break in the nation's history when the frontier closed. For the Turnerian school the settlement of the frontier provided the key to America's beneficent development—to the evolution of American democracy. The frontier became the key to America's exceptionalism.[3] The latest generation of western historians views the white advance across the continent as anything but beneficent for the nation, the physical environment, or the numerous minority elements on the western frontier. Theirs is a story of tragedy and irony, not triumph. As the subtitle of Limerick's book—*The Unbroken Past of the American West*—suggests, the "New Western historians" view the closing of the frontier as an irrelevant factor in western history, focusing instead on the "unbroken," unheroic, and unbenign conquest of the region. Their story is one of continuous racial oppression and capitalist excess. And when a historiographical debate hits the front page of a number of the nation's leading weekly news magazines, it becomes strikingly apparent that the topic has an appeal beyond the usual scholarly audience.[4]

These recent developments in western history have attracted wide attention partly because the West is still a place that fascinates most Americans, but more importantly, because the ongoing debate is vital to the question of American self-esteem. Although the present study is less western history than intellectual history, it is more than peripheral to the current debate.

The closing of the American frontier is its central focus, but the emphasis here is not when or whether the frontier closed—whether or not there was indeed a sharp break in western American development. Rather, the focus is on the anxieties aroused in those who perceived that the frontier was closing or had already closed. These "frontier anxieties" helped shape the period from the late nineteenth century through the New Deal, yet they have been largely ignored by historians.[5] That numerous Americans perceived that the frontier had closed, and acted on their perceptions, seems to have been missed.

A final prefatory note concerns the structural approach and methodology of the study. The tripartite division of the work—into "Before 1890," "The Closed Frontier," and "Postfrontier Anxiety"—is not meant to address the question of whether or not the frontier closed, or at what point (that theme is speculated upon in a very undeterministic manner in the epilogue). Rather, this division provides an imperfect but useful framework for categorizing *perceptions* of the closing of the frontier in the years covered. Until around the late 1880s or early 1890s, the frontier was generally thought to be closing. In 1890 the Census Bureau made its official declaration of the end of the frontier; the finality of its announcement seemed to set the tone for most observers. The nineties—years of economic crisis and political strife—saw the height of this frontier anxiety. As the new century opened, the economy became more stable, the nation had won an empire, and the sense of crisis had subsided. But after thrusting outward, the nation now turned inward to examine itself, and a number of intellectuals began to reflect on the closed frontier and to chart a new course in its absence. For the majority of those who addressed the frontier theme in the twentieth century, the frontier was a thing of the past.

No amount of statistical analysis of the continual westward movement of the nation's population or the rate of settlement of homesteads (which, incidentally, was highest in the decades *after* the official closing of the frontier) can provide an accurate reflection of how various intellectuals perceived the frontier's passing. We are dealing here with perceptions—often with myths. In this study I make an effort to categorize and synthesize expressions of frontier anxiety and to trace their effect on the events and debates of the times. Similarly, the phrase "the end of American exceptionalism" is used here in reference to the outlook of those who felt that with the frontier gone the nation's uniqueness would fade. Historians may certainly question whether those intellectuals were mistaken in subscribing to the notion of American exceptionalism (recent multiculturalist perspectives certainly raise doubts about the validity of such notions), but their faith in the notion of uniqueness clearly influenced the nation's culture and historical development.

My sincerest thanks go to my mentor, Charles C. Alexander, who suggested over five years ago that I examine the topic of concern over the closing of the frontier. Over the years he has offered expert guidance and much-needed encouragement. Thanks go also to Alonzo L. Hamby for all his help and advice. No one could ask for better, more concerned mentors. The Ohio University History Department chair, Bruce E. Steiner, has been a constant source of support. Thanks, too, go to Robert De Mott and Phyllis Field, who also read the manuscript, and to Warren French, who provided valuable insights.

I am especially indebted to a number of western historians. Walter Nugent and Elliott West both read the manuscript with great care and provided many excellent suggestions. Martin Ridge and Wilbur Jacobs gave encouragement and advice during my visits to the Huntington Library, provided me with feedback on portions of the manuscript, and generally made me feel confident about the value of this study. Encouragement was also provided by my former colleagues at the College of Wooster.

The ever-patient interlibrary loan staffs of Ohio University's Alden Library and the College of Wooster's Andrews Library deserve special mention for their assistance. I am also indebted to Ohio University for its financial support, particularly for the John Cady Fellowship that I received in the 1988–1989 academic year. Thanks, too, go to the Henry E. Huntington Library in San Marino, California, for the generous fellowship that enabled me to examine the Frederick Jackson Turner Papers. The College of Wooster was also kind enough to provide me with various faculty development funds to help bring this project to completion. Wooster's innovative Sophomore Research Program provided me the assistance of three hard-working, enthusiastic students, Amy Magnotto, Diana Cushman, and Christopher Brown, all of whom patiently checked citations and unearthed some interesting sources, too. And to the students in my "American West: Myth and Reality" seminars at the College of Wooster in the spring semesters of 1991 and 1992, who listened patiently when I answered too many of my own questions and offered valuable, insightful answers when I did not, I am grateful.

Finally, my warmest thanks go to my wife, Rebecca, and my mother, Evelyn, whose support and encouragement have helped make this a bearable task. My mother's transatlantic phone calls urging me to finish "the book," and before that "the dissertation," helped me to do both, and of the parties involved only the phone company can be sorry it's over. Rebecca's patience, understanding, and faith in the project were invaluable.

PART ONE.
BEFORE THE OFFICIAL
CLOSING

Our frontier, like the receding shadow-line of the sun dial that marks the hourly passage of time, has receded toward the West under the influence of the advancing sun of civilization, until at long distance it has reached the shores of the great Western Ocean, beyond which it can go no further. The recession of our frontier is the most important and the most interesting fact of our national history.

—*General Egbert L. Viele, geographer, 1882*

1. EDEN UNMARRED

Frederick Jackson Turner's contribution to the study of American history is perhaps unparalleled. His 1893 address, "The Significance of the Frontier in American History," is probably the best-known work of American historical analysis. But Turner's historiographical reputation has clouded historical perceptions. There have been excellent studies of the historical climate in which Turner conceived his essay, but these studies have, by their nature, reconstructed that climate only as it related to Turner.[1] Thus, pre-1893 expressions of concern over the closing of the frontier have been examined with an eye to their role in shaping Turner's thesis. Similarly, frontier-related concerns voiced after the appearance of Turner's essay are generally assumed to have been inspired by his thesis. The magnitude of the Turner phenomenon has obscured the significance of a widespread frontier anxiety pervading the last decades of the nineteenth century. Furthermore, reactions to the frontier's closing (or perceived closing) in the early decades of the twentieth century have been largely ignored by historians. Focusing rigidly on Turner, historians have debated at great length the finer points of his intellectual odyssey, the precursors of his frontier thesis, and its originality.

I do not question the originality of Turner's thesis—that the frontier molded the nation's character. No attempt is made to belittle Turner by raising the reputations of others at his expense.[2] Turner provided the most scholarly and memorable expression of the frontier's role in American development. His masterly synthesis of the American past renders whimsical any question of his originality. Ideas do not spring to mind fully formed, and Turner would certainly not have claimed that of his frontier thesis.[3] Instead, I suggest that Turner's writings were symptomatic of a wider frontier anxiety that emerged in embryonic form in the 1870s and became more pronounced in the succeeding decades. At the same time, this is not an examination of

3

Turner's precursors. To examine those who expressed anxiety over the closing of the frontier before Turner only as precursors of Turner is to ignore their significance in their own right.

My primary purpose in these early chapters is to outline the development of America's agrarian heritage and highlight some of the tensions of the 1880s as they related to anxiety over the closing of the frontier. While acknowledging, as some historians recently have, the presence of continuity in American western history, and realizing the pitfalls involved in "embracing frontiers that somehow close," it should be reiterated here that the current study is concerned with perceptions of the closing of the frontier. These perceptions, whether or not they were "technically" accurate, constituted historical reality, at least for those who expressed them, and it is their reality that I focus on in this study.[4]

I do not examine intellectual anxiety for its own sake, but rather because this concern seems to have influenced and helped shape the period under study. If the 1880s are viewed as a calm before the storm of the tumultuous nineties, an examination of frontier anxiety in those years suggests it was an uneasy calm at best.[5] When we consider that many Americans had, from their country's earliest years, viewed it as an agrarian paradise, a Garden of Eden far removed from the evils of the Old World, it comes as no great surprise that realization of the disappearing frontier of free land provoked a response from American thinkers. Contact with America's virgin soil, so the American tradition had it, meant release not just from poverty and oppression, but also from the immoral European mentality that bred these vices. But by the 1870s it was becoming starkly apparent, at least to a handful of intellectuals, that the continued existence of an American Eden was in peril.

Although there has been no major study of frontier anxiety in the late nineteenth century, what historical consensus exists suggests that it was almost exclusively a phenomenon of the 1890s. Perhaps because of the scholarly emphasis on Turner, or the historical assessment of the 1890s as a watershed, the historical field of vision has been too narrow.[6] Intellectual concern over the closing of the frontier did not appear suddenly in 1890 when the superintendent of the Eleventh Census declared that there was no longer an unbroken frontier line.[7] The Census Bureau announcement of 1890 has frequently been mentioned because it is a convenient device for historians who feel that frontier anxiety warrants mention—but not investigation—in their accounts of the late nineteenth century. It has also been used by those trying to account for the factors that influenced Turner's essay. But the Census of 1890 gave fresh impetus to ongoing concerns. In fact, the Census Report of 1880, as will be seen, also played a very significant role in the genesis of frontier anxiety.

As early as the 1870s, observers were expressing concern that much of the country's land had been settled or bartered away to railroad corporations and foreign syndicates. By the 1880s, a significant number of intellectuals had begun to question the nation's stability. Some began to respond to the gloomy state of affairs by seeking legislation to stem the tide of immigration. Worried by the threat of European-style overcrowding, they argued that America's changing status rendered it incapable of housing and transforming the world's unfortunates. In the same vein, and under the same rallying cry of "America for Americans," attempts were made to restrict and even eradicate alien landholding in the United States and its territories. The seemingly alarming growth of farm tenancy in the eighties heightened the anxiety further. To compensate for the apparent exhaustion of America's public lands, some intellectuals even proposed annexing or at least uniting with Canada. It seems reasonable to suggest that these frontier anxieties helped shape a minor crisis as the 1880s unfolded and formed a noteworthy prelude to the temperament of the anxious nineties.

In the minds of many, the frontier of free or cheap land had always been the wellspring of American democracy. An almost mystical faith in the country's written Constitution was linked to a belief that the frontier facilitated the continued existence and growth of democracy. Such notions concerning the link between America's democratic mode of government and its abundant resources were not new in the late nineteenth century. There would have been no frontier anxiety had there been no substantial agrarian heritage.

The image of the New World as an agrarian utopia peopled by sturdy yeoman farmers was a strong and enduring one,[8] based on the notion that America could remain indefinitely in a state of arcadian bliss and avoid the less idyllic circumstances of the Old World. And as American realities changed, the "myth of the garden" became a more influential symbol of America. This phenomenon is explained in part by the peculiar set of circumstances that fostered the myth.

For over a century after the United States' birth as a nation, its white inhabitants never ran out of land before more came their way. Whether from the Louisiana Purchase, or the annexation of the Floridas, Texas, and Oregon, or the Mexican cession of California and other territories, there was always land to settle, albeit with some exertion of force. Successive generations of Americans were never faced with the visible end of the frontier. And as long as there was a frontier, there was a perceived outlet for agrarian endeavor. This facilitated the presence of a pastoral vision even as commercial and industrial operations expanded.

The myth of the garden began to take shape after the colonies won their independence from Britain. With independence came the opportunity to expand westward and explore the interior of the continent. Benjamin Franklin was one of the first to comment on the significance of this opportunity. Franklin suggested in the 1780s that the westward movement of population would compensate for the vestiges of Europeanism that commercial activity had brought to the eastern seaboard. Franklin did consider the problems that might arise in the future when all the good land was taken, but this was not a pressing concern for him. With "at least 100 farmers . . . mostly tillers of their own soil" for every merchant, Franklin was confident that agriculture would remain "The Great Business of the Continent" for a long time to come.[9]

The French expatriate Hector St. John de Crèvecoeur, like Franklin, saw the vastness of the American continent as reason enough to allay any fears of European complexity taking hold in the near future. American society would for "many ages" retain its arcadian simplicity, he said. Crèvecoeur's *Letters from an American Farmer* (1782), which achieved great popularity in the last decades of the eighteenth century, directly attributed American virtues to the abundance of free land. He declared that on the new continent, the European "leaves behind him all his ancient prejudices and manners . . . [and becomes] a new man acting upon new principles." Such a transformation occurred in this new environment because the immigrant could cultivate thousands of acres of "unrented, untaxed lands."[10]

Thomas Jefferson expressed a similar sentiment when he wrote James Madison in 1787: "Our governments will remain virtuous . . . as long as they are chiefly agricultural; and this will be as long as there shall be vacant lands in any part of America. When they [the people] get piled upon one another in large cities, as in Europe, they will become corrupt as in Europe, and go to eating one another."[11] Although the Louisiana Purchase of 1803 helped alleviate Jefferson's concern, he was always gloomily aware that at some point in the future there would be no room for further continental expansion.

Many observers in Europe, too, seemed to recognize the centrality of the frontier to the survival and development of American institutions. One of the first to give vent to the theory was the German philosopher Georg W. F. Hegel. In a highly illuminating passage written in the early 1820s, Hegel stated that

> America is hitherto exempt from this [economic] pressure, for it has an outlet of colonization constantly and widely open, and multitudes are continually streaming into the plains of the Mississippi. By this means the chief source of discontent is removed, and the continuation of the existing civil condition is guaranteed. . . . Had the woods of Germany been in existence the French Revolution would not have occurred. . . . North America will be comparable with Europe only after the immeasurable space which that country presents to its inhabitants shall have been occupied, and the members of the political body shall have begun to be pressed back on each other.[12]

Alexis de Tocqueville recognized and contributed to the nation's agrarian heritage when he claimed, in *Democracy in America*, that "the soil of America is opposed to territorial aristocracy." Equality had, in Tocqueville's reckoning, been forced on Americans by the fortunate conditions they inherited on a sparsely peopled continent. Expressing a degree of confidence in the American political system, Tocqueville felt that this great advantage might be protected for some years to come.[13]

In the early to mid-nineteenth century, British conservatives used the factor of America's free land in formulating their arguments against democratic reform in their own country. One of the first such arguments appeared in 1823 in the *Quarterly Review* (a bastion of British conservatism). The piece suggested that the vastness of the frontier served as a safety valve for American institutions.[14] America's security and tranquility were guaranteed not by the country's political institutions, posited the *Quarterly Review* a few years later, but rather by "the inexhaustible fund of unoccupied land . . . offering a sure recourse . . . to every man who is ready and willing to labour . . . [and which] exempts the great body of the lower orders from what in other countries is the most usual and fruitful source of popular discontent and tumult, namely, the pressure of want."[15]

Similar arguments appeared periodically in *Blackwood's Edinburgh Magazine* (founded in 1817 as a Tory challenge to the Whig-dominated *Edinburgh Review*).[16] *Blackwood's* showed its true colors in reviews of Tocqueville's *Democracy in America*, arguing against legislation extending the franchise because of the geographical differences between Britain and America. The success of America's democratic experiment, one *Blackwood's* reviewer argued, depended upon the continued existence of vast open spaces that siphoned off society's misfits and malcontents. Great Britain had no such safety valve and hence was in no position to extend the franchise to the lower orders.[17] The American Eden remained unmarred for now, but a *Blackwood's* contributor prophesied in 1835, "wait till that huge receptacle of discontented multitudes is filled up, till hundreds of thousands are collected in great towns, till luxury and corruption have spread generally . . . then is the time to test the possibility of democratic institutions existing. . . ."[18]

Two decades later, in a letter to Thomas Jefferson's biographer Henry S. Randall, Thomas Macaulay gloomily predicted that when "the boundless extent of fertile and unoccupied land" was exhausted, America's institutions "will be fairly brought to the test."[19] Thomas Carlyle echoed Macaulay's sentiment in his 1850 work *Latter-Day Pamphlets*, warning Americans not to "brag" of their country's "model institutions and constitutions." Their "battle is yet to fight," Carlyle maintained, and would come when their lands filled up.[20] One writer in *Blackwood's* went so far as to predict "revolution" soon after America's "boundless extent of uncultivated land" became occupied.[21]

It was not just British conservatives who predicted disaster once the frontier closed. Running concurrent with their predictions in the antebellum period came those of southern apologists for slavery. In answer to the free-labor ethic of the northern states, southern proslavery intellectuals claimed that the supply of free land was the only foundation of free labor in the North. They looked forward to the imminent disappearance of free land and the hardships that would follow north of the Mason-Dixon line.[22] George Fitzhugh expressed these concerns most effectively when he pointed to the operation of a "safety valve" that allowed northern laborers to "escape to the West and become proprietors." But, Fitzhugh added, when the West was settled this artificial bulwark of democracy would disappear, and the North would have to adopt a slave labor system to control its unruly masses.[23]

Neither the cynicism of British Tories nor the attacks of southern defenders of slavery weakened the agrarian myth. From the late 1830s Horace Greeley had been urging the downtrodden to move west and seek their fortunes.[24] Abraham Lincoln, too, throughout his political career had praised the benefits offered by the vast areas of unoccupied land in the West.[25] Such optimistic outpourings held sway in these years. The Homestead Act of 1862 seemed to offer the poor city dweller the chance of becoming a self-sufficient yeoman farmer.[26] That the poor laborer had the resources to follow Greeley's advice went unquestioned for nearly a decade after the passage of the Homestead Act. The agrarian myth was more than holding its own in the 1860s. When a young Edwin L. Godkin in 1865 recognized the "favorable distribution of population" as the factor that "gave democracy its first great impulse in the United States," and one that was still promoting its spread, his observations were but the order of the day.[27]

However, by this time, a few observers were beginning to express concern over the state of the public domain and the future of the frontier safety valve. One of the first to comment on the situation was the commissioner of the General Land Office, the native Britisher Charles H. Pearson. In the mid-1860s, Pearson noted that it was "already impossible to find good land on [California's] public domain." And the situation in California, Pearson added, "is only the extreme instance of what is taking place all over the Nation."[28] Because much of the West was at best semiarid, the commissioner concluded that "the better part of America has been used up. . . . Americans will begin to be cramped for space by the time their population numbers twenty millions more, that is to say, in a little more than ten years hence."[29] Pearson viewed the American frontier within a world context, seeing it as "the great safety valve to a [European] labor system which is steadily worked at high pressure." With that safety valve closing, Pearson predicted that "the nation will soon be brought into close contact with all the social questions with which we in Europe are painfully familiar. . . . Democracy will then be put on its trial even more roughly than in the ferment of civil war." And England, along with the other European nations, would be forced "to seek fresh solutions of difficulties" with the closure of its transatlantic safety valve.[30]

For Pearson, trying times were just around the corner, only a decade or so away. For another observer, the young social critic Henry George, the time of trial was also imminent. For years George had been quarreling with Horace Greeley's famed advice to the downtrodden, and in 1871 he wrote a crushing indictment of public land policy.[31] His pamphlet, "Our Land and Land Policy," went too far against the grain of popularly held assumptions to have much impact at that early date, but it did lay down the fundamental points of his most famous work, *Progress and Poverty*, which would set the tone for the frontier anxiety of the ensuing decades. George adopted a Malthusian approach to population growth, reckoning on a 24 percent increase each decade. He weighed these findings against the remaining 450 million tillable acres of unsettled public land and concluded that within a generation people would "look with astonishment at the recklessness with which the public domain has been squandered."[32] George also offered a case study of land policy in California. He was angered at the presence of land monopoly in such a new state. Although California was a potential paradise for yeoman farmers tending medium-sized farms, its public lands, he said, had already passed into the hands of an exploitive class of landlords. George worried that the imminent polarization of classes resulting from this situation—not just in California, but all over the country—would eventually bring democracy to its knees. His words had little impact at the time, but George was not alone in the 1870s in expressing concern over the abuses of public land policy and the exhaustion of the public domain.

In 1875, the Prussian-born journalist and naturalized U.S. citizen Charles Nordhoff viewed the frontier's recession as a "serious calamity to our country." "Cheap and fertile lands," he said, "have acted as an important safety-valve for the enterprises and discontent of our non-capitalist population." Nordhoff added that "the eagerness of some of our wisest public men for the acquisition of new territory has arisen from their conviction that this opening for the independence of laboring men was essential to the security of our future as a free and peaceful state." Perhaps only one in every thousand poor laborers took advantage of the public domain, he concluded, but "it is plain that the knowledge that any one may do so makes those who do not more contented with their lot, which they thus feel to be one of choice and not of compulsion." Nordhoff felt that with these lands fully settled, America could not escape the pains that afflicted Europe.[33]

In the same year Brevet Major General William B. Hazen, in a pamphlet entitled "Our Barren Lands," declared that the region between the Missouri River and the Sierra Nevada mountains, and stretching from the Rio Grande to the Canadian border, was not worth "a penny an acre." Hazen's article was just one episode in a virulent war of words with George Armstrong Custer, who ridiculed notions of western aridity.[34] In a longer and less polemical article that appeared in the North American Review in the same month, Hazen declared that the country "was rapidly approaching the time when the landless and the homeless" would no longer be able to "acquire both lands and homes merely by settling them." Hazen had forcefully questioned the nation's confidence in the West. He argued that "the formation and rapid growth of new, rich, and populous states" would no longer "be seen in the present domain." Uncle Sam, he announced, was no longer rich enough "to give us all a farm . . . unless we take farms incapable of cultivation."[35]

More influential was John Wesley Powell's government-sponsored *Report on the Lands of the Arid Regions of the United States*, which surfaced in a very limited edition in 1878 and then in a larger press run the following year.[36] Powell, director of the United States Geographical and Geological Survey of the Rocky Mountain Region, had expressed concern over the future of white settlement in the lands of the semiarid West as early as 1873. Like Hazen, Powell had argued that the area between the Rockies and the Sierras lay under threat of constant drought. His report on his explorations of the region in 1873, delivered to the Secretary of the Interior the following year, had stated the "immediate and pressing importance" of "a general survey . . . for the purpose of determining the special areas which can . . . be redeemed by irrigation."[37] Little attention was paid to Powell's warning until the emergence of his *Report on the Lands of the Arid Regions*. In that work Powell made it clear that the semiarid regions of the West could not be cultivated by yeoman farmers working medium-sized holdings. The remaining lands had to be properly classified and changes would be brought to bear on public land policy to prevent prospective homesteaders from meeting with disaster.

Powell had swept aside hopeful fantasies about the West, offering hard realities in their place. His report helped spark a land reform movement and convinced the federal government to take action. In 1879 a Public Land Commission was created for the purpose of apportioning the remaining lands in a more rational matter. But despite Powell's warning, his realities proved too hard to swallow. Traditional assumptions held firm, and the land acts of the late 1870s continued to apply the old homestead principle to the semiarid lands of the West. Worse still, settlers poured into this region, taken in by the popular myth that rain followed the plough.[38] This ill-founded optimism was not dispelled until 1887, when the prolonged period of drought that Powell had predicted set in.

To at least a handful of observers before 1880, then, it seemed that the frontier was becoming less of a democratizing force in American life, and that tenancy and landlordism were fastening themselves on the New World as they had in Europe. But these expressions of anxiety did little to dampen the confident national mood of the immediate post-Reconstruction years. These naysayers were a tiny minority, and one that went largely unheard. The great "undeveloped" West was still, almost invariably, reckoned to be the nation's trump card, and agrarian mythology still confidently persisted. As far as most observers were concerned, the American Eden was still unmarred. But from 1880 on, there would be much worried commentary on the state of the public domain.

2. PROPHECIES OF GLOOM AND DOOM: THE ANXIOUS EIGHTIES

Although the censuses of 1860 and 1870 had indicated the presence of a number of large landholdings in the prairie states, it was not until 1880 that the full picture started to become clear. By that time the newly formed Public Land Commission had performed the monumental task of codifying all congressional legislation relating to the public lands.[1] Thomas Donaldson, one of the five members of the commission (along with John Wesley Powell), completed his massive official history, *The Public Domain*, in 1880.[2] More importantly, the statistics on tenancy had been gathered. The 1880 census revealed those statistics and suggested that tenant farming, even in relatively new states such as Kansas and Nebraska, had gained a foothold.[3] The 1880 Report was also the first to provide data on farm mortgages and the size of landholdings. Furthermore, it contained a series of maps showing the extent of the uninhabited area of the United States and its territories for every census year since 1790. Each map showed the density of population in different regions, and indicated the point the "frontier-line" had reached.[4] Those who consulted the Census could gauge that the United States had more tenant farmers than any European country, that many farms were too heavily mortgaged to be profitable, that large holdings were becoming more common, and that there was no longer an extensive frontier of free land that might serve to reverse the process. Although a particularly astute observer would hardly have been shocked to learn that a country the size of the United States would have more tenant farmers than much smaller European countries, this news nevertheless would have seemed alarming to most readers of the Census.

The appearance of Henry George's *Progress and Poverty* that same year brought that message home to more people.[5] George attributed nearly every aspect of the national character to the abundance of unfenced land. "This public domain," he said, "has been the transmuting force which has turned the thriftless, unambitious European peasant into the self-reliant Western farmer; it has given a consciousness of freedom even to the dweller in crowded cities and has been a well-spring of hope even to those who have never thought of taking refuge in it." George, like Charles Nordhoff, stressed that for every American, "there has been the consciousness that the public domain lay behind him," adding that the knowledge of this fact had given Americans a sense of generosity . . . independence, elasticity and ambition." Cheap land, he said, made America's institutions superior to those of other countries. But George's message was an ominous one. He charged that the republic had entered a new era in which land monopoly was becoming the norm. Commenting on California, he stated that it would be "difficult to point the immigrant to any part of the state where he can take up a farm on which he can settle and maintain a family."[6]

George allowed the American people no great credit for their democratic achievements, believing that any nation possessing an "enormous common" would have accomplished as much. But with the great pool of public land seemingly close to drying up, comparisons of conditions in America and Europe would no longer be so favorable to the former. In the same month that *Progress and Poverty* was published in New York, the *Atlantic Monthly* featured another pessimistic study that compared the effects of farm tenancy in England and America. The growth of the tenant farming system in America was deemed "an evil of the greatest magnitude." At least in England the rents were low and the land "thoroughly cultivated and improved." But in America, where rents were high and tenancy impoverished the land, there was "not one redeeming feature in the whole system."[7]

The ominous forebodings of 1880 were repeated and elaborated on as the decade unfolded. Efforts were made to locate the actual position of the receding frontier line.[8] The story of the rapid settlement of the West and the noble character of the pioneers was often recounted.[9] In fact, the "Garden of Eden," in its ostensible state of deterioration in the 1880s, was receiving as much attention as the prospering West had in any earlier decade. And the new question of concern that emerged was how to alleviate certain ills now that the frontier was seemingly less capable of performing that function.

Early in 1881 Henry George followed up on the success of *Progress and Poverty* with the publication of his second major work, *The Irish Land Question.*[10] He described the extent and terrible consequences of landlordism in

Ireland. The attack, however, was directed as much against the American land system as the Irish. Surely, America, he said, "with millions of virgin acres yet to settle," ought to be in a position to advise the British. But George claimed that such times had passed. America could not counsel other countries because her states were witnessing "the growth of a system of cultivation worse in its social effects than that which prevails in Ireland."[11] His conclusion, that private property in land was the root of the ills that existed in Britain and America, went too far against the grain of America's agrarian mythology not to cause a great stir. But if many Americans argued with his solutions, few who read his work could have been unaffected by his vivid accounts of the specific problems arising from land monopoly and his constant reminders that free or cheap land was a rapidly diminishing commodity.

Thomas Donaldson, writing in the *North American Review* in August 1881, stated that the supply of lands suitable for homesteading was "practically exhausted in the West." At this early date Donaldson, unlike George, was not overly alarmed by the tendency toward monopolization. He felt the taxation powers of state legislatures were great enough to break down extensive holdings and thus provide more land for homesteading.[12] Late in 1882 an editorial in *Century Magazine* expressed without qualification an even more optimistic opinion. The author urged young easterners to go west and take advantage of "career openings" in the sturdy yeoman farmer profession.[13]

However, from 1883, when the findings of the last census were officially published, hopeful evaluations of the West became rarer among experts on the public lands.[14] An article in the February 1883 edition of *Century Magazine* on "The Evils of Our Public Land Policy," by the economist Edward T. Peters, was indicative of the rising concern. Peters pointed to an alarming growth in the number of large farms. He calculated that between 1870 and 1880, the number of farms of more than 1,000 acres had risen from 3,720 to 28,578, more than a seven-fold increase. Though the system of large farming could be economical, any advantages reaped from it were "only to be had," said Peters, "by permitting gigantic monopolies of the soil, under which the lion's share of all benefits . . . fall into the hands of a few persons." Peters noted the abuses and failings of the existing land policies, which made the public lands "the easy prey of the monopolist," and concluded that with America fast becoming as densely peopled as any other country, it might be appropriate to fix the ominous motto "After us the deluge" to the nation's public land policy.[15]

The year 1883 also saw the publication of William Goodwin Moody's spirited attack on land monopoly, *Land and Labor in the United States*. Moody, an embittered social reformer, despairingly noted the post–Civil War transformation of many American farmers from proud landowners to poor tenants. He recounted the process by which the farmer's lands became heavily mortgaged, fell into the hands of railroads and banks, then were re-united as bonanza farms on which the former owner worked as a seasonal tenant. Moody saw the central elements of the agrarian myth—unoccupied land and the yeoman farmer—fast disappearing from the American scene and declared that his country "had taken immense strides" to place itself "in the position in which Europe is found after a thousand years of feudal snobbery."[16]

In 1884 Henry George lamented that the typical American farmer, cultivating his own medium-sized property and developing aspects of an independent and "manly character," was "the product of conditions under which labor is dear and land is cheap." As these conditions disappeared, the yeoman farmer would "pass away as he had passed away in England." Reserving for actual settlers what little arable land was left, as the Land Commission proposed in 1884, was, in George's opinion, "merely a locking of the stable door after the horse has already been stolen."[17] The Land Commission, however, had at least alerted the government to the theft. In a long supplementary section in the 1884 edition of *The Public Domain*, Donaldson made the alarming (albeit highly erroneous) claim that only five million acres of "purely agricultural lands" remained in public ownership in the West and then proceeded to attack Congress for allowing monopolization of the public lands.[18]

In 1885 the *North American Review* commissioned a special reporter, Thomas P. Gill, to investigate the problems of tenancy and landlordism. The report, which surfaced in January 1886, emphasized that America had more tenant farmers than England, Scotland, Ireland, and Wales combined. The claim was questionable and misleading, but one designed to strike an emotive chord in the American psyche. Gill compared America's great landlords to the absolute monarchs of past times. The small proprietor, he said, would become a "tenant-at-will," little better off than a serf.[19] The following month the *North American Review* featured another article on the same topic. Utilizing the findings of the 1880 Census, its author, Adam J. Desmond, pointed to the presence of more than one million tenant farmers in the United States. Desmond commented that this was "two hundred thousand more than Ireland had in the palmiest days of landlordism"—again, a striking though misleading and inaccurate comparison, but one that called into question the hallowed myth of the garden. Desmond's figures on tenancy were lower than Gill's, but his related comments were more revealing. After noting the favorable land-to-man ratio that America had possessed and squandered away to railroad corporations, Desmond voiced a widespread concern in claiming that the main beneficiaries of the subsequent sale of railroad lands were alien landlords.[20]

Alien landlordism had been a source of vehement public outcry in the prairie states throughout the 1870s. The most notorious alien landlord, the Irishman William Scully, had come to symbolize for westerners the evils of land monopoly. "Landlordism" and "Scullyism," along with "anti-Scully-ism" and "anti-alien land ownership," had become synonymous terms in the West before the major national journals picked up the issue in the eighties. Lists of alien holdings and recent acquisitions were widely published in western newspapers to document the full extent of the danger.[21] The threat posed by these new developments appeared to be very real as land became a more precious commodity. The issue played a part in the 1884 presidential campaign; both parties called for restrictions on alien landholding in their platforms. The sustained outcry led to the passage of federal legislation in 1887 and, soon after, action by certain states restricting alien landholding.[22]

Anxiety over the disappearing frontier had intensified opposition to all abuses of the public land laws and helped shape government policy in that area. During Grover Cleveland's administration, efforts began in earnest to restore to the public domain the land that had been fraudulently gained. The next Democratic party platform demanded the forfeiture of 100 million acres, or approximately half the land granted to western railroad corporations. In 1885 bonanza farming received a direct blow when an executive order mandated the removal of all fences from the public domain.[23] In 1887 the Dawes Severalty Act, the product of a complex mix of self-interest and genuine (albeit partially misguided) humanitarian sentiment, was passed, and millions of acres of Indian reservation lands were secured for future white settlement.[24] And two years later, on 22 April 1889, a small portion of the extensive lands of the Five Civilized Tribes in the Oklahoma Indian Territory was opened to white settlement for the first time. Thousands of land-hungry homesteaders poured into this region at the crack of the starter's gun.[25]

The land hunger of the sooner-boomers, while it certainly differed in nature from the frontier anxiety of intellectual observers, may not have been a completely unrelated phenomenon. Perhaps concern over the closing frontier was not confined to the nation's intellectuals. The well-developed agrarian movements that began to appear during this period and reached their height in the 1890s called for restrictions on land speculation, the size of holdings, alien acquisition of titles to American lands, and seizure of all lands forfeited by railroads and other corporations.[26] Frontier anxiety was certainly not the prime motivating factor behind either land hunger or agrarian protest. Nonetheless, a sense that the frontier was passing almost certainly lent greater urgency to the land hunger prevalent in the period, and may, too, have influenced, at least indirectly, the agrarian movements of the period as they called for the restoration of the public domain.[27] While these movements were sparked, first and foremost, by specific economic hardships, not frontier anxiety, they reacted vehemently to abuses of the land system. Moreover, agrarian leaders such as Ignatius Donnelly used concerns over the closing of the frontier in their rhetoric.

The cry of "America for Americans," directed at the alien landholder in the 1870s and more virulently in the 1880s, was also leveled against the destitute foreign immigrant. Immigration reached unprecedented numbers in the eighties. Worse still to many, it consisted of presumably inferior elements from southern and eastern Europe. The influx of the "new immigration," besides threatening protestant hegemony, seemed to coincide with the growth of urban squalor, political corruption, and industrial discontent; anxious observers had no trouble establishing a causal link. Much of this anti-immigrant feeling stemmed from racial assumptions that had surfaced more fully in the Social Darwinist framework of the late nineteenth century.[28] The historic traditions of American nativism—dormant since the fifties—reemerged in the eighties to restrict the influx of immigrants on the basis of their radicalism, religion, and race. Some anti-immigrant agitators often merely utilized the factor of the closing frontier to augment their arguments. But at the same time, it was not difficult to see a link between the diminishing opportunities for escape to the West and the onset of urban problems.

In 1881 a letter in the *New York Tribune* stated that the nation had "reached the point in its growth where its policy should be to reserve its heritage for coming generations, not to donate it to all the strangers we can induce to come among us."[29] Thomas Donaldson, too, suggested that the immigrant who could possess land immediately upon declaring his intentions of becoming a citizen had an unfair advantage over those who had been born or had lived in the United States for twenty-one years, and who had no prior right to the land.[30] Donaldson elaborated on his position in the 1884 edition of *The Public Domain*. Citing the arrival of nearly 800,000 new immigrants in 1882 in conjunction with his findings on the state of the public domain, Donaldson declared the inexpediency of proclaiming "to all nations of the earth that whoever shall arrive in this country from a foreign shore, and declare his intention to become a citizen, shall receive a farm on 160 acres.[31]

Many intellectuals believed in the assimilative power of free land; the melting pot notion was strongly linked to the nation's agrarian heritage. If given yeoman status, the shiftless immigrant would transform both his social position and his character. As Henry George put it, the "virtue of new soil" was that it created "wholesome human growth" from "degraded and dangerous materials." He saw the North American continent as the world's last great frontier. It was, for George, "that expansion over virgin soil" that gave freedom to American life and "relieved social pressure in the most progressive European nations." According to George, the closing of America's frontier would have calamitous effects on both sides of the Atlantic.[32]

In 1885 the evangelical missionary Josiah Strong proclaimed that the day was close at hand when the public land would be exhausted and immigrants would pour into the cities.[33] Although Strong ignored the fact that the city had been the immigrants' abode for decades, his perspective was not uncommon. With the assimilative capacity of the New World apparently declining, the continued acceptance of Europe's immigrants seemed an open invitation to Europeanization. Thomas Gill viewed the problem in especially dramatic fashion. Seeing that America was seeking no conquests to add to her domain, he wondered how she could continue to invite the "overflow population of the world to take possession of her territory . . . giving to everyone the privilege of citizenship, that allows even aliens to possess her soil." If America continued on this reckless course, Gill added, it would suffer the same consequences that followed the mistakes of Ancient Rome.[34]

The Norwegian-American Hjalmar Hjorth Boyeson, a professor at Columbia College and a recognized authority on immigration, shared the outlook common to those of his adopted country. Boyeson blamed the changing social conditions on the continuing flow of immigration and noted that "in spite of the magnificent dimensions of the continent," Americans were beginning to feel crowded. "Our cities are filling up," he went on, "with a turbulent foreign proletariat, clamoring for 'panem et circenses' as in the days of Ancient Rome."[35] Boyeson felt that the existence of the republic was threatened because the new immigrants were no longer being absorbed. With reduced opportunities in the New World, the new immigrant no longer had any respect for America's political institutions. And, not being animated by the American democratic spirit, the new immigrant would be even less assimilable. Boyeson postulated a vicious circle of ills that could be broken only by anti-immigration legislation.

By the latter part of the decade these expressions of concern had had noticeable effect. The legislative action begun in 1887 at both the federal and state levels and aimed chiefly at nonresident landlords also limited both the employment and landholding opportunities open to the less affluent immigrant.[36] Frontier anxiety was certainly not the only factor that helped alter perceptions on the question of the continued utilization of America's resources by Europe's underclass, and there were always those who argued against restrictions on the grounds that American institutions were holding up and could still speedily assimilate Europe's "poor apologies for mankind."[37] And there were, it must be stressed, those (probably the majority) for whom frontier anxiety was not the prime motivating factor, but rather a convenient notion that lent credence to baser, racist arguments. Nonetheless, frontier concerns, genuine or otherwise, most certainly did impact upon the immigration debate. And the seeds of discontent, apparent as early as the 1870s, took root in the 1880s and would bear ominous fruit in 1894, when the national Immigration Restriction League was formed. Meanwhile, in the same period, another factor was beginning to enter the equation. With less cheap land on the one hand and increasing land monopoly and steady immigration on the other, a few intellectuals considered increasing the public domain to offset the imbalance.

Concern over the closing of the frontier in the eighties had less effect on American foreign policy than land policy or immigration policy. There is little evidence to suggest (as one notable historian did) that from the 1870s the closing of the frontier convinced agricultural elements of the population to push the country towards a more active foreign policy in their search for overseas markets.[38] Other than Josiah Strong's prophetic announcement that "the pressure of population on the means of subsistence" in America would lead Anglo-Saxons on a heightened course of overseas expansion, frontier-related expansionist designs in the eighties were almost invariably directed towards Canada.[39]

The *Nation* and the *North American Review* in the early eighties featured a number of articles on the feasibility of annexing Canada, but until 1884 little mention was made of that country's vast resources in connection with America's diminishing land supply. When calls for annexation did begin to appear on those grounds, they came from both Americans and Canadians. Prominent figures in Canada's Liberal party often proposed closer relations with the United States as a solution for the lethargy of their own economy. They were usually well-to-do capitalists who felt American trade and investment were crucial to the expansion of Canadian business and industry. Their entrepreneurial designs were being stifled by the ruling Conservative party, which was favorable to Britain and shunned relations with the United States. The Conservative party under Prime Minister John Macdonald (1878–1891) followed a "National Policy" that was designed to prevent Canada's western prairies from falling into American hands.[40] The Liberals proposed everything from Canadian-American reciprocity treaties to outright annexation by America, and when their more moderate proposals made little headway, they finally succumbed to the supposed inevitability of Canada's drifting into America's orbit.[41]

It is significant that the Liberals used a "frontier argument" to entice the United States into taking action and that American periodicals published the argument frequently. In 1884 the *North American Review* featured a blatantly annexationist essay by Canadian physician and historian Prosper Bender. Bender talked at length about Canada's "immense tracts of virgin soil" and the "splendid opportunities that would be afforded to . . . the hard-pressed toilers of Eastern factories, mines, and foundries, as well as the cultivators of sterile and worn out lands, by the rich, virgin territory of the North West." He reminded the reader that "the available first-class land awaiting settlement in the Republic is of no great extent" and that it would all be taken up in the near future. Bender wondered how anyone could oppose the United States' simply "going up and possessing the land." He concluded that the constant stream of European immigrants could then be directed into Quebec and Ontario, thus relieving the buildup of social pressure in America's cities.[42]

By the middle of the decade a number of American journals, particularly the *Forum*, *Nation*, and *North American Review*, were featuring articles that pointed to the imminence of Continental Union.[43] Great attention focused on elections in Canada in the hope that the Liberal party would come out on top and establish reciprocity treaties with the United States. American political theorists assumed that Canadians would then see the benefits of better relations and press for a closer union. As it turned out, most Americans remained indifferent to these proposals, and most Canadians were hostile to them. But proposals for annexation continued to appear, and the closing American frontier was usually an integral element in the arguments.

Erastus Wiman, a prominent Canadian capitalist, was the driving force behind the Liberals' United States-oriented policies. His articles regularly appeared in the *North American Review* in the late 1880s. Wiman's arguments wavered between Continental Union and outright annexation by the United States, but always stressed the vastness of Canada's resources, which he said would serve to offset "the strange sense of limitation" being felt in the United States, where there was "no more new territory left to occupy." Like Bender, he suggested the possibility of America's unloading its immigration problem onto Canada. He envisioned a steady course from commercial union to political union, which, once achieved, would immediately take the pressure off American soil.[44] A few months later, in June 1889, Wiman was considerably less of a gradualist. He suggested that if the fishing disputes then going on between the two countries led to outright hostility, the United States would be justified in taking Canada by military force. Wiman hoped that Canada might free itself from all ties to Great Britain, and then willingly divide itself into perhaps thirty states. If not, he felt that the United States should perform the task. By 1890 he was asking in plain terms, "Has not the time for the capture of Canada come?"[45]

Few of those who addressed the Canadian situation at the end of the decade wrote as boldly as Wiman. The more common question was not "when shall we annex Canada?" but, "is union with Canada desirable?" Those who stressed the desirability of union rarely failed to mention Canada's extensive wheat fields, timber, and mineral resources.[46] The United States, of course, never came close to a Continental Union with Canada. Even reciprocity treaties were hard to come by in the late nineteenth century. Nevertheless, it is worth considering the intense interest with which American journals viewed Canadian affairs, and the frequency with which some Americans and Canadians proposed offsetting America's diminishing returns with Canada's abundance. The frustration that some Americans experienced at the disappearance of these possibilities might even be viewed as a prelude to the expansionist temper of the nineties.

Meanwhile, as anxiety over the closing of the frontier helped to shape concerns in specific areas, such as public land policy, immigration control, and the nation's position vis-a'-vis new territorial acquisitions, an increasing number of writers and intellectuals started to reflect on the disappearance of the old frontier West. Frontier anxiety had entered the general cultural milieu of the 1880s. At the start of the decade, young Frederic Remington came upon the realization that "the wild riders and the vacant land were about to vanish forever." As he later described the moment, Remington began "to try to recall some of the facts" about him, and "saw the living, breathing end of three centuries of smoke and dust and sweat." By 1881 Remington was chronicling in his art the closing moments of a more heroic age marked by a special breed of "men with the bark on."[47] Owen Wister (Remington's future friend and co-worker) journeyed out West a few years later, displaying supreme optimism about the region's future. But Wister's vision was marred by a fear, as he recorded in 1885, "that the prairies would slowly make way for your Cheyennes, Chicagos, and ultimately inland New Yorks, everything reduced to the same flat . . . level of utilitarian civilization."[48] Around the same time, the western humorist Edgar Wilson ("Bill") Nye, in an article entitled "No More Frontier," lamented that the march of civilization had taken all the joy out of pioneer life. Nye remarked that the Old West was so far gone that a single day's ride could get a man to where he could see daily papers and read them by electric light.[49]

There were good grounds for making such assumptions about the passing of the Wild West. Indeed, by the early 1880s William F. Cody was turning the saga into a highly lucrative entertainment spectacle. On 4 July 1882, Buffalo Bill Cody performed his first Wild West show—advertised as the "Old Glory Blowout"—outside North Platte, Nebraska. By the middle of the decade the famous Sioux leader Sitting Bull had become a featured performer, though he would end his days in a more fitting fashion just prior to the real Wild West battle of Wounded Knee in December 1890. But three and a half years before Wounded Knee, in May 1887, the New World came face to face with the Old as the Wild West show played in London to Prime Minister Gladstone, the Prince of Wales, and Queen Victoria herself—as symbolic an end to the Wild West as Sitting Bull's last stand. A flood of Buffalo Bill novels began to appear in that year. And by 1889, Cody's first imitator, Dr. W. F. Carver, a celebrated marksman, was touring Europe with twenty-five "performing Indians" hired from a reservation.[50]

But as the image of the cowboy was being promoted for profit, the people of western Kansas were streaming back east at the end of the decade with "In God we trusted, in Kansas we busted" chalked on their wagons. The agrarian myth was beginning to crumble even as the cowboy acquired mythic status. The noble pioneer was fast becoming a rootless vagrant.

Hamlin Garland had returned to the West in 1887 only to see its romance fading away. Garland later recalled in his autobiographical work *A Son of the Middle Border* (1917) that the yeoman farmer toiled incessantly for no reward and could no longer be consoled by the fact of his supposed separation from a more advanced, corrupt civilization. All that was left, in Edgar Watson Howe's estimation, was the bitterly futile agrarian existence that he portrayed in his first book, *The Story of a Country Town* (1883). That same year Mark Twain completed his *Adventures of Huckleberry Finn* (1884), acknowledging the end of the frontier as Huck naively pondered the possibility of lighting out for the Territory ahead of the rest. Twain's comic style was a far cry from the darker broodings of Garland and Howe, but his humor was as much a part of the emerging literary realist dissection of the agrarian myth.[51]

Meanwhile, Helen Hunt Jackson was taking a cynical view of the westward march of white settlement. Her *A Century of Dishonor* (1884) chronicled the crushing of Indian resistance that had characterized the Wild West, and she aroused sympathy for a dying culture in her novel *Ramona* (1885). Theodore Roosevelt was less concerned with the fate of the Indian but, reflecting sadly on the rapid disappearance of the "old race of Rocky Mountain hunters and trappers, of reckless, dauntless Indian fighters," formed the Boone and Crockett Club late in 1887 to preserve a little of the old frontier spirit.[52] *Century Magazine* provided a running commentary on the vanishing West in the last years of the decade. Roosevelt's "Frontier Types" series appeared from May to October 1888, and was followed by two more six-issue series, "Pictures of the West" and "Pictures of the Far West," all of which were more concerned with preserving the last fragments of pioneer culture than with telling the reader about any great "unknown West."[53]

As the decade came to a close, two European observers (both subsequently cited as important precursors of Turner)—an English Lord, James Bryce, and an Italian economist, Achille Loria—reflected on the problems they foresaw for the United States as a frontierless democracy. Loria described free land as a factor in the development of political institutions, and like Henry George, viewed the subject from a world perspective. By the late 1880s Loria found that developments in the United States provided a perfect proving ground for his theory, remarking that "the cessation of economic freedom, because of the total occupation of the soil, is destroying democratic methods, the glory of American times."[54]

Bryce viewed the West as "the most distinctly American part of America, because the points in which it differs from the East are the points in which America as a whole differs from Europe." But, Bryce suggested, the frontier fountainhead of American exceptionalism was drying up. He was hardly less pessimistic than Loria, commenting that the hardy, venturesome, self-reliant western pioneer type was fast disappearing from the scene as the West filled up. He stated that this region had provided a "safety valve" for eastern discontents, but was losing its effectiveness. As the frontier closed, "pauperism would become more widespread, wages would drop, and work would be harder to find; the chronic problems of old societies and crowded countries, such as we see them today in Europe, will have reappeared on this new soil. . . . It will be a time of trial for economic institutions."[55]

Also in 1889, in *The Winning of the West*, Roosevelt commented on the harsh, heroic lives of the Western pioneers "who have shared in this fast-vanishing frontier life."[56] A young historian, Frederick Jackson Turner, reviewed Roosevelt's work that same year and pointed to the West as a fruitful field for historical study.[57] In fact, before the Census Report of 1890 marked the official end of the frontier and prompted Turner to formulate his frontier thesis, frontier anxiety had affected the thinking of considerable numbers of Americans. That anxiety would become more acute in the nineties, but its earlier development was a factor of no small significance.

PART TWO.
THE CLOSED FRONTIER

Favorable has been the situation of the United States. . . . As free land becomes less abundant and less accessible, the wage-earning portion of our eastern population finds conditions of life forced upon it which at least hold down if they do not lower the standard of life. Pauperism is undoubtedly increasing with the increase of wealth, and extremes of condition and alienation of classes are familiar to all. Riots that call for military interference testify to the fact that we have not escaped, and are escaping less and less, the friction that accompanies all unfraternal arrangements among men.
—*Richard T. Ely, economist, 1893*

3. CRISIS IN THE NINETIES

In the 1890s a number of factors converged to produce a sense of crisis. Agrarian radicalism became a major political force in 1892 in the shape of the Populist party; a severe depression began in 1893 and continued into the latter part of the decade; labor unrest was rife, urban squalor more visible, and political corruption still rampant. The expansion of the country's industrial base had prompted the rapid development of a corporate business structure marked by huge trusts that seemed to threaten the existence of the small entrepreneur. To many, the former agrarian paradise seemed to have become an industrial hell.

The levels of frontier anxiety in the eighties and nineties seem to have paralleled the intensity and extent of the crisis in each decade. Most of the factors that contributed to the crisis of the nineties were present in the preceding decade—agrarian radicalism, the side-effects of rapid industrialization and urbanization, and downturns in the economy. But all of these developments—and the accompanying frontier anxiety—were more acute in the nineties.

Concern over the closing of the frontier was more than just another factor contributing to the sense of crisis. Just as frontier anxiety had helped shape intellectual debate in the eighties, it played a significant role in molding the greater forebodings of the following decade. The worrisome developments of the nineties were often attributed to the loss of the frontier. Furthermore, the events of the late 1890s that helped restore national confidence—victory over Spain and the expansionism that followed—were often justified by intellectuals expressing concern over the closing of the continental frontier. Just as the Tenth Census in 1880 had been a catalyst to the early development of frontier concerns, so the Census Bureau announcement of 1890 helped set the tone for the frontier anxiety that pervaded the last decade of the century. The transition from an older agricultural to a new, modern America was well under way in the 1880s, but the process accelerated rapidly in the succeeding decade. The official announcement in 1890 that a frontier line of settlement was no longer discernible seemed to symbolize the change. Besides announcing the end of the frontier, the Census Bureau Report for that year also showed that for the first time the value of U.S. industrial output exceeded the wealth produced on farms.[1]

The results of the 1890 Census were eagerly awaited. Articles on the forthcoming census appeared in the nation's leading magazines in the late eighties,[2] and it was hailed as the most detailed and complete effort yet undertaken. To those familiar with the state of the public domain, the findings of the 1890 Census were perhaps more a confirmation of prevailing concerns than a great shock. The Eleventh Census declared that the country had, up to 1880, featured a frontier line of settlement, but now that line was so broken up by bodies of population that such a settlement line no longer existed. Henceforth, it was declared, the westward movement of the line would no longer be discussed in census reports. The frontier was thus officially declared intransient.[3]

For at least a decade, of course, many observers had been lamenting the end of the frontier. Furthermore, by 1890 most of the remaining portions of the West had entered the Union. North and South Dakota, Montana, and Washington had all become states in 1889, and Wyoming and Idaho achieved statehood the following year. By the time the Census Bureau announcement concerning the frontier was published in 1891, only four territories—Utah, Oklahoma, Arizona, and New Mexico—were awaiting statehood.[4] It appeared obvious to many that there was no great uninhabited West left to explore, and the eagerness with which settlers poured into the newly opened Indian Territory in 1889 and 1890 seemed to bear testimony to the scarcity of cheap, tillable land.[5] Nonetheless, the Census of 1890 helped crystallize anxiety over America's future as a frontierless democracy. What many had feared, the census confirmed. Furthermore, the numerous articles that appeared in the early 1890s explaining the significance of "the great count of 1890," including one by the former superintendent of the Census, Francis A. Walker, suggest that the 1890 results reached a wider audience than the results of earlier censuses.[6]

During the nineties, the apparent exhaustion of the nation's supply of arable lands provoked fears among Malthusian-minded intellectuals who questioned the adequacy of the nation's agricultural capacity in the face of steady population growth. The closing frontier was also a common strain in the literary realism that had begun to develop in the late eighties and flow-ered more fully in the nineties. And of course Frederick Jackson Turner syn-thesized the prevalent frontier anxieties of the day in an essay that would, by the early twentieth century, spark a revolution in American historiogra-phy. As in the 1880s, efforts were made to ameliorate the effects of a closed frontier. The rapid exhaustion of the country's timber and mineral re-sources, along with an outpouring of sentimental reactions to the loss of the wild frontier (which had been so eagerly subdued), helped spark the last phase of the movement for land reform—the conservation movement. The immigration issue was very much alive throughout most of the 1890s, and arguments in favor of restriction were often based, as they had been throughout the 1880s, on the premise that the public lands were exhausted and immigrants could no longer be properly assimilated. Calls for the an-nexation of Canada were still heard in the early 1890s, but more signifi-cantly, arguments were heard throughout the decade for the acquisition of overseas territories to offset the problem of closed space in America and its accompanying sense of claustrophobia.[7]

An article in *Forum* magazine at the very beginning of the new decade indi-cated the growing concern over the perceived loss of the frontier. The au-thor, economist Rodney Welch, reacted cynically to the "well-meaning pro-fessional philanthropists, metropolitan clergymen, so-called economists, and newspaper writers" who each spring administered "Horace Greeley's cure for poverty" to every destitute man, woman, and child in the nation's overcrowded cities. Welch first considered the paucity of unsettled arable land left in the United States and then calculated the expenses involved in procuring, settling, and raising an adequate crop on an even halfway decent quarter section. He suggested that before enthusiastic philanthropists ad-vised a city laborer to go west and grow up with the country, they would do well to consider whether he had well in excess of $1,000 to cover the costs of such a venture.[8]

Welch went on to illustrate another fallacy of the agrarian myth when he pointed out that most city dwellers did not know the first thing about farm-ing, and even those who lived in squalid conditions generally had no desire to become yeoman farmers. The nation had passed that simple stage in its history when everyone had supposedly wished to partake of a pastoral exist-ence in the great garden of the world. "The pleasures of the country," said Welch, "like the joys of Heaven, are presented to the poor and wretched in overpopulated cities by persons rich in faith but destitute in knowledge." The average tenement dweller may not have enjoyed the happiest of lives, but what he endured was, "after all, preferable to existence in a dug-out which is seldom passed by man"—the only existence he was likely to find in the "great" West in the 1890s, according to Welch.[9]

A number of American writers, particularly William Dean Howells and Hamlin Garland, found the disappearance of the old America harder to accept than Welch did. These early literary realists were, as one literary critic has suggested, "'Jeffersonian,' bound to a preindustrial and precorporate way of life." They reacted cynically to the nation's faith in the agrarian myth, yet at the same time their writings were a tearful lament to a fast-fading agrarian America.[10]

Garland's trip home to Osage, Iowa, in 1887 prompted one of the first conscious literary reactions to the onset of capitalistic exploitation in the settled West.[11] The resulting book, *Main-Travelled Roads* (1891), comprised eleven sketches of prairie life that amounted to an angry reaction to the well-meaning philanthropists Rodney Welch had taken to task. Garland painted a grim picture of the "Golden West." In "Under the Lion's Paw," he told the heart-rending tale of a young, optimistic settler, Tim Haskins, who took his family out west only to find that there was no affordable land. Undeterred, Haskins decided to lease some land on the promise that he would be allowed to purchase it in a few years. For three years the Haskins family "rose early and toiled without intermission till the darkness fell on the plain, then tumbled into bed, every bone and muscle aching with fatigue, to rise with the sun next morning to the same round of the same ferocity of labor," only to be nonchalantly informed at the end of that period that their work had more than doubled the value of the land. Tim Haskins could either pay the new price or "git out."[12] Haskins's naiveté made the story more pathetic, but it was the disappearance of the frontier that made the owner's demand for the increment possible.[13]

In the preface to his next work, the novel *Jason Edwards* (1892), Garland reiterated the theme at length:

> For more than a half century, the outlet toward the free lands of the West has been the escape-valve of social discontent in the great cities of America. Whenever the conditions of his native place pressed too hard upon him, the artisan has turned his face toward the prairies and forests of the West. The emigrant not only bettered his own fortunes . . . but he bet-

tered the conditions of his fellows who remained, by reducing the competition for employment.

But to-day the dream—this most characteristic American emotion is almost gone. Free land is gone. The last acre of available farm land has passed into private or corporate hands. The nation has squandered the inheritance of the unborn as well as the living.[14]

Jason Edwards came to realize that free land was gone when he took his family out west to the cynically named "Boomtown," where all the land was in the hands of speculators. Edwards took out a mortgage but could not keep up with the high payments. When he pinned his hopes on the forthcoming crop, it was destroyed by a hailstorm. The beneficent West, it seemed, was nothing but a heartless wasteland where predictable exploiters and unpredictable nature combined to paralyze the hopes of optimistic settlers.[15]

William Dean Howells lamented the loss of the frontier in his first "utopian novel," A Traveller from Altruria (1894). While Garland had focused on the lack of free land as evidenced by the presence of land monopoly and speculation, Howells indicated his understanding of the deeper underlying factors—the pressure of industrial forces and the consequent narrowing of opportunity—that had seemingly come to the United States when the Western safety-valve closed.[16] Howells offered the reader a harrowing description of the changes that had befallen America between 1850 and 1890:

If a man got out of work he turned his hand to something else; if a man failed in business, he started in again from some other direction; as a last resort, in both cases, he went west, preempted a quarter section of public land, and grew up with the country. Now the country is gone; business is full on all sides, and the hand that turned itself to something else has lost its cunning. The struggle for life has changed from a free fight to an encounter of disciplined forces, and the free fighters that are left get ground to pieces between organized labor and organized capital.[17]

That sense of constriction and claustrophobia, of the country being full on all sides, was apparent in the more abstract descriptions in Henry Blake Fuller's novel The Cliff Dwellers (1893). Fuller asked the question, "Why is there more insanity and more self-murder to-day than ever before?" His answer was that "society has been, in general, loose-knit, so that each unit in it has had room for some individual play. [But today] society has a closer and denser texture than ever before; its finespun meshes bind us and strangle us."[18]

If society was becoming more "compact" and the West no longer acted as a safety valve, that was only part of the problem for some observers in the 1890s. The lack of available land awaiting settlement also provoked fears that not only would America cease to be the granary of the world, but it might, in the not-too-distant future, be unable to feed its own increasing population.

The Malthusian implications of the closed frontier were popularized by C. Wood Davis. A former Yankee businessman and the owner of large farming interests in Kansas, Davis produced a stream of articles for popular magazines in the early 1890s.[19] Davis contended that the existing depression (1893–1897) had resulted from the rapid development of America's fertile regions. Production had temporarily outrun consumption, and with the demand insufficient to meet the supply, agricultural prices had dropped. But the nation's arable lands were being occupied at a rate that insured their complete exhaustion before the end of the decade. America's farmers, Davis claimed, would experience a return to prosperity because population was increasing steadily, and less and less land remained for cultivation. As population rose, demand would rise to meet supply. But the optimistic elements of Davis's argument were more than balanced by his predictions that the public domain of the United States would not, when fully settled, be able to meet the increasing demand for agricultural goods and that "consumption must, as in Europe, be met from the products of a given and unexpanding area supplemented by an importation of food."[20]

In 1891 the ardent advocate of American annexation of Canada, Erastus Wiman, presented a similar argument in the North American Review. Wiman claimed that no more new wheat lands remained unoccupied in the United States. A "land hunger" now existed, he said, and was borne out by the fact that "if a farmer's son or a new-comer seeks to secure land that will probably produce bread, to do so he must displace an occupant already in possession, or go without."[21] Like Davis, Wiman saw the situation as beneficent for the depressed farmer class that had suffered from overproduction when there was free land but would experience increased domestic consumption and thus gain higher prices for goods now that the lands were fully settled. The change, Wiman concluded, would "put the American farmer on top," making him the most prosperous of all classes in the world. Wiman's piece did not, like Davis's, proceed to a pessimistic conclusion regarding the sufficiency of the nation's future agricultural production. Nevertheless, such a conclusion could easily be arrived at by way of a logical extension of Wiman's argument and was present in some of his earlier writings.

The Neo-Malthusian argument elicited quite a response in the early 1890s. It was used by eastern conservatives to placate discontented farming interests, who would, it was supposed, experience a change in fortune in the near future.[22] One essential element of the Davis-Wiman synthesis—the arid and unworkable nature of the remaining lands—was fiercely disputed by pro-irrigation spokesmen, who argued that these lands could, if properly irrigated, be brought under the plough and made productive.[23] And land companies, pointing to the rapid settlement of the Indian Territory (which Davis and Wiman both viewed as a reflection on the poor quality of the remaining land in the West), used the factor as a sales device.[24] These companies publicized the sure practicality of buying land before the shortage caused it to shoot up in value.[25] The pro-irrigation forces, on the other hand, often pointed to the recent land hunger as proof of the urgent need for government-sponsored irrigation projects.[26] In fact, as one historian has suggested, the "exhausted-land leitmotif" had, by the early 1890s, become an integral element in the discussion of agricultural depression and discontent and was very much a part of the social and intellectual climate of those years.[27]

It was from this climate that Turner's famous essay on "The Significance of the Frontier in American History" emerged. Turner had presented his frontier thesis in embryo in an earlier essay, "Problems in American History" (1892).[28] In that piece Turner admonished American historians for their constant focus on the Atlantic seaboard and lack of interest in "the colonization of the Great West." "This ever retreating frontier of free land," Turner said, "is the key to American development." That notion, as we have seen, had long been a factor in American thinking. But the historical profession had been so preoccupied with tracing America's cultural heritage back to its Teutonic origins that it had neglected the environmental forces that had shaped American life. Turner claimed that until historians studied the frontier phenomenon Americans would "have no real national self-consciousness." He went on to mention America's successive stages of development and the transition from savagery to civilization on each new frontier. In fact, almost every aspect of his more famous essay was present in "Problems in

American History." Everything that is, except an acute concern over the loss of the frontier. Turner did express a fear that the new immigration was becoming less assimilable than the old, but he did not yet lament the closing of the frontier.[29]

By contrast, the address Turner delivered the following year at the meeting of the American Historical Association (held in conjunction with the Columbian Exposition in Chicago), on "The Significance of the Frontier in American History," began and ended with the assertion that the loss of the frontier marked "the closing of a great historic movement"—"the first period of American history."[30] The essay was not just an original historical synthesis of the American past, but a classic expression of frontier anxiety.

Historians have hotly debated both the meaning and the validity of the Turner thesis.[31] But Turner saw the frontier not just as the key factor in American development but as a tremendously beneficent factor—and one that was no longer operative. For Turner the advance of the frontier had meant a steady movement away from the corrupting influence of the Old World. The frontier had, he said, "prompted the formation of a composite nationality for the American people." Immigrants were "liberated" and "Americanized . . . in the crucible of the frontier." Furthermore, the struggle of man against nature on the wild frontier had developed "the stalwart and rugged qualities of the frontiersman," making him more independent and individualistic. And individualism, Turner said, also promoted democracy, as pioneers set up anti-authoritarian political structures that breathed new life into the national body politic. Democracy had also been promoted by the abundance of opportunity secured by the store of free land. As long as there was opportunity, democracy could thrive. And "each frontier," Turner said, had furnished "a new field of opportunity, a gate of escape from the bondage of the past."[32]

Turner asserted quite forcefully that the great shaping force of American life was now gone. But he made few predictions about what a frontierless future would hold for the United States. The tone of his essay, like Roosevelt's *The Winning of the West*, was sentimental and nostalgic. It is worth mentioning, too, that almost all of Turner's historical studies focused on the early nineteenth century—when the frontier was still, supposedly, a fully operating force. Nevertheless, it was not hard to see that if the frontier had provided the foundation for a beneficent American exceptionalism, its loss could be catastrophic. Turner was a more modern-minded historian than is often assumed. He was certainly no mono-causationist when it came to explaining the development of American institutions and characteristics.

Nonetheless, his 1893 essay was driven by geographical (or environmental) determinism that did not allow for the artificial ameliorative factors in place of the closed frontier.[33] Although he expressed concern in "Problems in American History" that the new immigration was less assimilable and claimed in "The Significance of the Frontier" that the frontier had given Americans an expansive character, Turner did not feel that either immigration restriction or further territorial expansion could really offset the loss of the American frontier.[34] All in all, Turner's 1893 speech, despite its praise of America's institutions and virtues and its many poetic flourishes, was not an optimistic address, but a eulogy to a past age.

The same was true of another offering at the Columbian Exposition that summer. In the midst of the numerous technological testimonies to progress on display, there was one exhibit that must have seemed quite out of place. Roosevelt's Boone and Crockett Club had constructed a small log cabin—a reminder of pioneer times.[35] It is certain that the frontiersman's cabin attracted more attention that summer than did Turner's paper.[36] The young professor did not turn the historical profession upside down in 1893—the persistent conformity of historians to the Teutonic germ theory[37] rendered that much unlikely. In fact, his address was not readily accessible in print until the end of the following year.[38]

Despite its belated acceptance by historians, Turner's frontier thesis had, as Theodore Roosevelt assured him, "put into definite shape a good deal of thought that has been floating around rather loosely."[39] A complete "frontier synthesis" of the American past had indeed been lacking, but concerns of a similar nature to those expressed by Turner were being voiced with great regularity. In fact, at the fair that same year, at the Congress on Evolution (which heard a paper by Herbert Spencer), James A. Skelton, in an address that paralleled Turner's, proclaimed "this westward march of empire and freedom during the ages comes to an abrupt end. . . . The Columbian Exposition of 1893 celebrates both the beginning and the end of the Columbian epoch . . . and the beginning of a new epoch in which the race is again to be tested."[40] Roosevelt himself, addressing the State Historical Society of Wisconsin on the role of "The Northwest in the Nation" earlier that year, glorified the epoch of the "frontiersmen . . . the daring Indian fighters . . . [whose] life is now fast vanishing away." "There is," he added, "no longer any frontier," yet he expressed the hope that some of the frontiersman's hardy, heroic qualities might endure in future generations of Americans.[41]

In fact, the year of Turner's famous address was marked by a number of lengthy expositions on the significance of the closing of the country's frontier. Charles H. Pearson, who had made some pessimistic observations regarding the recession of the frontier back in the late 1860s, expanded his thoughts on the topic in *National Life and Character: A Forecast*, published at the beginning of the year. The book, Pearson stated, was prompted by his "observation that America was filling up." "The best part of the country has been taken up," Pearson remarked. He went on to suggest the possibility of socialism developing in the frontierless United States and the disappearance of individualism. Perhaps the best that could be hoped for, Pearson added, was "a general low level of content, and an exaltation of the patriotic sentiment."[42]

Richard T. Ely, prominent economist and colleague of Turner's, addressed the closed-frontier theme in his work *Outlines of Economics* (1893). Ely stated that the United States had enjoyed favorable circumstances in the past, but its favored status was passing. In one of the period's most substantial accounts of the closing of the safety valve, he explained:

> As free land becomes less abundant and less-accessible the wage-earning population finds conditions of life forced upon it which at least hold down if they do not lower the standard of life. Pauperism is undoubtedly increasing with the increase of wealth, and extremes of condition and alienation of classes are familiar to all. Riots that call for military interference testify to the fact that we have not escaped, and are escaping less and less, the friction that accompanies all unfraternal arrangements among men.[43]

The United States, Ely suggested, would have to change to meet these changing conditions just as other countries had: "All countries tend to fullness, and newness always disappears in time. That system which will not work in a thickly settled country is a condemned system, for it fails to work under what are now generally, and will soon be universally, the normal conditions of human life."[44]

Ely went on to outline Malthus's theory of population growth and his focus on population control. The Wisconsin economist declared that the United States would have to control its population size (which he reckoned to be doubling every twenty-five years); otherwise, "in a comparatively short period there would not be standing room on the surface of the earth for all the people."[45] In one particularly eloquent passage Ely reached the conclusion that the United States, with its newly acquired frontierless status, would have only one recourse for coping with the conditions that would arise:

> Everytime the sun rises it looks upon a larger population than ever before in the United States, and consequently upon a more complex industrial civilization. A force mighty, and it almost seems irresistible, is at work day and night, day and night, never ceasing, thrusting upon us more and more serious social problems. These problems can never be solved by the policeman's club or the soldier's bullet, for this quiet on-moving force laughs such repression to scorn. Only righteousness can solve them, for only in righteousness is there power to enable us to adjust ourselves to our new environment.[46]

In constructing his analysis in *Outlines of Economics*, Ely had relied heavily on the theories of the Italian economist Achille Loria, as laid out in his *Analisi della proprieta Capitalista* (1889). Turner, too, was well aware of Loria's work as he constructed his frontier thesis.[47] In fact, a good number of educated Americans must have been aware of Loria's theory of the land-to-man ratio in the early years of the decade. A very favorable review of Loria's book appeared in the *Political Science Quarterly* in December 1890.[48] A year and a half later, a thirty-five-page discussion of the principal elements of Loria's system appeared in the same scholarly publication. Like Ely after him, Loria had stated that America's favored condition could not last. The country's growing population, in conjunction with the diminishing fertility of its soil and the necessity of resorting to less fertile lands, Loria's reviewer explained, necessitated the implementation of a more intensive system of cultivation, which in turn would lead to the development of the institution of slavery.[49] And such dire consequences of a closed frontier were not only on the minds of the well-educated reader. In a Farmers' Alliance campaign song of the period, a rural youth pleads with his father to cast his ballot for farmers' rights before it is too late: "Free land will be gone and naught else can I do / But be to the rich man a slave."[50]

It was hard to escape such prophecies of gloom and doom in these years. One frequent bearer of apocalyptic visions was Ignatius Donnelly, the colorful Populist leader, author of the Omaha platform and longtime anticapitalist protester. In September 1893, Donnelly advised the farmers of Minnesota to hang on to their land "to the last gasp." "There are," he said, "no more Minnesotas on the planet; and every day the battle of life will grow fiercer."[51] A few months later he warned: "We have practically reached the limit of our available free land supply. That free-land has been the safety-valve of Europe and America. When the valve is closed, swarming mankind every day will increase the danger of explosion. Nothing can save the world but the greatest wisdom, justice and fair play."[52]

Around the same time that Donnelly was voicing his concerns, one of the last decent-sized tracts of Indian land, the Cherokee Outlet, was opened to white settlement.[53] Commenting on the event, the *Review of Reviews* declared that a new, less corrupt public land policy might be worth considering if there were more of these reservations available for settlement. But the publication stated quite categorically, "the time for such reflections is passed. . . . Because that which makes the opening of the Cherokee Outlet of significance is the fact that the end has practically come to the time when, as we used to sing, 'Uncle Sam was rich enough to give us all a farm'."[54]

As more intellectuals expressed anxiety over the loss of the western safety valve, it also became clear that free land was not the only victim of the continent's speedy settlement. Alice C. Fletcher, a Smithsonian ethnologist, lamented the disappearance of a distinct American Indian culture in her series "Personal Studies of Indian Life," which appeared in *Century Magazine* from 1893 to 1895.[55] In 1893 *Century Magazine* also featured Theodore Roosevelt's reminiscences of his times "in Cowboy Land" among the "hard-working, brave, resolute, and truthful" pioneer types.[56] Also in that year, Frederic Remington convinced the young Philadelphia author, Owen Wister, to collaborate with him on a series for *Harper's Monthly Magazine* to be called "The Evolution of the Cowboy."[57] The purpose of the series was to tell the story of the rise and fall of the great days of the open range. If Wister needed any more assurance in deciding to become a western writer, *Harper's* provided it in July 1893, sending him out west to write a series of "short stories of Western life which is now rapidly disappearing with the progress of civilization."[58] A few years later, in *The Story of a Cowboy* (1897), Emerson Hough lamented the disappearance of the colorful West of the rough-hewn cowboy—"the men of the wilder and freer West"—and the rise of the "smart and pretentious . . . [and] less picturesque . . . little city of the new West . . . [with its accompanying] horde of lawyers, doctors, merchants, thieves, and other necessaries."[59]

Nostalgia for the passing age of the cowboy and the wild frontier accounted for both Remington's rise to prominence in the nineties and the popularity of a fellow western artist, Charles Russell. Wister, too, harped on the heroism of a bygone age in numerous magazine articles during the decade.[60] The aged historian Francis Parkman expressed a similar sentiment in the preface to the 1892 edition of his classic work, *The Oregon Trail* (1849), writing that "the Wild West is tamed, and its savage charms . . . withered." He added that "if this book can help to keep their memory alive, it will have done its part."[61] The celebrated journalist Richard Harding Davis took a more cynical view in his book of reminiscences, *The West from a Car Window* (1892). Davis baited the "stay-at-home Eastern man" who "obtains false images of how wild the West really is." Many easterners had by this time been thrilled by William F. Cody's Wild West show. Davis declared that "A mild West show . . . would be equally accurate" as a description of life beyond the Rockies.[62] But in one sense, Davis's message was essentially the same as Remington's, Wister's, and Parkman's—the frontier epoch had reached its end.

Unlike Richard Harding Davis, who was a cynic when it came to cowboy culture (or at least the public's fascination with it), Theodore Roosevelt, like Remington and Wister, made a concerted effort to preserve the elements of the pioneer past that he held dear. In 1895, with Henry Cabot Lodge, he co-authored a short and popular book of *Hero Tales from American History*. The book extolled the frontier virtues of men such as Daniel Boone, George Rogers Clark, and the defenders of the Alamo.[63] But Roosevelt and Lodge shared more than fond memories of frontier America. Between the two of them they played a role in all three movements in the 1890s that were inspired in part by the perceived need to offset the loss of the frontier. Roosevelt was an ardent conservationist and territorial expansionist, Lodge a zealous advocate of immigration restriction and expansion.

4. INTERNAL SOLUTIONS: PRESERVING THE FRONTIER

Whether nostalgic reminiscences of a somehow wilder and freer frontier age that was passing away, or socioeconomic and political treatises on the present effects and future ramifications of the lost frontier, the closed-frontier theme had become an integral element in the intellectual life of the 1890s. As in the previous decade, it entered into and helped formulate the great debates of the day.

The attacks on land monopoly in the 1880s had made some impact on public land policy by the end of that decade. In addition, the General Revision Act of 1891 helped rectify some of the remaining abuses in the land laws.[1] But even though it repealed or limited previous land laws that had facilitated corrupt dealings, the General Revision Act could not turn back the clock to the time when the United States possessed a vast public domain. Even with the act on the statute books, the courts blocked any major surrender of railroad lands under the forfeiture laws. The ordinary homesteader now had a better chance of competing with the speculators and land companies for the remaining arable lands, but in sheer practical terms these reforms did not make a great deal of difference, because by the 1890s very little easily cultivatable land awaited settlement. The introduction of new dry-farming techniques and irrigation systems would promote homesteading in later years, as evidenced by the high rate of settlement in the early decades of the twentieth century. But for potential homesteaders in the 1890s, prospects were far from bright, not just because of the paucity of available homesteads but because the general depression of the nineties had an acute effect on American agriculture as a whole.

The movement for land reform entered its final stage in the nineties in response to the worsening state of the public domain. In some senses, land reform in the 1880s can be viewed as a response to the perceived closing of the

42

frontier. In those years much of the focus was on problems relating to the fair distribution of cheap and decent arable land. In the 1890s, with the supply of affordable, cultivatable land severely depleted, the focus became how to utilize poorer, semiarid lands, and how best to conserve the nation's other natural resources.[2] This new approach can be viewed as a response to the perception that the frontier had all but closed.

Throughout the 1890s the issue of whether the federal government should take on the responsibility of irrigating the semiarid western lands (lying beyond the ninety-seventh meridian from western Kansas to the Pacific) was hotly debated. Frontier-related arguments were evident on both sides of what was a very complex issue. Those like John Wesley Powell, who favored federally sponsored irrigation projects, argued that more land must be brought into cultivation to meet the growing demand for homesteads. To Powell and others it was a matter of creating a new frontier out of that small portion of the semiarid western lands—not more than two or three percent according to Powell—that were deemed potentially irrigable. This measure, it was hoped, would help offset the nation's growing land hunger.[3] The pro-irrigationists pointed to the mad rush into newly opened Indian lands as evidence of the acute land hunger in postfrontier America. In October 1893 the *Review of Reviews* acknowledged the disappearance of the traditional frontier of cheap, farmable land and asked the question "Where now shall the land hungry turn?"[4] Throughout the 1890s the same question was debated frequently in leading national magazines as irrigation advocates sought to convince the federal government to create a new western safety valve from the semiarid lands.[5]

Opponents of federally sponsored irrigation sometimes employed an argument similar to C. Wood Davis's Malthusian interpretation. They blamed the present agricultural depression on the overdevelopment and oversettlement of the continent, but differed from Davis in believing that the semiarid lands could be made productive.[6] They argued, however, that bringing more land under cultivation would only create a larger agricultural surplus and thus reduce prices further, making the situation even worse for the nation's farmers.[7]

The irrigation issue heightened anxiety over the depleted state of the public domain, but the debate often seemed to have more to do with complicated power struggles between individual western states and the federal government than with worries over the loss of the frontier.[8] Furthermore, the rhetoric of the pro-irrigation forces often served to bolster the myth of the garden, not explode it. One observer, in an effort to dissipate concern over the exhaustion of the public domain, questioned the prevalent notion that tillable land was scarce, pointing to "an empire of dry and partly-dry lands" in the far West that could, with a little irrigation, be apportioned into hundreds of thousands of profitable homesteads.[9]

Irrigating the semiarid lands turned out to be far more problematic than most land experts had expected. Even with major federal legislation—namely the Carey Act of 1894, which set aside certain proceeds from land sales to supply water, and the famous Newlands Reclamation Act of 1902, which made the federal government responsible for the provision of reservoirs and permanent irrigation works—settlers on the semiarid plains still faced hardships. However, though inadequate, these measures were clear victories for the pro-irrigation forces. The Newlands Act, especially, was widely heralded as a measure that would reopen the western safety valve. One newspaper in the state of Washington contended that the reclaimed desert lands would sustain a hundred million people. "The crowded conditions of the Eastern communities," the editorialist optimistically declared, "will be automatically relieved."[10] Crowded conditions persisted of course, but within two decades about 1.2 million acres of desert land had been reclaimed under the provisions of the act.[11]

The Newlands Act was a landmark measure in public land policy, and its passage indicated that fears over land hunger were more immediate than fears of overproduction. The role frontier anxiety played in the irrigation issue as a whole is difficult to determine. What is certain is that the pro-irrigationists' demands for federal assistance to settlers on an unprecedented scale (the federal government had always played a significant role in assisting western settlement) did little to enhance the image of the sturdy, independent yeoman farmer. Furthermore, the irrigation issue made it clear that wasteful or "extensive" cultivation of the soil would have to give way to more "intensive" forms of agriculture. This newfound understanding helped explode the myth of an infinitely abundant and exploitable nature that had characterized the open-frontier era.[12] This "Myth of Superabundance," as one conservationist recalled in the 1960s, lost more credence as the conservation issue developed in the 1890s.[13]

It is probably more accurate to talk of conservationism in the nineties as an issue than as a movement. The term "conservation" held very different meanings for different groups. In fact, the question of how best to conserve the nation's remaining natural resources was a source of even more heated controversy than the debate over irrigation. Two distinct, though by no means antithetical, schools of conservationist thought had emerged by 1890. On the one hand, nature writers such as John Burroughs and John Muir sought to preserve nature for aesthetic purposes. For them nature was a sanctuary, a place where people could find beauty and simplicity in an increasingly ugly and mechanistic society. To the other school, nature was more a workshop than a temple. For these more utility-minded conservationists—such as University of Wisconsin economist Richard T. Ely and Gifford Pinchot, chief forester in the Department of Agriculture (1898-1910)—nature was a commodity to be used carefully and efficiently. A fundamental difference in outlook obviously separated the "utilizers" from the "preservers," but both groups were reacting to the same set of circumstances. It was clear to all conservationists that the continent's resources could not be infinitely exploited. It was clear, too, that the land had been subdued rather than nurtured. Nowhere was this more apparent than in the depleted state of the "Great American Forest," the woodland wilderness.

As one historian has suggested, the frontiersman had done battle with the wilderness, and the more he conquered the more he was praised. As long as nature's gifts seemed limitless, the pioneer had free rein to exploit them. Throughout the nineteenth century, prime timberland had sold for as little as five cents an acre. Loggers simply burned over twenty-five million acres of forest each year and managed to cut four-fifths of it in less than a century.[14]

A few perceptive individuals had outlined the dangers of this unchecked exploitation of natural resources long before 1890. The first noteworthy work of conservationist thinking by an American was George Perkins Marsh's *Man and Nature*, published in 1864. Another early and very active conservationist was Wisconsin Senator Carl Shurz, who was appointed Secretary of the Interior by President Hayes in 1877. The creation of Yellowstone National Park in 1872 and the rise of forestry associations in the 1870s and 1880s reflected the gradual awakening of the need for conservation. But it took a spree of unparalleled recklessness under the auspices of particularly inept post–Civil War chief executives to bring matters to a head.[15]

In the 1890s, with the frontier officially closed and the nation's stock of virgin forests rapidly dwindling, there was a noticeable change in attitude toward nature. As the process of urbanization and mechanization accelerated in the last years of the century, wild country clearly inspired quite different reactions than it had in earlier decades. As one historian has remarked, citizens were now more likely to approach wilderness "with the viewpoint of the vacationer . . . than the conquerer."[16]

After 1891 conservation became a major political issue.[17] In that year Congress passed the Forest Reserve Act, which gave the president the authority to set aside timberland as national preserve. President Benjamin Harrison took full advantage, creating six forest reservations in the 1891–1892 fiscal year. By the end of his administration, Harrison had set aside more than 13 million acres of forest land.[18] This course of action appealed to both Congress and the president on strictly utilitarian grounds. They argued that these forested lands were essential to the water supply and that timber supplies must be used more economically. However, when leading publications such as *Century Magazine* and the *Atlantic Monthly* lent their support to Harrison's actions, they stressed both the practical aspects of conservation and the aesthetic qualities of wilderness.

A flood of articles on the topic appeared in these two magazines during the 1890s, a good number of them contributed by the nature writer John Muir.[19] In this decade, Muir was the nation's foremost publicist for the benefits of wilderness. He lamented the departure of wilderness from the great central plain, but delighted in the knowledge that "thousands of tired, nerve-shaken, over-civilized people" were beginning to discover "that wilderness is a necessity." He declared the usefulness of mountain parks and reservations, "not only as fountains of timber and irrigating rivers, but as fountains of life."[20]

This theme of the perils of overcivilization, always at the center of Muir's writings, was an integral element in Turner's work, too.[21] Though the frontier was Turner's nominal subject—and in his mind the great regenerative force in American life—it was the woodland wilderness that he associated most strongly with the frontier. In his 1896 article "The Problem of the West," Turner contended that it was "out of his wilderness experience" that the pioneer had "fashioned a formula for social regeneration." "This forest philosophy," he declared, "is the philosophy of American democracy."[22] Theodore Roosevelt, too, stressed the importance of contact with wilderness, feeling that the modern American was in danger of becoming an "overcivilized man."[23] It was Roosevelt who would bring a degree of coherence to the conservation movement in the early years of the twentieth century, stressing both the aesthetic and the practical benefits of wilderness preservation.

The fear of overcivilization was a factor behind many of the expressions of frontier anxiety in the late nineteenth century. In the mid-1880s, Henry

George had coupled his constant reminder that the western safety valve was closed with his concern that the city dweller, because he was "utterly divorced from the genial influence of nature," would deteriorate "physically, mentally and morally."[24] Such notions were fairly widespread by 1890 when a school-garden movement got under way in several cities to promote the very qualities—physical, mental, and moral growth—that George saw declining. The movement sought to inculcate an attachment to agriculture in city children who would then, it was hoped, migrate to farms under the sponsorship of the government, thus relieving social pressure in the cities. The school-garden movement expanded after 1893, when the depression set in. In Detroit, the idea of cultivating vacant lots originated as a relief measure for the idle poor. A few years later the same system was implemented on a wider scale in Philadelphia, and by 1898 the Salvation Army was setting up farm colonies in Colorado, California, and Ohio for the nation's urban poor.[25]

Along with the school-garden movements and the early back-to-the-land movements, the 1890s witnessed the emergence of nature studies in the educational curriculum. Those years also saw the formation of a number of nature-oriented associations, among them Muir's Sierra Club in 1892 and the American Park and Outdoor Society in 1897.[26] The decade also saw a boom in the construction of parks in and near large cities. These new facilities were, the *Atlantic Monthly* claimed, essential "as a means for cultivating the esthetic sense of the people."[27] Landscape architects such as Frederick Law Olmstead and Charles Eliot proposed that, in addition to the city parks, patches of "wild forest" be preserved close to metropolitan areas. In them, Eliot contended in 1891, men could find relief from the "poisonous struggling . . . of city life."[28]

Renewed interest in nature's splendor and faith in its regenerative powers were hardly enough to offset the level of frontier anxiety present in the 1890s. Conservationism and the change in outlook that accompanied its emergence addressed the issue of the loss of the frontier, but attention all too often reverted to fears of overpopulation and the inability of a frontierless America to assimilate the steady stream of foreign immigrants.

Concern over the loss of the frontier played a part in the immigration debate in the 1890s, just as it had in the preceding decade. But with the western safety valve now officially closed, fears over the assimilative capacity of the New World were, for much of the nineties, more readily expressed than in the eighties. Arguments for immigration restriction did not always stem directly from the notion that a frontierless America was unable to house new arrivals. Factors of race and religion were also at the forefront of that debate.[29] Nevertheless, frontier-related concerns surfaced in many of the restrictionist arguments and were clearly the sole inspiration of a good number.

Francis A. Walker was among the best-known and most respected of the restrictionists. The former superintendent of the Census, Walker was openly racist in his arguments, declaring his preference for the old immigrants from northern and western Europe over the new southern and eastern European immigrants. Through clever statistical manipulation, Walker argued that immigration served to curtail native population growth. Thus, he claimed, the native stock of Teutonic origin was gradually being replaced by a degraded foreign stock.[30] Walker's argument was ingenious as it stood, but was made even more effective when he contended that a frontierless United States could no longer assimilate and Americanize these "alien breeds."[31]

Walker made the exhaustion of the public lands a central element of his thesis in an 1892 article in the *Yale Review*. Walker drew a parallel between changing public attitudes towards the nation's timberlands and the changing outlook on the immigration question:

There was a long time in the life of the United States when "the axe of the pioneer" was perhaps the best emblem of our civilization. Primeval forests had to be swept away . . . [so] that the fertile soil beneath might be open to cultivation. To-day all the reason of the case which made the removal of the original tree-covering of the soil a matter of felicitation has disappeared.

"There was a time, a long time," he went on, "when every able-bodied man coming to our shores . . . brought an added strength to the young nation. . . . A continent was to be wrested from savage nature . . . and every one's help was welcome in the great work." But conditions had changed, and the country was no longer in a position to extend a welcome to the downtrodden masses of Europe:

A generation or less ago, a vast extent of free public lands offered to every new-comer a home and a farm simply for the seeking. . . . such a resort to the soil, so open, so free, hardly allowed a labor problem to exist. To-day, the tracts of public land worth taking up . . . are few and far between. . . . Reluctant as we may be to recognize it, a labor problem is at last upon us. No longer can a continent of free virgin lands avert from us the social struggle which the old world has known so long and so painfully.[32]

The tide of population pouring into the country had to be stemmed, Walker stated, because the country was rapidly filling up and its great assimilative force—the frontier—was spent. Furthermore, the new immigrants were by their very nature less assimilable than the older, Teutonic elements had been. Poles, Bohemians, Hungarians, Russian Jews, and South Italians were, he claimed, "ignorant, unskilled, inert," lacking in "social aspiration." Without a frontier it would simply be impossible to Americanize these elements. Walker advocated various restrictive measures, including a "money test" requiring payment of a $100 fee per immigrant upon arrival. This he felt would keep out all but the most worthy elements and reduce the immigrant flood to a trickle. America, Walker concluded, would do best to return to its original role as a "city upon a hill," offering the example of noble government and purpose to the world. To achieve that much, the city could no longer allow itself to become a boarding house for all comers.[33]

Walker made the same points a few years later in an *Atlantic Monthly* article, this time placing even more emphasis on "the important fact of the complete exhaustion of the free public lands." "Fifty years ago, thirty years ago, vast tracts of public land were open to every person arriving on our shores," he said. "To-day there is not a good farm within the limits of the United States . . . which is to be had . . . under the Pre-emption Act, or . . . the Homestead Act." He concluded that a situation in which "immediate occupation of the soil is impossible" for 95 percent of the population should not be compounded by the arrival of more land seekers.[34]

Walker was the most eloquent of the restrictionists; his status as former superintendent of the Census made him also one of the more influential. Furthermore, Walker's post as professor of economics at the Massachusetts Institute of Technology afforded the restrictionist outlook a degree of academic respectability.

The Republican Senator Henry Cabot Lodge was also at the forefront of the movement for immigration restriction. In promoting his case, Lodge presented a blend of racial and frontier-related fears similar to Walker's. Lodge's descriptions of the "ultra-socialists and anarchists" went hand in hand with his description of the changed conditions in postfrontier America. Writing in the *North American Review*, Lodge looked back to the days when America, realizing the need to develop its vast territory, welcomed immigrants with open arms. He declared that "when all the region beyond the Alleghanies, or even beyond the Mississippi, was still a wilderness, the general wisdom of this policy could not be gainsaid." But with these lands becoming increasingly full and the southern and eastern European elements becoming steadily more difficult to assimilate, more stringent policies on immigration would have to be imposed.[35]

A few months later Albert Shaw, the recently appointed editor of the *Review of Reviews* and one of Turner's old Johns Hopkins University associates, reiterated Lodge's and Walker's arguments. Shaw attributed the recent clamor for restriction to the change in character of the immigrants and the fact that "the free homestead area in the United States is practically exhausted."[36] Although Turner himself never advocated restriction, he did state in his 1892 essay, "Problems in American History," that "there is no longer that quick reception and Americanization of these immigrants which we see in earlier days."[37]

Turner's tentative assessment of the situation reached few people in the early 1890s and could not have had much impact on the immigration debate.[38] Shaw, on the other hand, was the editor of a respected publication that boasted a circulation of 70,000.[39] He saw to it that articles linking the immigration problems with the closing of the frontier were favorably assessed in the *Reviews of Reviews* and contributed editorials along those lines himself.[40] Shaw also allotted a good deal of space to one of the most prominent expositors of this approach, Josiah Strong.[41]

In his 1893 work, *The New Era; or, The Coming Kingdom*, Strong proclaimed "the importance to mankind and to the coming kingdom of guarding against the deterioration of the Anglo-Saxon stock in the United States by immigration." "There is now being injected into the veins of the nation," he said, "a large amount of inferior blood every day of the year."[42] Strong made it quite clear that the loss of the frontier was a crucial consideration in the immigration issue; he declared that "the widening waves of migration . . . meet to-day on our Pacific coast. There are no more new worlds. . . . The time is coming when the pressure of population on the means of subsistence will be felt here as it is now felt in Europe and Asia."[43]

Although spokesmen for restriction, such as Lodge and Strong, had made the exhaustion of the public lands an integral part of their arguments, racial assumptions were clearly a driving force behind them.[44] A number of other thinkers, however, based their arguments for restriction wholly on frontier-related factors and subordinated racial considerations completely. Writing in *Forum* in 1891, William Gibbs McAdoo, then an unsuccessful Tennessee streetcar owner and lawyer, downplayed the centrality of racial considerations. McAdoo stated that "a large number of people in the United States, who have no latent prejudices against foreigners as a class, are at this moment seriously considering the wisdom of a stringent restriction. . . . they affect to believe that the phenomenal assimilative powers of the Republic have at last reached their limits."[45] Another restrictionist made exactly the same point, declaring that "the exhaustion of the public lands" was the only justifiable reason for discriminating against the new immigrants.[46] After 1893, as the depression set in and labor's position worsened, labor editors such as John Swinton adopted the same land-exhaustion theme in an effort to promote immigration restriction without alienating the largely foriegn-born union membership. Swinton declared that the supply of labor was outstripping demand and capitalists were exploiting the situation by hiring workers at lower rates. There was, he concluded, no escape to the West now that the "free lands of other years are fenced in."[47]

Aspiring politicians such as McAdoo and labor editors such as Swinton may have displayed political good sense as much as anxiety over the exhaustion of the public lands when they downplayed the explosive race issue.[48] It is interesting, however, that both sides in the controversy over immigration restriction asserted that the subject of land exhaustion was an integral issue in the debate. One writer who strongly favored continued immigration claimed in the *Forum* that there was "incalculable room for immigrants." "The argument," he posited, "upon which the proposition for taxation or exclusion is based seems to be mainly that our free land has been disposed of by the government, and that we no longer have any land to give away. That may be admitted. What has it to do with the question?" The author went on to argue that the disposal of land by its original owners "has no necessary connection with the occupancy or productive use of the land."[49]

At the same time the *North American Review* featured an article co-written by John B. Weber, United States Commissioner of Immigration, and Charles S. Smith, president of the New York Chamber of Commerce. The two men argued that continued immigration could only be harmful to the development of the country if a "change of conditions had been reached." They stated quite firmly that no such change had occurred, that the nation's resources had "hardly been touched," and that "the point of exhaustion" had "certainly . . . not been approached."[50] Addressing themselves more specifically to the notion that the closing of the western safety valve ought to preclude further immigration, Smith and Weber pointed out that overcrowding in the cities resulted not from the loss of the frontier but from emigration out of rural districts. Most immigrants, they argued, still went west.[51] They concluded with the assertion that the continent's assimilative powers were still intact, and that it "did not take long to graft Americanism upon sound, vigorous European stock."[52] As late as 1897 the *North American Review* featured an article that endorsed a policy of unrestricted immigration on the grounds that America's density per square mile was still very low compared to Europe's, and its assimilative powers still enormous.[53]

These objections to the restrictionists' line of reasoning clearly suggest that the land-exhaustion theme was an influential factor in the immigration debate. The majority of intellectuals who addressed the topic in this period did not offer an optimistic assessment of the nation's assimilative capacity. Most deemed the frontier closed. But concern over the closing of the frontier could not prevent restrictionist sentiment, which had been on the rise in the 1880s and early 1890s, from waning when prosperity returned in the last years of the century.[54] In fact, the restrictionists, although they created quite a stir in the nineties, made few actual gains. A strengthening of the immigration laws in 1891 led to the imposition of stiffer health standards and outlawed the solicitation of labor abroad. There was a sharp decline in immigration after 1892—from the record high of 790,000 immigrants to 216,000 in 1897.[55] But this had more to do with the worsening economic climate in the United States than with any new legislation. Moreover, the restrictionists failed to achieve their main legislative goal—passage of a literacy test, a measure which would have dramatically reduced the number of entrants.

By the end of the century immigration was again approaching the half-million mark annually,[56] but by then fewer people seemed concerned over this rise in immigration. A "splendid little war" with Spain had restored national confidence, and the old melting pot concept had regained prominence. Surely, it was assumed, a nation capable of bearing the "white man's burden" in far-off dependencies could have no trouble assimilating its own foreign stock.[57] Yet, while the expansionist fervor of the late 1890s helped subdue fears over the nation's assimilative capacity, those same expansionist designs were themselves generated in part by the understanding that the continental frontier was gone.

5. EXTERNAL SOLUTIONS: NEW FRONTIERS

A host of factors—economic, social, political, cultural, religious, and psychological—helped forge America's expansionist temperament in the late 1890s.[1] The need for overseas markets, some historians have suggested, played a part in precipitating the nation's outward thrust. With the country's industries and farms producing more than could be consumed domestically, it was only natural that some business leaders, and even a few thoughtful agrarians, would demand "new economic frontiers."[2] And as the major European powers scrambled for overseas colonies in the late nineteenth century, some Americans naturally felt their country should be sharing in the bounties of the "New Imperialism."[3]

Yet purely economic factors are rarely the sole determinant of foreign policy, and they are definitely inadequate when it comes to explaining the events of the late 1890s. The decade of the 1890s can be viewed as a "watershed" in American history.[4] While the business class lauded economic growth, others saw a downside to the development of capitalism. For many Americans those years marked the nation's transition from a simple, self-contained, predominantly agrarian society to a more complex, increasingly urban, and industrial one. The "old America" seemed pure, free of the ailments that beset the Old World, while the "new America" was at best a tarnished Eden, at worst the replica of its progenitor. Such gloomy images were clearly present in the 1880s, but became more common and more acute in the 1890s.

The United States was undergoing profound demographic change. The population had grown from 39 million in 1870 to 63 million by 1890.[5] Concurrent with the increase in numbers, many Americans saw a deterioration in character as new immigrants poured in from southern and eastern Europe. Changes in the social landscape accompanied the demographic explosion. The meteoric rise of the poorly governed urban metropolis and the rapid expansion of the country's industrial base, accompanied by the growth of business trusts and labor unions, all marked a radical departure from Jefferson's agrarian utopia. The agrarian protest during the decade, along with instances of industrial violence, such as the Homestead and Pullman strikes and Coxey's March, constituted a level of social unrest that would have seemed almost unimaginable a few decades earlier. What's more, the safety valve of free lands seemed to have closed. The loss of the western safety valve (which, in actuality, had never operated in the direct manner that proponents of the agrarian myth imagined) could serve as an explanation for every adverse development of the period.[6]

The frontier had been viewed as the greatest, most benign force in American life—the source and lifeblood of qualities such as independence, opportunity, self-reliance, and manliness. The understanding that America was frontierless helped to spark such diverse movements as conservationism, literary realism, and nativism. Spokespersons for these movements had agonized over or attempted to offset the loss of qualities that the open frontier had supposedly generated. But many observers deemed "internal solutions" insufficient as replacements for the western safety valve. Attention frequently turned to "external solutions"—to the creation of new territorial frontiers.

When proponents of expansion sought these frontiers in the 1890s to offset the loss of the domestic frontier, they did so for a variety of reasons. Some felt new arenas would have to be found to nurture the manly virtues that had, according to popular perception, been fostered on the rugged western frontier. Some reckoned that the energies exerted in developing the continent would become a dangerous surplus if new fields of action were not found.[7] A number of these commentators deviated from the commonly held assumption that the existence of an internal frontier had facilitated self-containment and isolation from world affairs. They argued that the very presence of a moving frontier had imbued Americans with an expansive character, which made continued expansion inevitable after the domestic frontier closed. Others simply sought new territories to relieve their Malthusian concerns.[8]

There was no single, overriding frontier-based argument for expansion. Yet various manifestations of the closed-frontier theme surfaced frequently in expansionist rhetoric, which, building on the precedents set in the eighties, became more acute and common as the crisis of the nineties deepened.[9]

The United States' interest in Canada carried over into the early 1890s, with Erastus Wiman still at the forefront of the movement for annexation. His views continued to receive a good deal of exposure in American journals, particularly the *North American Review*. [10] Writing in that journal in August 1890, Wiman reiterated his theme that "the boundaries of the great Republic" were "all fused and determined." He stressed the absolute necessity of gaining "more breathing space for this vast and growing aggregation of humanity." Employing his usual Malthusian argument, Wiman stressed that population growth was so rapid and the exhaustion of the arable lands so constant, "that without new and cultivatable territory the sources for the supply of food products will soon be below even the local demand." The obvious solution, he argued, was the appropriation of Canada's vast wheat-growing region north of the Minnesota line. [11]

The *Review of Reviews*, under Albert Shaw's editorship, also made much of Canadian opportunities in the light of land exhaustion in the United States. An editorial in August 1891 discussed the possibilities of using the Canadian northwest as a wheat-growing district when the United States had fully exhausted its own supply of arable land. [12] The following month another editorial declared that "the territories of Canada must, "in the face of land hunger at home," attract the surplus population of Europe, and even large numbers of people from the United States themselves." [13]

Similar articles and editorials appeared periodically in the *Review of Reviews* up to the mid-1890s, although they were, for the most part, less optimistic about the possibilities of union or annexation after 1891. [14] In that year Canada's Liberal party lost again to the British-oriented Tories in the general election, and any American hopes for a Canadian-initiated movement toward union (never a real possibility anyway) began to fade. [15]

Canadian prospects dwindled, but the territorial designs on that country had set a precedent for the more ambitious designs of the nineties, which were often formulated by intellectuals of far greater stature and reknown than those who had addressed the Canadian issue. Influential expansionists such as Josiah Strong, Theodore Roosevelt, and a host of others placed great emphasis on the loss of the continental frontier, and their arguments did not go unheard.

Trying to establish direct causal links between currents of thought and concrete foreign policy decisions is always a tricky venture. Furthermore, it is always difficult to determine the role that intellectuals play in molding public opinion, and equally difficult to measure the effects of public opinion on policy making. "Public opinion" is an ambiguous term. In short, it is impossible to measure exactly the importance of frontier anxiety in formulating either the expansionist outlook or the actual expansionist actions of the nineties. But the closed frontier theme had become a staple of American literature by the early nineties and helped shape the debates over public land policy and immigration. The theme surfaced regularly in books, journals, newspapers, and speeches. It would be safe to assume that most Americans believed their country no longer possessed a frontier, and were in many cases worried by that state of affairs. It would also be fairly safe to assume that the writing of men such as Roosevelt, Strong, Wilson, and Mahan had some influence on the policy-making process.

The Protestant minister Josiah Strong had first linked the closing of the frontier with the need for overseas expansion in his tremendously popular work *Our Country* (1885). Strong elaborated on the theme in his second major work, *The New Era; or, The Coming Kingdom* (1893). Drawing on Lord Bryce's reflections on the American character, Strong emphasized the significance of "the process of settling the western wilderness." This process had "operated to intensify Anglo-Saxon energy and aggressiveness." The "colonizing tendency of this race," Strong explained, "[has been] developed by the westward sweep of successive generations across the continent." The frontier process had been God's way of "training the Anglo-Saxon race for an hour sure to come in the world's future." With the closing of the internal frontier, "with the pressure of population on the means of subsistence" now becoming a reality in the New World (as it had already in Europe and Asia), that hour had arrived. The world, Strong concluded, was now about to enter a new stage of its history—"the final competition of races."[16]

Strong pointed to the qualities that had been exhibited by Anglo-Saxons in developing the resources of such a vast continent. In Strong's estimation, God had blessed them by affording them "the greatest physical basis for Empire!" Now that the nation had mastered its own frontier, it was ready to embark on the divinely ordained conquest of new ones. "Having developed [in the course of its westward march] peculiarly aggressive traits calculated to impress its institutions upon mankind," Anglo-Saxons were sure to extend their dominance over the entire globe.[17] And, Strong's analysis suggested, if such expansionism did not occur, if that Anglo-Saxon energy and aggressiveness continued to well up in a frontierless continent, disastrous consequences would result.

Josiah Strong was an avowed expansionist; his role in shaping the expansionist temper of the decade was fully in accord with his intentions.[18] But expansionists could find similar, frontier-related justifications for their designs in the writings of other intellectuals such as Frederick Jackson Turner and Woodrow Wilson, who did not share Strong's intentions.

Turner was hardly an advocate of overseas expansion in the 1890s.[19] In fact, the closest Turner came to advocating such a course of action in that decade was in an address to the Madison Literary Club in February 1891. In that address, which few could have heard or been aware of, Turner stated that the colonization of the United States was over. But he added, "the United States . . . had developed colonizing energy in settling the West." And because the country's industries produced more than its populace could consume, there was "an important incentive to the possession of colonies in the fact that thus they can furnish themselves with consumers of the home product." Turner added that the recent Pan-American Congress was evidence of the United States' desire to procure substitutes for colonization by attaching South America's economic life to its own.[20] But even here, Turner was simply seeking to account for a process he saw unfolding. He was neither endorsing nor condemning the course the country seemed to be taking.

But while Turner was not himself an expansionist, those who wished to could find historical justification for expansionism in his writings. As Turner posited most clearly in his famous 1893 essay, the frontier experience had facilitated the growth and development of democracy and had been the source and sustainer of almost every beneficent facet of the American character. It was easy to infer from all this that the national character would be adversely affected if the frontier process ended. Advocates of expansion could draw assurances from Turner's synthesis that such a course was inevitable. Turner stated in 1893 that "the people of the United States have taken their tone from the incessant expansion which had not only been open but has even been forced upon them." He added that it "would be a rash prophet who should assert that the expansive character of American life has entirely ceased."[21]

There was much for imperialists to draw on in Turner's 1893 essay, yet the main thrust of the piece was not expansionist. Turner stated that the American intellect would "continually demand a wider field for its exercise," but he also asserted that such extracontinental adventures would not offset the loss of America's own frontier. When Turner posited that "such gifts of free land [would never again] offer themselves," he was not offering the nation a mandate for expansion into territories that would have to be taken.[22] Instead, he was lamenting the end of the frontier process proper—the westward march across the continent. For Turner there was no course of action that could adequately compensate for the loss of the continental frontier.[23]

The same philosophy was evident in Turner's more readily accessible piece, "The Problem of the West." Written for the *Atlantic Monthly* at the request of editor Walter Hines Page, this essay reached a far wider audience and was reviewed in a number of big-city newspapers.[24] Once again Turner stated that the dominant fact in American life had been expansion and that this movement had been checked with the occupation of the country's free lands and the settlement of the Pacific coast. Turner added that it would take a rash prophet to predict that "these energies of expansion will no longer operate." Recent demands for a vigorous foreign policy he viewed as indications that the country would continue to expand.[25] Again Turner was simply presenting his understanding of what had unfolded and what was likely to. He was hardly offering a clear case for expansionism. In fact, Turner's concluding remark, that "the problem of the West means nothing less than the problem of working out original social ideas and social adjustments for the American nation," suggested that internal solutions, not overseas expansion, were more viable responses to the closed frontier.[26] Turner would spend much of the remainder of his career unsuccessfully searching for such remedies.

While expansionists might find justification for their designs in Turner's writings (even though he never endorsed such a course), they had easier access to similar arguments in the writings of Turner's good friend and former Johns Hopkins associate Woodrow Wilson. By 1893, Wilson was well established as a professor of jurisprudence and political economy at Princeton and as a writer on political and historical topics. At Johns Hopkins the two men had frequently discussed the role of the West in American history, both agreeing that it was a factor that had been unduly neglected by historians. Wilson later disclaimed all originality for such thoughts, declaring, perhaps a little too modestly, that everything he ever wrote on the topic had come from Turner.[27] Whether that was true or not, Wilson provided some justifications for expansionism in his writings.

In *Division and Reunion* (1893), Wilson approximated Josiah Strong's reasoning as he offered a firm rejoinder to those Europeans who criticized the American tendency to equate "mere bigness and wealth" with greatness:

The obvious fact is that for the creation of the nation conquest of her proper territory from Nature was first necessary; and this task, which is but recently completed, has been idealized in the popular mind. A bold race had derived inspiration from the size, the difficulty, the danger of the task. . . . Expansion had meant nationalization; nationalization had meant strength and elevation of view. "Be strong backed, brown-handed, upright as your pines; by the scale of a hemisphere shape your designes," is the spirited command of enthusiasm for the great physical undertaking upon which political success was conditioned.[28]

Wilson added that the expansion of the country, besides being an impetus to the growth of nationalism, ensured the "expansion of democratic feeling and method."[29] Thus, one might suppose, continued expansion would facilitate the continued development of these beneficent qualities.

In 1893, in *Forum*, Wilson remarked further on the benign influence of America's "intense and expanding western life." It was this factor, said Wilson, that had settled the slavery question. Furthermore, it was this frontier experience that produced "the typical Americans"—such as Washington, who, Wilson said, had got his experience and his notions of what ought to be done for the country through his contact with the wilderness—his life on the western frontier. He added that Washington "had conceived the expansion of the country much more liberally than others of his generation" and had "looked confidently forward to many a great national enterprise which even yet we have not had the spirit to undertake."[30]

Wilson's frontier-based historical synthesis seemed to provide a clear justification for continued expansion. In reality, though, Wilson had simply allowed his rhetorical prowess to get the better of his good sense. Like Turner, he felt that the frontier had shaped the expansionist character of the American people, but he was not confident that the loss of the internal frontier could be offset by further expansionism. Wilson refused, in the 1890s, to join the believers in grand process—the unqualified expansionists—though they could draw profitably from his writings.[31]

Those who linked the closing of the frontier with the probability of further expansion did not always exhibit the subtlety of Turner or Wilson, or even Strong. To many who shared Malthusian fears, it was simply a question of offsetting domestic land exhaustion through the acquisition of new territories. Thus professor John W. Burgess of Columbia argued in 1890 that a few thousand savages in the Polynesian Islands had no right to reserve for themselves lands capable of sustaining millions of civilized men.[32] Similar arguments were voiced in a number of leading journals. The fertile lands of Cuba and the Hawaiian Islands were particularly enticing targets. Their agricultural potential, it was argued, necessitated their acquisition by the land-hungry United States.[33]

The factor of the closed frontier also emerged in senate debates over a naval appropriations bill in 1895. Lauding the merits of the bill, Delaware Senator Anthony Higgins declared, "we have already arrived at the end practically of our land for homesteads. . . . 'Uncle Sam' is no longer rich enough to give us all a farm." The youth of America would have to seek fortunes in other fields besides agriculture, particularly manufacturing and commerce, and the nation would develop a growing interest in and dependence on foreign commerce; thus it would take a strengthened navy to secure the nation's future.[34] Senator Orville Platt of Connecticut restated the case in more emphatic terms. "Vast and boundless as our possessions are, they are occupied," he declared.

> From the Atlantic to the Pacific we have dotted all our land with villages and towns and cities. We are reclaiming the desert. . . . Our activity at home is unparalleled, but something else is needed. The opportunity for the adventurous spirit of our citizens to have free course is being limited as we are settling up our lands, and it is to the ocean that our children must look, as they have looked to the boundless West, for the opportunity to develop their ambition and their talents.[35]

But the closed frontier arguments for expanding the navy paled in comparison with the expansionist arguments of the back seat admiral and popular prophet of imperialism Alfred Thayer Mahan. Mahan applied the doctrine of "closed space" to the world as a whole, but his main interest was in the implications of that doctrine for the United States. Writing in *Harper's Magazine* in 1895, he declared that "more and more civilized man is needing and seeking ground to occupy, room over which to expand and in which to live." Displaying the common Anglo-Saxon superiority complex blended with Social Darwinism, Mahan added that "like all natural forces, the [expansionist] impulse takes the direction of least resistance, but when in its course it comes upon some region rich in possibilities, but unfruitful through the incapacity or negligence of those who dwell therein, the incompetent race or system will go down, as the inferior race has ever fallen back and disappeared before the persistent impact of the superior."[36] Such had been the case, he said, with the United States' own dealings with the American Indian. "There is," he said, "no inalienable right . . . to control the use of a region when it is done so to the detriment of the world at large . . . the redundant energies of civilized states, both government and peoples, are finding lack of openings and scantiness of livelihood at home, that there now obtains a condition of aggressive restlessness."[37]

Mahan noted that the United States did not yet share this tendency of civilized states toward expansion, although it ought to. "The force of circumstances," he said, "had imposed upon her the necessity [of doing so]."[38] A policy of isolation was no longer practical now that the continent's resources had been developed. The United States would have to join in the colonization of the uncivilized portions of the world—and of course would need a bigger and better navy to do so.[39]

Mahan reiterated his argument in *Harper's* a few years later. He declared that civilized man's energies had, during the nineteenth century, been devoted "to the development of the resources of each country. . . . Everywhere there was a fresh field. . . . Energies everywhere turned inward, for there, in every region, was more than enough to do." Consequently, he determined, there had been relative peace in this century. But "all such phases pass," he concluded, and America would now have to adopt an expansive, twentieth-century outlook in order to prosper.[40]

The notion that overseas expansion was necessary in the postfrontier age elicited strong responses from those who opposed such a course of action. Just as some writers had argued in favor of unrestricted immigration of the ground that there was "incalculable room" in America for newcomers, so some anti-expansionists held that the nation's energies ought to remain focused on internal development. James Bryce argued in the *Forum* late in 1897, as war fever rose, that it would be wrongheaded for the United States to gain Pacific colonies. He stated that the nation still possessed "an enormous territory of unequaled natural resources . . . capable of easily supporting much more than twice its present population. . . . Thus the United States needs no transmarine domain in which to expand."[41]

The next June, as the nation pondered the question of what to do with the fruits of the recently won war, an editorial in Lyman Abbott's *Outlook* argued that there was no need for expansion because, unlike Europe, the United States was underpopulated. "America," the author of the piece stated, "has surplus acreage, and needs new peoples to develop its undeveloped resources. The seventy million people of the United States are totally inadequate to fell its forests, cultivate its fields, open up its manifold wealth, utilize its untold natural resources."[42]

Other writers in the nineties, while opposed to American expansion, agreed that this policy had evolved quite naturally out of the nation's past. As early as 1893 an American socialist, William D. McCracken, argued that the United States was initiating an undesirable foreign policy that had resulted in large part from the fact that the country's natural opportunities were already preempted. "The supply of desirable free land is exhausted," he said, "and that of cheap land so far reduced, that it can already be manipulated by monopolizing or speculating agencies." In McCracken's reckoning, the United States was beginning to follow a policy that was a natural outgrowth of capitalism. Opportunities at home had been fully monopolized, so the search for new ones would naturally take place abroad. McCracken, however, was not greatly worried because the various proletarian elements in the world were bound to realize their common interest and tear down the whole capitalist system anyway.[43]

In 1898 a British professor at Cambridge University, William F. Reddaway, expressed strong concern over the expansionist tendencies of the United States, mainly because he perceived a threat to British colonies. Reddaway, too, attributed this new course of action to the loss of the frontier. "Hitherto," he wrote, "the internal development of the Union has been favored by the existence of relatively inexhaustible supplies of land. With fertile territories crying out for settlement, a foreign policy has been superfluous."[44]

Since the early 1880s William Graham Sumner had been exploring the role of free land in shaping social and political institutions,[45] but his first substantial offering on the topic, his article "Earth Hunger," did not appear until 1896.[46] By this time Sumner was a widely read essayist and professor of law at Yale, and a notoriously harsh exponent of Social Darwinism. But while many Social Darwinists used this philosophy to justify American expansionism, arguing that the fittest, most highly developed races would naturally conquer the weaker ones, Sumner was vehemently opposed to imperialistic ventures.[47] His opposition was partly grounded in his observations on America's favorable land-to-man ratio.

In "Earth Hunger," Sumner argued that the ratio of population to land determined the possibilities and limitations of human development. He applied his thesis to the world as a whole, but the bulk of his attention centered on the development of the United States, where an abundance of land and relative sparsity of population had helped ensure the existence of democratic institutions. Americans, he said, had experienced particularly favorable social and economic conditions. More land meant a higher standard of living for the laboring classes, who were few enough in number to demand as much in wages as they could earn themselves farming their own land. Furthermore, Sumner added, in such a situation "each man has plenty of the 'rights of man' because he need only 'be' to be a valuable member of society." Sumner noted that Americans understood all this and that their march across the continent bore out their understanding. Their desire for more land and the ensuing economic and social benefits—their "economic earth hunger"—was only natural.[48]

Economic earth hunger, Sumner said, was inevitable, unavoidable, even commendable; if uncivilized peoples tried to stand in its way, they would perish. Philanthropy might delay their fate, but it could not avert "the forces which carry us all along like a whirlwind." But "political earth hunger"—"the appetite of states for territorial extension as a gratification of national vanity"—was another thing entirely. This course of action, this chasing "of all the old baubles of glory, and vanity, and passion," would, Sumner said, destroy democracy.[49]

Sumner's distinctions between economic earth hunger and political earth hunger were, at times, a little hazy. He justified the expansion across the continent, including the acquisition of Mexican territory, on the grounds that it had resulted from economic earth hunger along with the occasional manifestation of a less reprehensible form of political earth hunger. But when it came to those territories that American imperialists were eyeing in the nineties, he perceived a particularly dangerous brand of political earth hunger at work. Despite the occasional lack of theoretical clarity in his arguments, Sumner was adamantly critical of the recent designs on Canada, Mexico, Cuba, and Hawaii. He saw absolutely no need for such acquisitions. "The United States," he ventured, still enjoyed "a privileged position such as no other community of men ever has occupied in the world's history." Its earth hunger was satisfied for the present, because the propertyless classes could still, under a relatively favorable land-to-man ratio, live in comfort and acquire property.[50]

Sumner repeated his argument soon after the United States had won its war in 1898 in his sarcastically titled essay, "The Conquest of the United States by Spain."[51] This time Sumner's reasoning was crystal clear. He chided the American people for believing that their freedom and enlightenment were the result of a conscious choice and attacked the popular notion that the nation's prosperity proved its exceptionalism. These assumptions would in time "meet with harsh correction," Sumner said, because the United States was in a protected situation: "It is easy to have prosperity where a few men have a great continent to exploit."[52] Democracy needed no defense in this situation, because it was rooted and founded in economic circumstances, but this protected position would pass away as the continent filled up and the struggle for existence became more acute. And the one course that would hasten the disappearance of those advantages was imperialism. Sumner posited that victory over "a poor, decrepit, bankrupt old state like Spain" was no cause for an outburst of patriotic and, still worse, imperialistic urges. "Expansion and imperialism are a grand onslaught on democracy," he said, because they hasten the advent of plutocracy, thus bringing about circumstances that "make the weak weaker and the strong stronger."[53]

Those who, like Sumner, opposed further expansion were in the minority. However, their arguments suggest that the closed-frontier leitmotif was an integral part of the debate over expansion. The issue of whether to retain the Philippines prompted Senator Albert J. Beveridge of Indiana to advance his views on the matter. In a speech entitled "The March of the Flag," which marked the opening of the Indiana Republican campaign in September 1898, Beveridge combined his thoughts on America's divine mission to civilize inferior races with the argument that expansion had always been a staple activity of the American people.[54] The nation's history, Beveridge said, had been one of "statesmen who flung the boundaries of the Republic out into unexplored lands and savage wilderness; a history of soldiers who carried the flag across blazing deserts and through the ranks of hostile mountains; even to the gates of sunset; a history of a multiplying people who overran a continent in half a century." And Beveridge's argument that expansion had, from the birth of the Republic, been the conscious design of American statesmen and should continue to be so was voiced repeatedly by others as the decade wore on.[55]

Of all the Anglo-Saxon nations, Beveridge contended in his next speech on the Philippine question, the American people had been chosen by God to "lead in the regeneration of the world." And the fact that America's expansion overseas had come hot on the heels of the consolidation of the continent seemed to him an obvious sign of divine intent.[56] If the United States retained the Philippines, it would be fulfilling its divinely ordained responsibilities. But if that was not enough to convince the skeptic, Beveridge added a more utilitarian argument, too. In the face of land exhaustion at home, the Philippines—Beveridge called them the "garden of the seas"—would prove a useful landed resource.[57] And so, too, according to Beveridge, would Cuba with its "15,000,000 acres of forest unacquainted with the axe." These lands, he argued, had to be saved for "liberty and civilization," and their availability was timely for Americans in light of their own closed frontier.[58]

Among those intellectuals who formulated frontier-based arguments for expansion, Brooks Adams came closest to establishing a direct link between the closing of the continental frontier and the need for overseas markets. Turner had touched on this topic, but stopped short of actually advocating expansion.[59] Adams, on the other hand, directly endorsed a policy of commercial expansion. His ambitious work *The Law of Civilization and Decay* (1895) argued that the center of world trade had followed a westward movement from the ancient crossroads in the East to Constantinople, Venice, Amsterdam, and finally London.[60] This movement unfolded in accord with laws relating to the density of industrial and commercial operation. A few months after the victory over Spain, his essay on "The Spanish War and the Equilibrium of the World" appeared in *Forum*. Adams argued that the recent war was an indication of the acute intensification of commercial competition. The prize at stake in this war, and the wars that were bound to follow, was the seat of commercial exchanges—"the seat of empire." The social center of civilization, Adams contended, had been advancing steadily westward for more than a thousand years. If Americans could now develop and increase their commercial activities overseas—west of the Pacific continental boundary—then their country would become the center of world trade and commerce. Adams's point to Americans was that if they wanted the fruits of world commerce, they would have to expand beyond their own frontier. Failure to do so would prove catastrophic because "the civilization which does not advance declines; the continent which, when Washington lived, gave a boundless field for the expansion of Americans has been filled."[61]

Adams elaborated on this theme in his next essay, "The New Struggle for Life among Nations" (1899). He declared that civilization had always advanced by two processes—the individual and the collective. The eastern races had tended toward collective systems, the western toward individualistic ones. The Anglo-Saxon was the most individual of all races and had reached this high fortune under conditions that fostered individualism to a supreme degree. These conditions had prevailed when the world was vacant, but now that population was becoming denser, the qualities of the pioneer would cease to command success and collectivist systems would prevail. Thus America, in its pioneering period, had been intensely individualistic and, luckily, had not remained a self-contained country. Expansion beyond her continental boundaries had averted the onset of collectivism, but now that the nation had launched itself on that expansionist course, there could be no turning back. Any cessation of economic expansion would facilitate the arrival of collectivism. Individualism might disappear with the amalgamation of gigantic trusts. The government would either be absorbed by these trusts or absorb them itself. The only competition between eastern and western races "would be for the most perfect system of state socialism."[62]

Adams had formulated a very effective justification for expansionism. Although he had fitted the closing of the continental frontier into a world context, he appealed to core American values that had, supposedly, developed out of a pioneering past. Theodore Roosevelt adopted an approach similar to Adams's, although, as with most writers on the topic (Turner and Wilson are examples), his "frontier" was peculiarly American. Roosevelt's most famous work, *The Winning of the West*, was in effect a study of American imperialism and its march across the continental mainland.[63] That expansion over the internal frontier had, Roosevelt asserted, fostered the "Pioneer Spirit" and produced a "rugged and stalwart democracy." The frontier experience, he declared, had cultivated a "vigorous manliness for the lack of which in a nation, as in an individual, the possession of no other qualities can possibly atone."[64]

Roosevelt was no stranger to the "outdoor life." He thought of himself as a "wilderness hunter" of sorts and was greatly alarmed that "his breed" seemed to be dying out as the untamed West disappeared. To Roosevelt these hardly, self-reliant qualities of the outdoorsmen were vital to the national health, and beginning around 1895, he began to display great uneasiness about the state of the American character.[65] In the absence of pioneer qualities, the American people were in danger of becoming soft. "Unless we keep the barbarian virtues," he said, "gaining the civilized ones will be of little avail."[66]

Finding ways to counteract the dangerous deterioration of manliness that accompanied the transition from a pioneering country to a developed one was of paramount importance to Roosevelt. His book of *Hero Tales from American History*, coauthored with Henry Cabot Lodge, was an attempt to provide the next generation with suitable role models. But role models were not enough in Roosevelt's estimation; action, too, was required. And what better action to regenerate frontier virtues than a war? Thus Roosevelt wrote in 1897, "In strict confidence . . . I should welcome almost any war, for I think this country needs one."[67] William James later protested: "He [Roosevelt] gushes over war as the ideal condition of human society, for the manly strenuousness which it involves, and treats peace as a condition of blubberlike and swollen ignobility, fit only for huckstering weaklings."[68]

James was right, of course, but Roosevelt got his war anyway, and he led his own regiment of "Rough Riders" in the famous charge up San Juan Hill (actually Kettle Hill) to help win it. Then, when the war was over, Roosevelt deified the Rough Riders in print. Their success, he said, stemmed from the fact that their pioneer virtues were still intact. They had come from the four territories that still remained within the boundaries of the United States, "from the lands that have been most recently won over to white civilization, and in which the conditions of life are nearest those that obtained on the frontier when there still was a frontier." They were, he went on, men who had "left their lonely hunter's cabins . . . to seek new and more stirring adventures beyond the sea."[69] Speaking before Chicago's Hamilton Club in April 1899, Roosevelt urged all Americans to take heed of the Rough Riders' example, to lead lives of "strenuous endeavor," and not shirk the responsibilities of empire:

> The timid man, the lazy man . . . the overcivilized man, who has lost his great fighting, masterful virtues . . . whose soul is incapable of feeling the mighty lift that thrills 'stern men with empires in the brains'—all these, of course shrink from seeing the nation undertake its new duties. . . . These are the men who fear the strenuous life, who fear the only national life which is really worth leading.[70]

By 1900 the United States had acquired an empire which stretched from the Caribbean to the Orient, much to Roosevelt's satisfaction. The impetus to expansion had come from many sources. Social Darwinism had played a part, justifying the conquering of supposedly inferior races by a higher civilization. Religious missionaries, too, had played a part, popularizing the notion of an American mission to Christianize the world. Economic factors also influenced the policymakers of the late nineties; foreign markets were vital to a country whose output greatly exceeded domestic demand. And, even as the country produced more than it could consume, Malthusian-minded thinkers worried that the day was at hand when the country would be unable to feed itself. The social and intellectual malaise of the nineties also helped create an environment conducive to expansionist designs. The arguments for America's *fin de siècle* expansion were many and varied. The consciousness (whether false or otherwise) that America no longer had a frontier emerged in many of them. Social Darwinists such as Beveridge,

Christian missionaries such as Strong, and economic expansionists such as Brooks Adams all displayed an uneasiness over the loss of the frontier. To many, that loss seemed to underlie the whole complex of doubts evident in the late nineteenth century.

PART THREE.
"POSTFRONTIER ANXIETY"

Undoubtedly the vast areas of cheap and fertile land which have been continuously available for settlement have contributed, not only to the abundance of American prosperity, but also to the formation of American character and institutions: and undoubtedly many of the economic and political evils which are becoming offensively obtrusive are directly or indirectly derived from the gradual monopolization of certain important economic opportunities.

—Herbert Croly, editor, progressive theorist, 1909

Whenever the light of civilization falls upon you with a blighting power, and work and pleasure become stale and flat, go to the wilderness. The wilderness will take hold of you. It will give you good red blood; it will turn you from a weakling into a man. . . . When your pack train leaves the dusty road and 'hits the trail,' you will acquire new courage to live your life. You will get new strength.

—George S. Evans, California trail rider, 1904

6. THE FADING FRONTIER

As the new century dawned, the prevalent tone seemed to be one of confidence. The nation had conquered its internal frontier and had ventured
outward to extend the boundaries of the republic. Early in 1901, Woodrow
Wilson, addressing the problem of what to do with the country's newly acquired territories, emphasized the closed frontier. The country had for
nearly three hundred years followed a single law, he said, "the law of expansion into new territory." And although the nation's continued expansion
into noncontiguous territory might be something of a departure from its traditional frontiering, the ideals and principles that had been worked out in
the course of that process would ensure the satisfactory resolution of any
problems that might arise.[1] Later that year Wilson seemed more assured that
the nation's extracontinental expansion was in keeping with its original
democratic purpose. He remarked that crossing the seven thousand miles
that separated the Philippine Islands from the Pacific coast was not an aber-
ration for the nation, but a simple addition to the three thousand miles that
its frontier had travelled across the continent. Wilson was not by any means
justifying the recent annexation of the Philippines, but simply lauding the
spread of democratic ideals beyond the nation's continental boundaries.
The future president's outlook was bright as his "Missionary Diplomacy"
began to take shape.[2]

Wilson's frontier-related rationale for extracontinental expansion was
echoed by President Theodore Roosevelt in an address at St. Louis in May
1903. Roosevelt emphasized the benign nature of the westward march across
the continent. Although he did not make specific reference to the Philippines, Roosevelt did stress that the nation had "never tried to force on any
section of [its] new territory an unsuitable form of government."[3]

There were those who doubted the wisdom of Roosevelt and Wilson,

71

though. Commenting on Roosevelt's speech, the *Nation* countered that the acquisition of the Philippines "was a violent break with all our best American traditions . . . [and] wholly out of line with our historic expansion."[4] A few years earlier an article in the *Arena* took an eminently practical approach to the Philippine question, arguing that the monies invested in this overseas venture would have brought better returns if invested in reclamation projects in the semiarid West. What rationale could there be for overseas expansion, the article asked, if hundreds of millions of acres awaited reclamation in California, Arizona, Wyoming, and other semiarid states. Why extend the frontier beyond the continental boundaries when there were still frontiers within to be conquered?[5] This sentiment was voiced again by Benjamin O. Flower, the *Arena*'s editor, in May 1901. Drawing on the findings of William E. Smythe, the nation's leading advocate of reclamation, Flower concluded that "vast . . . virgin fields" were salvageable and that government money would be better invested in that venture than in subduing islands thousands of miles away.[6]

The argument raged back and forth in the early years of the century. The debate featured few expressions of genuine "frontier anxiety," but often featured frontier-related arguments. Despite the objections of the anti-expansionists, their adversaries held sway. Coming to terms with the nation's entry upon the world stage did not prove too difficult; the majority sentiment was highly optimistic. The old frontier may have been lost, but a new age had seemingly begun.[7] The nation, as Theodore Roosevelt was fond of reminding his countrymen at the beginning of the new century, stood on the threshold of great and glorious times and had only to "rise to the greatness of its opportunities."[8] The inaugural editorial in *World's Work*, founded in November 1900, exemplified this mood of confidence: "It is with the activities of the newly organized world, its problems and even its romance—that this magazine will concern itself . . . the keynote [of American life] at the century's end is the note of joyful achievement; and its faith is an evangelical faith in democracy that broadens as far as social growth invites. The republic has been extended, held together, again extended, and it is still the house of refuge and the beacon of civilization."[9]

Another magazine, the *Independent*, ventured a similar sentiment, commenting that the frontier had gone, and with its passing a certain picturesqueness had disappeared from American life. And, the publication went on, "the frontier will not return. A glimpse of it may be caught here and there on the plateaus of Arizona and New Mexico, but even there the new conditions are being established." But reminiscences ought not to be tainted with sadness because, it was confidently concluded, "a new era has begun."[10] The novelist Frank Norris reached a similar conclusion in an article in *World's Work* in February 1902, "The Frontier Gone at Last."[11] Norris, subscribing to the popular notion of racial determinism, traced the westward march of the Anglo-Saxon race around the globe. The march of this world frontier, Norris ventured, seemed to have ended at the Pacific continental boundary, but a gun blast on the first of May 1898, in the Bay of Manila, signaled the frontier's advance across the Pacific. The natural end of the frontier was finally reached, Norris said, when American marines arrived in China in the summer of 1900 to intervene in the Boxer Rebellion. "[T]he Anglo-Saxon in his course of Empire had circled the globe and brought the new civilization to the old civilization, had reached the starting point of history."[12] But, Norris asked rhetorically, with the frontier now finally gone, with all wildernesses conquered, what would absorb the "surplus" and "resistless" energy of the race? Luckily, there was a force powerful enough to make wars of conquest unnecessary and obsolete—Trade. Norris drew a few peculiar analogies as he developed this point:

> The desire for conquest . . . was as big in the breast of the most fervid of the crusaders as it is this very day in the most peacefully disposed of American manufacturers. Had the Lion-Hearted Richard lived today he would have become a 'leading representative of the Amalgamated Steel Companies'. . . . Had Mr. Andrew Carnegie been alive at the time of the preachings of Peter the Hermit he would have . . . been first on the ground before Jerusalem.[13]

"Eastward the course of commerce takes its way," Norris added, but war and divisiveness need not accompany it. Though parallels might be drawn between the captains of industry of the twentieth century and the captains of armies in ages past, the postfrontier age of commerce had the potential to ignite a "new patriotism," one that would "include all peoples." Norris concluded confidently that with the frontier gone at last, "Americans, supreme in conquest, whether of battleship or of bridge-building," might well come to realize "that the true patriotism is the brotherhood of man." He added that "The whole world" might become "our nation and simple humanity our countrymen."[14]

While there was an undercurrent of opposition to the confident outlook on expansionism espoused by Roosevelt, Wilson, and a host of others, there also existed an undercurrent in American thought that ran counter to the postfrontier optimism of commentators such as Frank Norris. Some observers saw evidence that the deleterious effects of a closed frontier were finally being realized in America. In its opening issue of the new century the *Arena* featured a symposium on "The Trust Question." The opening article began with a statement that "for the first time in our history, the American people as a mass is awakening to questions that elsewhere in the world are as old as greed." The article went on to claim that "the same misery that wearies life under the despotisms of Europe is being fastened upon us." The reason for this unhappy turn of events was that the country had at last passed out of the fortunate state that had accompanied the existence of its wide, unsettled domain. America had been blinded, the article went on, by its fallacious belief that free institutions were the fundamental basis of its happy state. Confident in the transforming power of its institutions, America had invited the crowded populations of Europe to take advantage of its lands, but in doing so the nation had squandered the very foundation of its democracy—the vast public domain. Now the country had millions of men working at starvation wages and millions more not working at all. The diseases that had long afflicted Europe were now rampant in America; "the hideous red hand of anarchy" had been raised in the New World. And "the Trusts," the article went on, "are a natural outgrowth of the diseased conditions," the unavoidable consequence of a fully settled domain.[15]

The economist and political scientist Richard T. Ely, Frederick Jackson Turner's friend and colleague at the University of Wisconsin, discussed the topic of the country's new problems in the postfrontier age in his 1903 work, *Studies in the Evolution of Industrial Society*. Ely argued that America had managed to offset the harmful side effects of rapid industrialization because of its "great body of unoccupied land," but the nation's supply of free land had all but disappeared. Now the country would have to find a new way to deal with those who were dissatisfied. In the absence of the frontier, the potential problems of the future had become the actual realities of the present. New economic and governmental directives were now needed to replace the frontier.[16] Ely concentrated more on explaining how current realities had come about than on how their concomitant problems might be resolved, but there were others who offered solutions as well as explanations.

For the reclamation enthusiast William E. Smythe, the solution to the nation's problems was cooperation. In his 1905 work, *Constructive Democracy: The Economics of the Square Deal*, Smythe stressed unequivocally that virgin land was the key to the nation's health and well-being. Smythe felt that the needs of the "surplus man" could still be met by the resources of the continent so long as the government turned its attention to the irrigation of the semiarid western plains. But for his irrigation scheme to be a success, the country would have to realize the benefits of cooperation. "Cooperation is the watchword of this new century," he wrote. "The extent of cooperation among human beings is the measure of their civilization. 'Thou shalt cooperate!' is the legend written on the face of the desert in terms of imperious command. Mankind must accept it, or the closed gates will never open; and mankind must keep faith with it, or disappear from the land."[17] The time had passed, Smythe added, when the common man could create opportunities for himself, or when private capital could ensure the creation of opportunity. The new age would have to be one of "constructive statesmanship" centered around the principle of cooperation. To ensure the successful settlement of the semiarid lands, the government would have to fund irrigation projects and provide loans to individuals, and individuals would have to cooperate amongst themselves rather than compete for personal gains.[18] Smythe's central argument was echoed by Algie M. Simons, editor of the *International Socialist Review*, in his book *The American Farmer* (1902). Regarding the task of "conserving and controlling and subjecting to the will of man the waterfall of half a continent," Simons charged, "it will at once be apparent that nothing is adequate to this task but the co-operative energies of the whole nation."[19]

Smythe's book touched on a number of other issues related to the land issue. On the topic of extracontinental expansion, he echoed the thinking of Benjamin O. Flower, commenting wryly that "it is better business to dig ditches in the West than to dig graves in the Philippine Islands."[20] On the issue of immigration, Smythe believed that once the West was irrigated, its resources would be sufficient to meet the needs of all immigrants who came in good faith. But in Smythe's estimation, "Asiatic elements" did not fit into this category. The Chinese, he said, were unassimilable because, unlike the Europeans, they were in America only for the purpose of sharing in its wealth and sending the proceeds back to their native land.[21] Smythe was not alone in his anti-Asiatic stance,[22] but it was clear that the argument against Chinese immigration, which led to exclusionary laws in 1888, 1892, and again in 1902, had little to do with anxiety over the loss of the frontier and much to do with simple racist inclinations.[23]

Yet there were, in the early years of the century, those who linked the immigration question to the frontier. One writer in the *Atlantic Monthly*, in October 1900, reasoned that the loss of the frontier marked the end of an era in the nation's economic history, and that immigration would now become a major problem, but offered no tangible solutions to the dilemma.[24] Edward Alsworth Ross, a renowned social scientist and ardent "Nordicist," elaborated on this theme in his first major work, Social Control (1901). Ross explained how the "pitiless sifting" of conquering the West had shaped the American character and made the powerful Nordic stock even more hardy and virile. But with the untamed West gone, the nation was destined to become more settled, more urbanized, and, by consequence, more decadent. The great Nordic race was destined for moral and physical softness. The Anglo-Saxon homogeneity of rural, protestant America was being diluted by the inferior immigrant strains from southern and eastern Europe. The implication of Ross's observations was clear—block the streams that were diluting the Nordic stock and its purity and greatness would be preserved.[25]

Ross was apparently unaware of the writings of Frederick Jackson Turner when he wrote Social Control, although by 1902 he had read Turner's 1893 essay.[26] Ross would have found much food for thought in Turner's newspaper contributions at the beginning of the new century. Turner was at a loss for constructive solutions to the problem of immigration, but certainly not averse to commenting on the nature and acuteness of the dilemma as he envisioned it. Writing in the Chicago Herald Tribune in September 1901, Turner focused on the difficulty of assimilating "non-English stock" now that the "free lands . . . are gone." But restrictive legislation was a difficult course to take, Turner added, in the light of "American respect for the New World as a refuge for the oppressed."[27] A year later the paper published another article by Turner on the topic of "Jewish Immigration." Turner's piece was, for the most part, a fair and balanced account, but it concluded with the assertion that "Russian and Polish Jews . . . Italians, Slovaks . . . and other immigrants of Eastern Europe" were particularly unassimilable elements that "have made New York City a great reservoir for the pipe lines that run to the misery pools of Europe."[28] Turner, like others in the period, was too liberal-minded to propose restrictive legislation as an answer to the problem. The Progressive theorist Walter Weyl, for example, also pointed to the changing origin of the immigrants and to the difficulty of assimilating them without a frontier. Weyl stated quite clearly that the time had passed when unrestricted immigration could be beneficial to the country, yet could not bring himself to openly advocate restrictive measures.[29] But such proposals were heard on occasion during the first decade or so of the century.[30]

Once in a while, arguments in favor of a more restrictive approach to immigration included lengthy analyses of the changing land-to-man ratio in the United States. A prime example is sociologist Henry Pratt Fairchild's article "Some Immigration Differences," which appeared in the *Yale Review* in 1910. At the root of Fairchild's argument was the notion that the safety valve was no longer operative. Surplus inhabitants could no longer move to thinly settled regions, so they piled into the cities. Fairchild's argument was facile in many ways, to say the least, but it is worth pointing out that he touched on many of the issues that would become integral to the heated debate among historians a generation later over the operation of the safety valve.[31] Edward Alsworth Ross reiterated his major argument in the *Century* a few years later. Ross charged that the absence of two variables freed the United States from any ethical obligations to an unrestrictive immigration policy. Those variables were "oppression," which he said, "is now out of fashion over most of Europe," and the "public lands," which, he reminded his readers, were gone. But there was of course another factor at the forefront of Ross's thinking. He complained that "Europe retains most of her brains, but sends multitudes of the common and the sub-common." Like other Nordic supremecists who began writing in this period, Ross expressed fear over the injection of "sub-common" blood into the veins of the American nation.[32]

It is also worth mentioning that there were occasional calls against immigration restriction on the grounds that the country was still far from fully settled,[33] but such arguments were much rarer in the postfrontier period of the early twentieth century than they had been in the late nineteenth century. The surprising thing, perhaps, is that comparatively few calls for immigration restriction were heard in the early years of the twentieth century. An immigration bill would pass Congress in 1915, but President Wilson, partly for humanitarian reasons and partly out of political expediency would veto it. Although restrictive legislation would be enacted at the beginning of the 1920s, the Progressive era witnessed a relative decline in nativism. Perhaps, as one notable historian has suggested, the clamor abated "partly because the spirit of Progressivism was too rooted in humanitarianism to embrace such nativistic sentiments."[34]

The writings of Frederick Jackson Turner in the early part of the twentieth century seem to parallel a more general shift away from the confident mood that characterized the century's opening to one that became more cognizant of the nation's growing problems as the decade wore on. In December 1901, writing in the *International Monthly*, Turner announced confidently that "democratic aspirations remain[ed]," indeed were held "with passionate determinism," in spite of the loss of the frontier. The country's heartland—the Middle West—had the potential to "reconcile popular government and culture with the huge industrial society of the modern world."[35] Two years later Turner elaborated on the theme of the lost frontier in an article for the *Atlantic Monthly*, "Contributions of the West to American Democracy." He pointed to the concentration of capital and labor and to the emergence of socialist proclivities in American political life; both trends had developed contemporaneously with the recession of the frontier. Echoing the thinking of William E. Smythe, Turner stated that the old, individualistic pioneer methods were becoming redundant, and that the remaining western lands demanded cooperative activity for successful settlement. With the free lands gone, Turner concluded rather ambiguously, the nation would have to turn to "the realm of the spirit, to the domain of ideals and legislation" for the preservation of democracy. Turner's confidence had become a little jaded, his optimism less assured.[36]

By the beginning of the next decade Turner's optimism was even less apparent. In a commencement address at Indiana University in 1910 entitled "Pioneer Ideals and the State University," Turner concentrated more fully on the developing problems in postfrontier America—the process of industrial consolidation and the growth of class antagonism. The solution he offered to these problems—centering around the capacity of the state universities to sustain pioneer ideals of democracy—almost certainly reflected the speech's setting rather than Turner's conviction.[37] Later that year, in his presidential address to the American Historical Association, Turner reflected again on the disappearance of the old "pioneer individualism" and the growing manifestation of "the forces of social combination." Hitting on the theme that would become central to the rhetoric of the New Deal a generation later, Turner expressed the hope that the forces of government would replace the landed frontier and become the new guarantor of American democracy.[38]

In his articles and addresses during this period, Turner wrestled with the problem of how to offset the loss of the frontier and arrived at a variety of solutions, none of which proved satisfactory to him.[39] For the rest of his life Turner agonized over this dilemma, but in his private writings in the early twentieth century he devoted far more space to outlining the problems of the postfrontier age than to constructing solutions for them. The problems of corporate concentration, the "new immigration," socialism and syndicalism, class stratification, and the pressure of population on the means of subsistence were among Turner's greatest concerns. On a more general level, he worried that the American experience was beginning to approximate its European counterpart, and that there was a general decline in optimism in the newly frontierless nation.[40] Similar observations were being made by other thinkers in the early part of the century as they sought to account for the origins of the problems that the Progressive movement would address.

Herbert Croly, who at least indirectly influenced Theodore Roosevelt's "New Nationalism" platform and later cofounded the New Republic, was responsible for perhaps the most influential sociopolitical treatise of the Progressive era. His book The Promise of American Life (1909) provided both a searching analysis of the American condition in the early twentieth century and a constructive program for the resolution of the nation's problems. The natural circumstances of American life, Croly argued in a vein similar to Turner's, had enabled the nation to avoid for many years the complex social problems that plagued Europe. The "virgin wilderness," he explained, had played a significant role in encouraging an "easy, generous, and irresponsible optimism." "The land," Croly stated (without due deference to its indigenous inhabitants), "was unoccupied, and its settlement offered an unprecedented area and abundance of economic opportunity. . . . The vast areas of cheap and fertile land have contributed, not only to the abundance of American prosperity, but also to the formation of American character and institutions." But concurrent with the passing of the frontier came the "monopolization of certain important economic opportunities." And "many of the economic and political evils" that were becoming "offensively obtrusive" were, in Croly's estimation, the result of this growth of monopoly in the postfrontier age.[41]

Americans had been able "to slide down into the valley of fulfillment," Croly said. Getting ahead had been relatively easy; understandably, the national mood had been one of supreme confidence. Croly quoted James Muirhead, an English observer of American life, who in 1893 pointed to America's "childlike confidence in human ability and fearlessness of both the present and the future." Accompanying this general mood of confidence, Muirhead noted in much the same vein as Turner and many others, had been a heavy emphasis on the individual. But for Croly there were deleterious side effects of all of this. "The automatic fulfillment of the American national Promise is to be abandoned, if at all, precisely because the traditional American confidence in individual freedom has resulted in a morally and socially undesirable distribution of wealth." The frontier age, then, though seemingly beneficent, had by its very nature fostered certain harmful qualities that were magnified by the new realities of postfrontier America. Now, in the absence of the country's natural advantages, the supremacy of the individual would have to be subordinated to the "demand of a dominant and constructive national purpose" if the promise of American life were to be realized.[42]

A year after the publication of Croly's book, Theodore Roosevelt, writing in the *Outlook*, addressed the problems of postfrontier America. Roosevelt's article, "The Pioneer Spirit and American Problems," was in many ways typical of his approach. He praised "the pioneers that pushed the frontiers of civilization westward." The ranchmen, miners, cowpunchers, muleskinners, and bull-whackers, as usual, received honorable mention. But Roosevelt acknowledged, too, that the pioneer days were largely over, and that the more complex life of the new era required "a greater variety of good qualities than were needed on the frontier." Life, he argued, would have to become more social, and the "general welfare" would have to become the preeminent concern of the new age. While still lauding the patently individualistic pioneer virtues, Roosevelt hinted that they needed to be curbed whenever they became inconsistent with the public welfare. Roosevelt stopped far short of condemning the individualistic urges of the frontier age and even ventured that the "pioneer spirit" was essential to the nation's continued growth in the twentieth century. But he did acknowledge that unbridled individualism was incompatible with the realities of a more complex postfrontier America.[43]

The sociologist Robert Tudor Hill, in his book *The Public Domain and Democracy* (1910), addressed more fully the issue that Roosevelt had skirted. The nation, Hill argued, had entered a new age in which "enterprise is largely collective and co-operative, and should be directed toward the larger benefit of communities." The problem, Hill added, was that "those individualistic elements so strongly encouraged during the past decades of national development" still persisted. "How much expression of individual liberty can be allowed," Hill asked, "and general social welfare be preserved?" The nation was faced with a serious dilemma—how to secure the wider social welfare when the country's citizens were still acting upon the private impulses that had suited the needs of an earlier, less complex age. Hill had no answer to the dilemma, but there were those who did.[44]

While Croly's magnum opus was receiving a good deal of attention in the years immediately following its publication, Walter Weyl was toiling arduously over his landmark work, *The New Democracy* (1912). Weyl's book, like Croly's, consisted of an analysis of the origins of the nation's problems coupled with a constructive plan for social democracy. Like Croly's book, Weyl's would become the object of Theodore Roosevelt's praise during the 1912 presidential campaign. And at Croly's request, Weyl would later assist in the founding of the *New Republic*. The two shared much, but Weyl's evaluation of the role played by the frontier in the nation's development was even more critical than Croly's. Croly had pointed to the false optimism and excessive individualism fostered by the open frontier, but stopped short of condemning the frontier experience outright. Weyl had absolutely nothing positive to say about the pioneer period (an aspect of his thinking that Roosevelt could not have found praiseworthy).

In *The New Democracy* he argued that the frontier experience had provided a catalyst for the predacious materialism integral to the American character. By accentuating the worst aspects of the national character, the frontier experience had prepared the way for plutocracy. The frontier age, in short, had been antithetical to the development of true democracy: "The subjugation of the continent from the Appalachians to the American Desert, and beyond, and the search for the wealth which was its embodiment, must set its stamp upon the acquisitive, imaginative, and starkly individualistic American; it must set its stamp upon the feeble, faltering, starkly individualistic state. The nation was compelled to develop along lines hostile to the highest political evolution."

The "open continent," Weyl went on, had "intoxicated the American," had given him "an enlarged view of self," and had "dwarfed the common spirit." It had also "created an individualism, self-confident, short-sighted, lawless, doomed in the end to defeat itself, as the boundless opportunities which gave it birth became circumscribed."[45]

Worse still, the whole process of settling the vast continent had, in Weyl's estimation, fostered a set of attitudes that stood as a barrier to reform in the postfrontier age: "To-day we cannot tear down a slum, regulate a corporation, or establish a national education system, we cannot attack either industrial oligarchy or political corruption, without coming into contact with the economic, political, and psychological after effects of the conquest [of the continent]." Rampant, unbridled, individualistic profit-seeking had led naturally to corporate consolidation, which facilitated the maximization of profit. The corporations had "secured themselves against the time when tens of millions of homeless men would press upon the no longer boundless, but strictly bounded, territory."[46]

Weyl also outlined some of the environmental consequences of the "rape" of the continent in The New Democracy. Because the task had been performed so zealously, so enthusiastically, Weyl was hardly surprised that the individualistic ethos that fueled the endeavor outlived the open frontier. It was fully logical to him that the frontier age was followed by the "monopoly age"—the era of plutocracy. Weyl was too realistic to have expected anything better, but he did express the hope that a new socialized democracy would supplant plutocracy. This new public-spirited democracy could temper the unchecked individualism of the frontier age and channel it towards positive social purposes. Weyl wanted a kind of national "socialization" similar to Croly's model and a far cry from outright socialism. Weyl's book was essentially optimistic, and in this it typified the spirit of Progressivism. The country, Weyl explained, was wealthy enough, and its middle class sizable enough, to guarantee the establishment of this new, thoroughgoing social democracy.

Not long before his death in 1919, Weyl's optimistic belief that a New Democracy could be realized within the existing socioeconomic structure— without violent upheaval—gave way to pessimism and disdain for "bourgeois reform movements"; Weyl decided to join the Socialist party. Jack London had taken that same step a decade and a half earlier. And in constructing his theories London, like Weyl, made much of the notion of the closing of the frontier.

Jack London is best remembered for his best-selling novel The Call of the Wild (1903), a product of his "primitivist/individualist" phase. But by the time it was published, London had already entered a new phase of his career in which he championed the socialist cause.[47] The inevitable clash between the classes was imminent in America, London argued late in 1903 in an article entitled "The Class Struggle," because conditions in the country had finally changed. The American frontier had served as a safety valve for the discontents of the working classes, ensuring social fluidity and consequently stunting the growth of class consciousness:

> The capitalist class and the working class have existed side by side for a long time in the United States; but hitherto all the strong, energetic members of the working class have been able to rise out of their class and

become owners of capital. They were enabled to do this because an undeveloped country with an expanding frontier gave equality of opportunity
to all. In the almost lottery-like scramble for the ownership of vast un-
owned natural resources, and in the exploitation of which there was little
or no competition of capital, the capable, intelligent member of the working class found a field in which to use brains to his own social advance-
ment.

"But," London continued, "the day of an expanding frontier . . . is past.
Farthest West has been reached. . . . The gateway of opportunity after opportunity has been closed, and closed for all time." The openness of the
frontier had been replaced by a stultifying claustrophobia:

> Rockerfeller has shut the door on oil, the American Tobacco Company
> on tobacco, and Carnegie on steel. After Carnegie came Morgan who
> triple-locked the door. These doors will not open again and before them
> pause thousands of ambitious young men to read the placard: NO THOR-
> OUGHFARE.
>
> And day by day more doors are shut, while the ambitious young men
> continue to be born.[48]

Jack London's sociological study of slum conditions in the East End of
London, *The People of the Abyss*, was published in the same month as "The
Class Struggle." The book, at least on one level, was an extended examination of a claustrophobic closed frontier society and its effects upon the inhabitants.[49] And in his essay "How I Became a Socialist" (1903), London explained how this claustrophobic reality of postfrontier America had
transformed him. "I was not looking for Socialism at the time of my conver-
sion, but I was fighting it. I was a rampant individualist, I was proud to be
one of nature's strong-armed noblemen."[50] Then a change of place triggered
a change of heart: "I fought my way from the open West [of yesteryear],
where men bucked big and the job hunted the man, to the congested labor
centers of the East, where men were small potatoes and hunted the job for
all they were worth."

Dropping down from the proletariat into the "submerged tenth"—the
"Social Pit"—London examined how his individualism had been hammered
out and socialism hammered in. It was not even a conscious transformation,
London said, simply the inevitable consequence of a changed environment.
He had not, he claimed, been influenced by propaganda, had not read so-

cialist works. He had simply been transformed without knowing it and had returned "to California and opened books . . . and discovered that [he] was a Socialist." He was nineteen years old at the time.[51]

London was even more absolute in his frontier thinking than Turner, who, though he had stated quite categorically in 1893 that the frontier had been the irreplaceable environmental wellspring and guarantor of democracy, despairingly sought after substitutes for the rest of his life. For London the matter was cut and dried—the frontier had provided the opportunities that had staved off class war for the first century or so of U.S. history, but in its absence that conflict was inevitable. There could be no solutions to the closed frontier within existing socioeconomic structures. There could be no social democracy of the kind proposed by Croly and Weyl. Only full-fledged socialism provided a workable answer. For the laboring classes, socialist thinking was the natural by-product of the closed frontier. Even Andrew Carnegie, the archetypal rags-to-riches capitalist of the day, "might have risen to be president of his union, or of a federation of unions . . . had he been born fifty years later."[52] The current climate, London contended, already contained all the ingredients of class struggle. The question now, he concluded, concerned only the outcome of that struggle.[53]

Another well-known socialist and sociologist of the period, Algie M. Simons, also stressed the closing of the frontier in relation to the need for a socialist state. In his book *Social Forces in American History* (1911) Simons noted that "this ever moving frontier has been the one distinctive feature of American society. . . . While the frontier existed . . . [t]he competition crushed, unemployed, or black-listed worker of capitalism moved west" to take advantage of the "greater opportunities for self-employment." With the frontier now gone, Simons went on, the United States was experiencing the polarization of classes that marked older societies. His hope was that a "democratically controlled government of the workers" would replace the frontier as the guarantor of opportunity.[54]

London's and Simons's socialist beliefs placed them outside the progressive mainstream, which was reformist rather than revolutionary in nature. Most thinkers who addressed the issue of the closed frontier did not arrive at the extreme remedies that they did, but in a sense their thinking was typical of a significant undercurrent of American social thought in the early twentieth century.

In the light of the perceived absence of the frontier, a whole range of social commentators began to assess the national condition. They fed off Turner no more than they fed off the writings of untold others who had addressed the same question. The nation's agrarian heritage—its garden mythology— had been an essential formative component of the frontier anxiety of the late nineteenth century. That frontier anxiety had in turn set the tone for assessments of the national condition in the postfrontier age. In the new century, regardless of whether the landed frontier was technically closed or not, a host of writers applied a "postfrontier perspective" to the national state. In their estimation, the frontier was no longer in the process of closing; it was quite categorically closed. Some, such as Weyl, might be relieved at this; while others, such as Turner, agonized over it. One writer in the *Atlantic Monthly* ventured the opinion that Progressive reform was an effort to adjust the country to the realities of the postfrontier age: "Pension systems and methods of welfare work are being developed which would have been resented by the individualists of frontier times. Instead of free lands, trade-schools and technical education are to afford our youth opportunities for getting a start in life."

The article in question, "The Influence of the Passing of the Public Lands," written by William J. Trimble, one of Turner's students, echoed the thinking of Walter Weyl (and incidentally foreshadowed much New Deal thinking). Trimble argued that the individualistic democracy of the public land era had to give way to the new "socialized democracy" of the postfrontier age.[55] Trimble's and Weyl's rejection of individualism was more complete than Turner's, and certainly more so than that of Theodore Roosevelt, who clung tenaciously to the "pioneer spirit." Jack London and Algie Simons, on the other hand, went further than any of them, rejecting capitalism outright in favor of full-fledged socialism. But all were dealing with the same basic theme—the relation of the individual to society in postfrontier America. All were, in one degree or another, commenting on the necessary transition from individualism to cooperation in the absence of the frontier.

The theme of the closed frontier, then, was a common and a significant one during the Progressive era, and not just in the writings of socioeconomic and political theorists. It was a significant part of the rationale behind conservationist thinking and the back-to-the-land movement; it also became a staple of the literature of the early twentieth century. "Postfrontier" anxiety, in fact, was as important a part of the cultural milieu of the early twentieth century as frontier anxiety had been in the climate of the late nineteenth century.

7. BACK TO UNTAMED NATURE

By 1900 agriculture produced only 20 percent of the nation's income.[1] According to Census Bureau definitions, the United States was still predominantly rural at the beginning of the new century and would be up until 1920, but it was obvious that the nation was no longer predominantly agricultural. Yet the declining importance of agriculture hardly coincided with a decline in the fortunes of the nation's agriculturalists. The early years of the twentieth century were generally good years for American farmers. With the agricultural demand of a growing population rising to meet the decelerating level of supply, farm prices rose. Between 1870 and 1900 the number of farms more than doubled (from 2.66 million to 5.74 million), and the country's improved acreage doubled as well (from 408 million to 841 million acres). In contrast, the period from 1900 to 1920 saw a smaller, though not insignificant, increase in the number of farms (up to 6.45 million) and in the amount of improved acreage (up to 959 million acres).[2] Perhaps the positive effects of a closed frontier were being felt by the American farmer, just as Malthusian thinkers such as Erastus Wiman and C. Wood Davis had claimed they would back in the 1880s and 1890s.

Although one set of statistics might support the notion that the frontier was closed, it did little to prevent hundreds of thousands of homesteaders from taking up land in the high plains in the first twelve or so years of the new century. Even after that point the homesteading urge did not abate. Many homesteaders who were unable to procure well-watered lands in the United States moved into the adjacent Canadian prairies (part of the same "ecological frontier," if not the frontier of American folklore) for almost another two decades until the termination of the Dominion's land policy in 1930. The homesteading urge was certainly as acute as ever in the early twentieth century.

Whatever the case—whether the homesteaders or the Malthusians were right about the status of the frontier—many of those who addressed the condition of American farming in the early twentieth century wrote from a distinctly postfrontier perspective. As one expert on the public domain, Charles Moreau Harger, put it, western land values might be rising and the life of the farmer improving rapidly, but the "promised land" was passing. The practice of "frontiering" was no longer a factor of any consequence in American life. With land values in states such as Nebraska rapidly rising to the levels common in older states, what incentive was there to go west, Harger wondered.[3] Agnes C. Laut, another authority on the public lands, writing in Century in 1909, declared that the great east-west migration across the continent had come to an end and the only remaining frontier was the Canadian Northwest. Claiming that almost 400,000 American farmers had moved to free homesteads in the region during the last six years, Laut declared that this was "The Last Trek to the Last Frontier."[4] Canadian immigration officials were quick to exploit this postfrontier theme, advertising Canadian lands as the "last best West" and organizing "Free Land Clubs" all across rural America.[5]

While the Canadian Northwest did provide a new frontier for large numbers of American homesteaders, to most writers of the era the presence of this "last best West" seemed more an indication of the end of the "American frontier" than its prolongation. The same can be said for Alaska, which was also heralded as a final frontier in the early years of the new century. An official U.S. Department of Agriculture article in the National Geographic Magazine reported that Alaska could furnish 200,000 family homesteads of 320 acres a piece, but that hardy pioneer types would be required for the task of settling in so harsh a climate.[6] The beginning years of the new century were marked by an outpouring of works on the old frontier as well as Hiram Martin Chittenden's three-volume work on The American Fur Trade of the Far West and Agnes C. Laut's Pathfinders of the West, works on the Lewis and Clark expedition, the history of the Mississippi Valley, the old New York frontier, the Great Plains, the discovery of Puget Sound.[7] The reason, probably was the understanding that the frontier period was over and its history could now be recorded.

Besides this outpouring of historical works on the old frontier, the early years of the century saw an increased interest in nature. There was tremendous interest in tamed nature—gardens, gardening, and bird-watching in particular.[8] There was also a general fascination with rural life that fueled a Country Life Movement in the first two decades of the century. The Commission on Country Life, chartered by President Roosevelt in 1908 and effectively dissolved by Congress and President Taft the following year, reflected the larger Country Life Movement in its recognition of the deficiencies of rural life as well as the attraction of the Jeffersonian agrarian mystique.[9] The "nature" in the Country Life Movement was a tamed and subdued nature. The tremendous popularity and attractiveness of the theme was reflected in the massive sales of Gene Stratton-Porter's nature novels: *Freckles, The Girl of the Limberlost* (1909), *The Harvester* (1911), and *Laddie* (1913). Each sold more than a million copies. Stratton-Porter's novels would make the best-seller list again in the late teens and the first half of the twenties. With birds, animals, and flowers often adorning the margins of her stories, Stratton-Porter conjured up a beautifully tranquil, serene, and beneficent natural environment for her mass audience.[10] The tamed nature of Stratton-Porter and the Country Lifers obviously had a profound effect on the American imagination.

Perhaps the motivation for nature writers and nature lovers in the period stemmed from a sense that the agrarian arcadia was fading. But more interesting in the present context is another brand of back-to-naturism that can be more clearly linked to the understanding that the frontier age was passing. This second tendency was focused on the primitive, untamed, dangerous wilderness. It reflected a need on the part of the generation that had witnessed the taming of much of the nation's woodland wilderness to seek danger and adventure in what primitive nature remained.

Writing in the *Overland Monthly* in 1904, the naturalist George S. Evans lauded the "primitive" and "elemental" charms of the wilderness. "The wilderness still exists," Evans declared. Even though the continent had been plundered, primeval nature could still be found in parts of the far West. There were still places where "the rocks have equanimity, the mountains ruggedness, the trees sturdiness, the wind savagery." Evans added that while the civilized man had none of these qualities, contact with the wilderness would foster them. Man would be at one with the environment and take on its elemental qualities, and leave behind his "stupid, conventional society." Evans concluded his paean to rugged wilderness on a note that would have met with the full approval of disciples of primitivism, such as Theodore Roosevelt.

The pastimes of men in the wilderness are of the manly order. Those who delight in the chase here can pass hours filled with exciting incidents. To pit your human ingenuity against the ingenuity of the animal, to capture him at his own game, is invigorating and refreshing. . . .

Whenever the light of civilization falls upon you with a blighting power, and work and pleasure become stale and flat, go to the wilderness. The wilderness will take hold of you. It will give you good red blood; it will turn you from a weakling into a man.[11]

By the early twentieth century appreciation of wilderness had, as one historian notes, "become a national cult."[12] Anxiety over the loss of the frontier had prompted many Americans to seek in the woodland wilderness an antidote to the perils of civilization. The Boy Scout movement (officially founded by the Englishman Sir Robert Baden Powell in 1907) was first conceived by the popular American nature writer Ernest Thompson Seton in 1902. Seton later reflected on the importance of the Boy Scout movement for postfrontier America. Looking back to the time when every American boy had grown up close to nature, he lamented that the country had undergone an "unfortunate change" since then. Urbanization and industrialization had resulted in "degeneracy," Seton declared, and getting the youth of America back to "the simple life of primitive times" at regular intervals would provide a sure remedy to the dangers of overcivilization.[13]

Jack London's ideological transformation from ardent individualist to full-fledged socialist in a sense symbolized the passing of the frontier era. And prior to his ideological awakening, London, in an effort to escape "the encroachments of [the] steady, sober, and sternly moral civilization" that accompanied the postfrontier age, sought adventure in the primordial wilderness of the Alaskan Klondike region.[14] London sought gold in the Klondike, too, but returned home the following year with only artistic riches to cash in. In the distinguished Western magazine *Overland Monthly*, in 1899, at the rate of five to seven dollars a story, London began to do just that.[15] In his first Alaskan tale, "In a Far Country," he lauded the benefits to be earned by giving up "the comforts of an elder civilization, to face the savage youth, the primordial simplicity of the [Alaskan] North."[16] The theme was repeated in story after story and the Alaskan tales were collected in *The Son of the Wolf*, published the following year. The finest treatment of the theme came in London's masterpiece, *The Call of the Wild* (1903), in which the transformative powers of a primeval wilderness environment were graphically apparent. In this enormously successful story, a domesticated canine becomes the "great primordial beast" after a time in the Klondike. When the process was reversed in London's *White Fang* (1906), the result was less artistically satisfying, London's commitment to the theme less apparent, and the book markedly less successful.[17]

But even as London described the benefits of contact with Alaska's untamed forest wilderness, he sensed that this last frontier was passing. Alaska, like his native California, would cease to be a frontier. "Exploration and transportation will be systematized. . . . The frontiersman will yield to the laborer, the prospector to the mining-engineer . . . the trader and speculator to the steady-going modern man of business," he wrote in 1900.[18] London's socialist transformation seemed quite logical to him in light of the passing of the frontier, but his admiration for the individualism of the pioneer era led him to a rejection of socialism in the last years of his life. London, in these years, entered what has been called his "agrarian phase."[19] Marked by novels such as *Valley of the Moon* (1916) and *The Little Lady of the Big House* (1916)—which were in a sense more like Gene Stratton-Porter's novels than his own earlier wilderness writings—London espoused a return to the soil, to the simple life of the farmer or rancher.

While London's intellectual odyssey was hardly a common one, his initial preoccupation with experiencing what there was left of untamed wilderness in postfrontier America was shared by many. "The wilderness," novelist Harold Bell Wright proclaimed in 1916, is "a land where a man, to live, must be a man." A few years earlier Joseph Knowles, a part-time illustrator, had plunged naked into the Maine woods to prove his manhood and experience the rejuvenating powers of the wilderness, and in doing so had made headlines in the Boston *Post*. Knowles's reversion to primitivism captured the attention of Bostonians and received newspaper coverage all across the eastern United States. A public fascinated with Knowles's adventure bought 300,000 copies of his personal account, *Alone in the Wilderness*. The same fascination with wild nature and its redemptive powers ensured the success of Edgar Rice Burroughs's *Tarzan of the Apes* (1914) and its numerous sequels.[20] After journeying through the national parks of northwestern Montana, one writer in *Harper's Magazine* reflected on the "strange joy . . . of facing anything . . . so indestructibly stupendous" as untamed nature. "In this exquisite solitude," the writer continued, "it was utterly impossible to bring the mind to think of civilization and its complexities." In this "man's world," he wrote, "women gave up their ancient prerogative of screaming after an hour or two, in sheer weariness (all but the 'womanly woman,' who keeps it up for a day), a set expression of terrified resignation taking the place of oral appeal."[21]

The theme appeared month after month in articles and stories in popular magazines in the first decades of the century. Another writer in *Harper's Magazine*, in 1907, declared ruefully that the only "really important opportunities for pioneer exploration are confined to Canada and Alaska."[22] The following year the magazine's readers were treated to an account of one explorer's experience "Wintering among the Eskimos" of Canada.[23] In deference to the public's appetite for tales of wilderness adventuring, *Harper's*, in the first two decades of the century, featured accounts of journeys "Through the African Wilderness," experiences in "The Wilderness of Northern Korea," expeditions "Through the Heart of the Suriname Jungle," "Along the Unchartered [Peruvian] Pampaconas," "Through the Guiana Wilderness," to the "Frontier of the Forbidden Land" (the Central-Asian plateau), and to the Arctic.[24] And Theodore Roosevelt, as might have been expected, added his name to the list of explorers and adventurers as he journeyed through the African wilderness after vacating the presidency in 1909, and then through the Brazilian wilderness after his failed run at the office in 1912.[25]

After the death of Captain Robert Falcon Scott and his associates on their Antarctic expedition in 1912, Roosevelt posed the question, "Is Polar Exploration Worth While?" As might have been expected, the ex-president answered with a resounding "yes," pointing to the "courage, hardihood, shifty self-reliance and unshifting fixity or purpose" that such endeavors produced.[26] Roosevelt's concern about the stultifying effects of settled, civilized society never subsided. In an address a few years earlier he had reiterated the theme, declaring that "one of the dangers of civilization has always been its tendency to cause the loss of virile fighting virtues, of the fighting edge. When men get too comfortable and lead luxurious lives, there is always danger lest the softness eats like an acid into their manliness of fiber. The barbarian, because of the very conditions of his life, is forced to keep and develop certain hardy qualities which the man of civilization tends to lose."[27] That Roosevelt harped on this theme in the early decades of the twentieth century was hardly surprising. It is, however, interesting that his utterances were representative of so widespread a strain in American thought in the period.

The public's appetite for tales of wilderness exploration, great as it was, could not match its hunger for cowboy tales. In a sense the yearning was the same: The rugged wilderness served as a mental antidote to the supposed corrupting influence of civilization in the postfrontier age. And the cowboy, too, in all his mythic grandeur, served as a symbol of a simpler, more rugged frontier age. The image of the cowboy was a creation of the postfrontier mind, and incidentally, one that bore little resemblance to the grim realities of that character's existence.

This nostalgic longing for a bygone age received particularly ironic expression from the Right Reverend Ethlebert Talbot, Episcopalian bishop of central Pennsylvania, in *Harper's Monthly* in 1905. The Reverend looked back fondly on his last eleven years as first bishop of the missionary district of Wyoming, even lamenting the absence of stagecoach robberies in the new, civilized West.[28] The most widely read piece of nostalgic longing for the "Wild West" in the period, though, featured an upholder of the law, a stern and rugged yet moral man—the Virginian. Owen Wister's novel *The Virginian* (1902) was reprinted fifteen times in the first eight months after its publication and sold more than any other book during 1902–1903.[29] The book captured the attention of a public that thirsted after the wild frontier. As Wister clearly outlined in the preface, his novel was a paean to a "Wild West" that had passed from the realm of reality into the realm of romance.

> It is a vanished world. No journeys, save those which memory can take, will bring you to it now. . . . [W]here is the buffalo, and the wild antelope, and where the horseman with his pasturing thousands? . . . [H]e will never come again. He rides in his historic yesterday. You will no more see him gallop out of the unchanging silence than you will see Columbus on the unchanging sea come sailing from Palos with his caravels.[30]

Andy Adams's *The Log of a Cowboy* appeared a year after Wister's book and featured more of the real West and less of the mythic. Adams, a bonafide cowboy himself, in writing unromantically of the hardships of the trail drive, had produced a book that latter-day critics would praise highly. But it was the colorful Virginian, not the nameless range rider, that captured the attention of the public. It was not the daily toil of real cowboys that enamored the public, but the "half-wild freedom . . . danger and excitement" of western life as experienced by the fictional cowboy hero.[31] The western novel genre that Wister had created grew in popularity as the frontier passed into memory. Zane Grey's westerns, beginning with *Riders of the Purple Sage* in 1912 and numbering more than fifty in all, would dominate the best-seller lists from the teens through the mid-twenties.[32] Cowboy stories became a mainstay of the magazine literature of the period, too, particularly in magazines such as *Scribner's* and the *Overland Monthly*.[33] These publications devoted a good deal of space to articles that lamented the passing of this great heroic breed from the American scene.[34] Paralleling this theme was an inter-est in the passing of the cowboy's legendary adversary—the Plains Indian.[35]

Accompanying this preoccupation with the rugged wilderness, rugged cow-boys, and vanishing Indians was a mood of anxiety over the passing of the pioneer spirit. This theme became a mainstay in the magazine literature of the early twentieth century. Writing in the *Outlook* at the beginning of the century, Charles Moreau Harger lamented that "Romance in pioneering is fast disappearing from the West" and the terms "settler" and "claim" would in a few years be "marked obsolete."[36] A few years later Harger reiterated the theme, declaring that "the pioneer of the plains is a reminiscence. His white-hooded prairie-schooner is little more than a dream":

> Unfused, forlorn and gray it stands,
> A faded wrech cast far ashore;
> The Mayflower of the prairie lands
> Its journey o'er.

Harger went on to suggest that a "new Westerner" might emerge with all the commendable rugged qualities of the old pioneer and some new, more pro-gressive qualities to boot. This new Westerner would be a "clear-headed, stout-hearted, frank-faced man of the plains; the product of years of trial, of experiment, of triumph."[37] It apparently escaped Harger that in his effort to describe the nature and characteristics of this new breed he had simply painted a rather traditional picture of the old frontiersman.[38] Perhaps it was difficult for Harger to offer a more attractive western image than the one that had already been built up over generations. It seems likely that his prime motivation was concern over the passing of the pioneer spirit, rather than heartfelt optimism regarding the promise of a new and improved west-ern type.

Harger was not alone in trying to show that the old western spirit was not passing from the scene. The muckraking journalist Ray Stannard Baker, in the early years of the century, focused the bulk of his journalistic energies on the corruption of the railroads, but also addressed the problem of the pass-ing of the frontier. Writing in *Century* in 1902, Baker claimed that there was still a wide-open space—"the Great Southwest"—where, "in spite of human enterprise . . . men can go and have it out with themselves, where they can breathe clean air, and get down close to the great, quiet, simple life of the earth." "Here in the desert," he wrote, "there yet remain places of wildness and solitude and quiet; there is room here to turn without rubbing elbows."[39] Baker tackled the theme again in an article entitled "The Western Spirit of Restlessness," which appeared in the Century in 1908. Baker pointed out that the pioneer had long since crossed the Rocky Mountains and reached the Pacific Ocean. Nonetheless, he argued, the American character still held something of that adventurous nature that had marked the frontier age. "The Western spirit of restlessness" was not yet dead, but the fact that it was manifested only by roving "floaters," traveling around the West with no particular objective, hardly amounted to strong evidence that the frontier spirit was alive and well.[40]

In 1914, in the American Monthly Magazine, Baker addressed the problem of the closing of the frontier one more time. In "The New Pioneering and Its Heroes," Baker was unwilling to admit that the frontier's closing made any real difference to the nation's development. He clutched at straws, stating first that there was still a genuine frontier wilderness where real pioneers could still be found, and that he had experienced its wonders on a trip through Wisconsin and Minnesota. What Baker described bore little resemblance to untamed wilderness, and the characters he spoke of seemed quite tame for pioneers. Seemingly realizing as much, Baker went on to admit that "pioneering of the old sort" was indeed a "passing phase."[41] But, he argued in a vein similar to Harger's, there was a new pioneer spirit. In an effort to explain himself, Baker stated that this new spirit was marked not by the cry of "Westward Ho!" but by a new cry that might be called "Inward Ho!" or even "Downward Ho!" Men would now have to "look for a miracle of adventuring, for the joys and hardships of pioneering, not to the West, the South, nor the North, but within the common soil upon which they stand."[42] All this suggested that the frontier was closed—that there was nowhere to go, no place for pioneering, no alternative to working the soil where you stood—instead of suggesting that a new pioneering spirit was about to take hold of the country.

Baker, like Harger, seemed resigned to the grim fact that the pioneer age, with all its attendant glories and beneficence, had come to an end. But neither writer seemed willing to concede that past wonders had been irrevocably lost. In an article in the Atlantic Monthly in 1917, Harger contended that the pioneer days had passed but the pioneer spirit lived on in the West, and then proceeded to describe a settled, community-oriented, and decidedly unadventurous way of life that bore absolutely no resemblance to the heady pioneering lifestyle that he lauded.[43]

Like Frederick Jackson Turner in this period, Baker and Harger seemed unable to come fully to terms with the closing of the frontier—which they all so readily admitted. Their dilemma was not uncommon. A writer in *Harper's Magazine* in 1916 contended that the buffalo, the cowboy, and the Indian might have passed, but there was still an untrammeled Old West. That this Western wonderland, uncorrupted by the scourge of "paternal regulations and effete conventionalities," could be found only in a "few out-of-the-way corners" of central Oregon lent little credence to the claim, though.[44] An article in the *Overland Monthly* the same year asked the question "Is the Old West Passing?" "Every few months," the author declared, "we read in some magazine a more or less poetic lament over the passing of the Old West." The article proceeded at some length to demonstrate that the Old West and its "distinctively Western types" had not passed from the scene; the eastern traveler simply had to go to far greater lengths to locate them—which hardly augmented the author's argument.[45]

A writer in the *Yale Review* in 1917 declared that Americans' fascination with untamed wilderness in the postfrontier age bore testimony to the survival of "the pioneering instinct." The author, the prominent critic and later literary historian Henry Seidel Canby—whose name was hardly suggestive of pioneer lineage—declared, quite erroneously: "We are the descendants of pioneers—all of us." Canby then went on to claim that "if we have not inherited a memory of pioneering experiences, at least we possess inherited tendencies and desires."[46] The novelist and historian Emerson Hough made the same point in *The Passing of the Frontier* (1918). The frontier, "our most priceless possession," had passed, Hough declared, but "it has not been possible to eliminate from the blood of the American West, diluted though it has been by far less worthy strains, all the iron of the old home-bred frontiersman."[47] In reviewing Hough's book, Hamlin Garland reiterated the same sorrowful lament over the loss of the frontier and expressed a similar confidence about the preservation of pioneer traits in the future. Garland, whose earlier anguished commentaries on the closing of the frontier seemed to offer little hope for the future, closed his review proclaiming that "in a sense the frontier of American progress will never pass."[48] Appearing at the height of American participation in World War I, Hough's book made it clear to the parents of American soldiers on the battlefields of Europe that their sons were carrying on the frontier tradition of courage and perseverance in the face of adversity.[49]

A few years after the war, novelist Willa Cather related the frustrations of a western farmhand, Claude Wheeler, in *One of Ours*. Wheeler's frustrations stem from the destruction of the old heroic West. Sitting on the statehouse steps in Denver, looking up at a statue of Kit Carson, the character declares his grim realization that the West is no more: "The statue . . . pointed Westward; but there was no West, in that sense, any more. . . . Here the sky was like a lid shut down over the world."[50] In contrast, the war in Europe represented a release from the claustrophobia of the closed-frontier West—a "sunrise on the prairie"—and Wheeler shipped overseas to be like the heroic pioneers.

The United States, of course, did not enter World War I for discernibly "frontier-related" reasons, and American combatants were hardly seeking an outlet in the trenches of France for pioneering urges that could not be vented in the "claustrophobic," postfrontier United States. But the literature of the period does reflect a preoccupation on the part of many American thinkers with the theme of the closing of the frontier. Whether manifested in wilderness novels and excursions, nostalgic tales of a wilder West, or reflections on the presence of the pioneer spirit in the postfrontier age, the theme was a prevalent one in the first two decades of the twentieth century, and one that would retain its prominence in the decade to come.

For those Progressive theorists who addressed the theme of the closing of the frontier, the goal was generally to curb the excesses of frontier individualism and work towards a more cooperative society. The efforts of most literary figures who tackled the theme were seemingly less constructive, consisting largely of attempts to hang on to the frontier past with all its attendant individualism.

For conservationist thinkers in the period, Ray Stannard Baker's cry of "Downward Ho," or "Inward Ho," reflected an understanding of the need to use the nation's resources more practically. Increasing recourse to large-scale irrigation and to dry-farming techniques in the early decades of the century bore testimony to changed conditions.[51] The existence of the frontier and its seemingly inexhaustible resources, Theodore Roosevelt told the Presidential Conference on Conservation in 1908, had freed whole generations of Americans from responsibility for the needs of their successors. "When the American settler felled the forests," he said, "he felt there was plenty of forest left for the sons who came after him. When he exhausted the soil of his farm, he felt that his sons could go West and take up another. The Kentuckian or the Ohioan felled the forest and expected his son to move west and fell other forests on the banks of the Mississippi."[52]

Roosevelt's realization of the desperate need for wiser use of the nation's resources after the closing of the frontier prompted an uncharacteristically harsh condemnation of pioneer individualism. Roosevelt sounded remarkably like Walter Weyl when he advocated an abrupt turnabout, away from the mentality that secured "the right of the individual to injure the future of us all for his own temporary and immediate profit."[53] William J. Trimble echoed the same sentiment in 1914, in his article on the "Influence of the Passing of the Public Lands." Trimble declared, "The sooner we as a people become conscious that we are in a new economic era, the better it will be for us. We have come to the time when we may no longer waste; we must conserve."[54] The same theme was reiterated time and time again in the Progressive era. Because "land and resources have been cheap," Robert Tudor Hill declared in *The Public Domain and Democracy* (1910), "very little attention has been given in their disposal to wide social interests."[55] The solution to the problem was clear in the minds of most conservationists—a new emphasis on cooperative endeavors, coordinated by the national government to serve the interests of the wider public, must mark the natural resource policies of the postfrontier age.

The thrust of conservationist thinking was markedly different, then, from the lamentations on the passing of the Wild West and the pioneer spirit that marked much of the literature of the period, and very different in kind, too, from the efforts to rekindle the "primitive virtues" in what could still be found of the primordial wilderness. For some, such as Theodore Roosevelt, these seemingly contradictory tendencies were both eagerly subscribed to. In a sense, that was hardly surprising. While for some the closing of the frontier necessitated the reordering of priorities, for others it prompted a mournful longing for the past. That both responses could emanate from a single mind, as was the case with Roosevelt, with Frederick Jackson Turner (who lauded the pioneer spirit but realized that it must adapt to the realities of the postfrontier world), and with Jack London, was understandable. Coming to terms with the perceived loss of the frontier was so difficult because its presence had been regarded as a crucial component of the American way of life. The frontier may have passed, but its influence—or at least, the influence of the myths that had sprung up around it—remained a central presence in the cultural climate of the early decades of the century.

8. RUGGED INDIVIDUALISM REVISITED

During the 1920s there was a vast outpouring of writing on the American frontier, fueled in part by the publication of Frederick Jackson Turner's collection of essays, *The Frontier in American History* (October 1920). Turner's essays met with a mixed response from the historical profession, but largely unqualified praise in newspaper and magazine coverage.[1] Equally important was the prevailing mood of the postwar years. The traditional image—a "lost generation" of intellectuals wandering from bar to bar and bedroom to bedroom in melancholy alienation from mainstream American culture—is a stereotype. Yet, like all stereotypes, it does contain a few grains of truth. The 1920s are not best characterized as the age of the lost generation, but there was, as one historian has perceptively noted, a nervousness and anxiety that pervaded the age.[2] The image of the frontier, it seems, provided a kind of solace for some in the uncertain postwar years. As one writer reflected at the beginning of the 1930s, "authors were world-weary and war-weary, [and turned] to the West to celebrate the passage of an heroic age."[3]

The nervousness of the "twenties generation" stemmed in part from an uncertainty about the merits of rapid modernization and technological progress. The 1920 Census classified the nation for the first time as predominantly urban, though its definition of "urban"—settlements of 2,500 or more—hardly mirrors today's classifications. The advent of the urban skyscraper served as a symbol of the transition, and the advent of new mass production techniques promoted spiraling growth in the automobile industry. The nation had become more "citified" and more mobile. But the march of the modern age in America sparked apprehension about the future and a tendency to cling to a simpler, seemingly more virtuous past.[4] The qualities of woodland wilderness and of heroic, unbridled pioneer individualism served as a kind of antidote to fears of impersonal technological progress in the 1920s.

This longing for wilderness and pioneer virtues—for the open frontier—had been prevalent in the first decades of the century, too. The frontier was not, as some suggested, "rediscovered" in the 1920s.[5] But in the 1920s these "frontier longings" were less frequently accompanied by concerns over the dangers of excessive individualism in a postfrontier world than they had been in those earlier decades. The emphasis in the Progressive era on the need for cooperation would return again in the New Deal years, but in the 1920s the focus was on the merits of individualism. Herbert Croly's blueprint for *The Promise of American Life*—a social democracy attuned to the needs of postfrontier America—went unrealized in the 1920s. If Croly's book and Walter Weyl's *The New Democracy* were among the more representative works of the Progressive era, then Guy Emerson's less remarkable little book, *The New Frontier* (1920), marked the spirit of the 1920s and the dormancy of the progressive, regulatory state.

Guy Emerson, a Harvard law school graduate, director of publicity for the Liberty Loan drives, and later Vice President of the National Bank of Commerce in New York, never achieved the kind of recognition for his writing on the frontier that Turner did (and rightly so). Interestingly, though, his book and Turner's *The Frontier in American History* were often advertised together in press releases.[6] That much was surprising in one sense, because the two books, despite their common titles and Emerson's acknowledgement of an intellectual debt to Turner (which was very great indeed), were quite different in tone and outlook. Turner's collection of essays was at root a pessimistic book, glorying in the past, but offering little substantive hope for the future. Emerson's book, on the other hand, was a supremely optimistic work that focused on the future. Writing to Turner just prior to the publication of *The New Frontier*, Emerson apologized for quoting so heavily from Turner's writings, noting that it had been almost impossible to improve on his language and that there was "nothing to add to what you have said on the subject of the Frontier."[7] But Emerson had added something to Turner's ideas which Turner himself had never and would never be able to add—an unwavering optimism concerning America's future as a frontierless democracy. Press releases for *The New Frontier* featured a passage from the book that reflected the author's bright outlook:

And we still have our frontier. It is a frontier industrial, financial, commercial, political, social, educational, artistic, diplomatic, religious. Let us not forget that the old frontier constantly presented problems without precedent. It seemed to be impossible of conquest and settlement. But settled it was. If we do not forget and abandon its strong lessons, its great hopes, its splendid dreams, if we do not lose our grasp upon its vigor and common sense, if we do not forsake our priceless heritage . . . we shall find that we are immeasurably nearer the settlement of the new wilderness, that we are steadily pushing forward the fighting line of the new frontier.[8]

Turner's collection of essays centered on the formative role of the frontier and the West in the development of the nation and dealt, less sure-handedly, with the implications of the closed frontier. For Emerson there was no dilemma; the qualities of the frontier were still shaping the nation's development, and chief among those qualities was individualism. Emerson saw no need to temper frontier individualism in a closed frontier environment. For him, the frontier had never really closed. Individualism was alive and well and the only concern was keeping it unbridled and unhampered.

While the Great War to save the world for democracy had proved a great disappointment for Progressive theorists like Croly and Weyl, and in the judgement of some historians, dealt a death blow to the Progressive movement, for Guy Emerson the war provided living proof of the strength of America's pioneer virtues. The frontier spirit, Emerson charged, had "shone from the faces of two million men who carried the fresh strength and youthfullness of America to war-jaded Europe." That same quality of sturdy individualism and rugged self-reliance was manifested again, Emerson contended, in the reelection of Calvin Coolidge to the governorship of Massachusetts in 1919. Such triumphs signaled the vitality of American "liberalism" (a liberalism very different from that envisaged by most Progressives, to be sure).[9]

The "physical frontiers" of America might be gone, but "the great frontier of American character" was alive and well. The only danger, in Emerson's estimation, was that the "machinery of organization and government" might stifle the "intense individualism" that had been nurtured on the old frontier.[10] The solution, Emerson proposed, was not to temper individualism to meet the needs of a closed-frontier society, but to glory in the individualistic spirit—to keep the frontier alive by keeping its spirit alive. The physical frontier was easily replaced with new frontiers of business enterprise. For

Turner the solution was not that simple, and he would wrestle with the question of democracy's fate in the postfrontier age throughout the twenties, just as he had in earlier decades.

Yet no matter how vast the gulf separating Turner's anxiety from Emerson's blinding optimism concerning America's postfrontier future, Emerson seemed unaware of it in his periodic letters to Turner in the period.[11] Turner's 1893 essay, Emerson said, "has done more to correct my point of view than anything I have read." He spoke of the need for every intelligent thinker to read *The Frontier in American History*, adding that the volume "stands by itself in its importance and influence in shaping American ideals for the future, because even though the physical frontiers have gone we cannot in substantial measure fail to be children of our past."[12] In fact, Turner would argue almost as much a few years later in an essay entitled "The Children of the Pioneers" (1925). "Pioneer spirit and conceptions," Turner wrote, "prevailed even in . . . [large Midwestern cities] long after the era of especial hardships of pioneering passed away." But while Emerson was convinced that the frontier spirit would endure, Turner was not. He concluded the essay on a pessimistic note, pointing to the dangers of standardization and of the loss of individualism and originality.[13]

Unlike Turner, future president Herbert Hoover shared Emerson's confidence; he did not see the loss of the physical frontier as a cause for anxiety. An article entitled "American Individualism" by Hoover, then Secretary of Commerce, appeared in *World's Work* in April 1922.[14] That same April more than half of the 500,000 coal miners across the nation went on strike, and three months later the miners were joined by 400,000 railroad workers. With the nation facing the prospect of industrial paralysis, Hoover's essay was hastily published in book form the following December "with an immediate and pressing purpose": a Hoover associate named Edgar Richard had suggested that the book would help dissipate public fears and restore confidence.[15]

Turner's influence on Hoover's thinking was obvious. Turner had, in fact, sent Hoover a copy of *The Frontier in American History*. Hoover reciprocated by sending Turner a copy of *American Individualism*, which Turner summarized as "a noble statement of the fruits of our past and the promise of our future."[16] Yet despite Turner's conventionally deferential and enthusiastic response to the writing of a major statesman, his nagging doubts concerning the future prospects of a frontierless nation certainly outweighed his occasional optimism. Turner, though he admired Hoover, indeed voted for him in 1928, certainly never wrote anything that came close to matching the unbridled optimism that Hoover displayed.[17] In *American Individualism* Hoover lauded the individualistic pioneer spirit that had been nurtured on the frontier and concluded optimistically:

That spirit need never die for lack of something for it to achieve. There will always be a frontier to conquer so long as men think, plan, and dare. . . . The days of the pioneer are not over. There are continents of human welfare for which we have penetrated only the coastal plain. The great continent of science is as yet explored only on its borders, and it is only the pioneer who will penetrate the frontier in the quest for new worlds to conquer. The very genius of our institutions had been given to them by the pioneer spirit. Our individualism is rooted in our very nature.[18]

Hoover acknowledged that new social conditions existed now that the "vast plains of the West" had been settled. But, like Emerson, he concluded that this was no cause for alarm and no need to modify frontier individualism. "Salvation will not come to us," he said, "out of the wreckage of individualism." Attacking the "cooperative-based" progressivism of Croly and others, Hoover charged that the real danger was not the changed conditions of the country vis-à-vis the loss of the frontier, but "the perpetual howl of radicalism . . . [which] assume[s] that all reform and human advance must come through government." These radicals, he added, "have forgotten that progress must come from the steady lift of the individual." If the nation's emphasis remained squarely on the preservation of individualism, its social problems would be easily overcome and a "social system as perfect as our generation merits" would be achieved.[19]

An equally optimistic appraisal of the nation's postfrontier fortunes, though addressed to a smaller audience than Hoover's or Emerson's commentaries, was Robert D. Dripps's speech "New Pioneers for New Frontiers." Dripps, the executive secretary of the Buffalo Bill American Association (which was chaired by General John J. Pershing), delivered the address in 1924 to explain the purpose of the newly formed organization. That purpose, Dripps stated at the outset, was "to keep alive the spirit of the American pioneer." The passing of the "physical frontier" was no cause for concern, he said, because "mental and spiritual frontiers" remained. That "same longing for freedom and individual initiative that constitute the frontier spirit" was alive and well. In a vein similar to Hoover's and Emerson's, Dripps outlined the sinister force that constituted the great adversary of the pioneer spirit: "the gradual process which has been going on during the past few decades, looking toward an increased centralization of Government, and involving the gradual unloading on the Government of functions, of duties and responsibilities, which had always been regarded as resting upon the individual citizen."[20]

The present generation was the first to have had no "first hand contact" with the frontier, Dripps noted, but that shortcoming was easily alleviated. By merely studying "the type represented by the pioneer, the frontier, the scout; to picture to ourselves the actual living conditions of these people, the difficulties which confronted them, the ways in which they met these difficulties and the reaction of the whole process on their own character and philosophy of life" would be enough to bolster the mental and spiritual frontiers of the population. Once this much was done the ogre of big government would have no chance; it would, in short, be crushed by the spirit of the frontier even in the frontier's absence. And the character whose example could provide the necessary nurturing of those frontiers of the mind was Buffalo Bill, who had provided a "dramatic representation [of] the essential things in that [pioneer] era to the next generation." William Cody was no Barnum, according to Dripps, but the archetypal pioneer, and everyone needed to catch some of his spirit. Sounding like Theodore Roosevelt, Dripps declared a need for "more Americans of the physical type, of the virility and muscular strength and energy of the pioneer." And he promised that his organization would work to promote that type, "encourag[ing] self-reliance and individual initiative . . . and patriotism," and thereby ensuring the nation's future greatness.[21]

Few observers in the 1920s reacted to the end of the physical frontier with the confidence of Hoover or Emerson or the Buffalo Bill American Association. Most writers simply expressed a longing for a simpler, more rugged, more individualistic frontier past. A collection of essays edited by Duncan Aikman entitled *The Taming of the Frontier* was typical of this nostalgic bent. Each of the ten essays focused on the "standardization" of life in a western city since frontier times. In his introduction Aikman described the essays as "protests against our sterile urban conformities."[22] Together the essays served as a chronicle of the emasculation of American individualism. Describing the taming of El Paso, Owen P. White lamented the arrival of civilization in the early 1870s. This one-time utopia of individualism and frontier ruggedness was rapidly succeeded by a stifling uniformity—the citizens now "showered daily . . . changed their clothes by the clock, and began to play golf." "This was the end," White declared.[23] Bernard De Voto similarly described the arrival of civilization in his hometown of Ogden, Utah. "Once the frontier marched through Ogden with its chariots and its elephants," he wrote. "Once there were demi-gods and heroes . . . desire and splendor—something of courage and adventure, something of battle, life a hot throbbing in the veins . . . a city shouting its male-ness to the peaks." But now, he concluded disparagingly, "there are culture clubs and chiropractors."[24]

Others essays in Aikman's collection described the ominous onset of civilization in Denver, St. Paul, Portland, Kansas City, Cheyenne, and Los Angeles. For San Francisco and San Antonio the accounts were not quite so gloomy because there still remained some opposition to the strictures of civilized society in those places.

Willa Cather painted a similarly woeful picture in her novel *A Lost Lady* (1923). Cather's earlier novels, particularly *O Pioneers!* (1913) and *My Antonia* (1918), had focused on the strength of the pioneer spirit. In *A Lost Lady* Captain Forrester, the representative of the old pioneering types, comments sadly on the end of their era and the end of their dreams. "All of our great West has been developed from such dreams," he says. "We dreamed the railroads across the mountains," but "all of these things will be everyday facts to the coming generation." Forrester can do no more than sigh, like an "old Indian" resigned to the inevitable.[25]

Cather presented her thoughts on the closing of the frontier more directly through the reflections of another of the novel's leading characters, Neil Herbert:

> The Old West had been settled by dreamers, great-hearted adventurers who were unpractical to the point of magnificence; a courteous brotherhood, strong in attack but weak in defence, who could conquer but not hold. Now all the vast territory they had won was to be at the mercy of men . . . who had never dared anything. They would drink up the mirage, dispel the morning freshness, root out the great brooding spirit of freedom. . . . The space, the colour, the princely carelessness of the pioneer they would destroy and cut up into profitable bits, as the match factory splinters the primeval forest.[26]

For Cather the closing of the frontier was cause for concern because the spirit of the frontier was being replaced by something new and far less benign. In the novel Cather looked back nostalgically to a more colorful, more heroic time, and on that level her book was typical of the writings of the period on the frontier and the West. But Cather's book was unusually pessimistic. For most of those in this period who addressed these topics, the prevalent themes were nostalgia and hope—hope that the pioneer spirit could endure. Cather, though, mixed nostalgia with despair—despair that both the age and its colorful qualities had passed and were irretrievable.

Typical of the nostalgic predilections of the time were the cowboy novels of Emerson Hough, *The Covered Wagon* (1922) and *North of 36* (1923), which lauded the colorful individualism and heroism of the cowboy, and Bernard De Voto's *The Crooked Mile* (1924), *The Chariot of Fire* (1926), and *The House of Sun-Goes-Down* (1928), which chronicled the westward movement and the influence of the frontier on the American character. Owen Wister reminisced about the good old days *When West Was West* (1928). Philip Ashton Rollins searched for "the spirit of the Old West" in his 1922 work, *The Cowboy*. Rollins found that spirit residing in the cowboy, and his discovery amounted to one of the most unqualified paeans to the West of that decade or any other. The western spirit, Rollins wrote, "was a spirit that begat personal service and extreme self-reliance. . . . It was a spirit that gave to a man an intense individualism, and not only a hatred of class distinctions . . . but also a bitter antipathy to all social usages of limitation of personal action except those which either were prescribed by universal fundamental law or were in the Western code."[27] The cowboys of the Old West, Rollins went on, were generous to friends and strangers alike, "and without expectation of reward." The big-hearted spirit of the West was manifested, he said, in the little sagebrush fires all across the prairies that promised warmth and comfort to every lonely, hungry stranger. The lost West that Rollins painted seemed too good to be true (and it was), but it reflected what many people wanted to believe. Rollins closed his account with a heartfelt appeal for the preservation of the cowboy spirit in the national memory: "These by-gone, virile, warm-hearted men of real idealism, of high courage and brave achievement, of maturest force and child-like simplicity, of broad tolerance, if often of violent prejudices, these builders of an empire, may not, through the drama's stressing of their picturesqueness, be forgotten as to their bigness and be recorded by some definitive historical treatise in the future as having been mere theatric characters."[28]

The popular magazines of the period were doing a good job of keeping alive—or perhaps better, marketing for popular consumption—the spirit of the Old West. Cowboy stories, homesteading tales, and accounts of pioneer exploits abounded in publications such as *Scribner's, Harper's,* and even the more intellectually charged *American Mercury* during the 1920s.[29] As in the two decades prior, this fascination with the heroes of the Old West was coupled with a fascination with woodland wilderness, its dangers and its charms.

Theodore Roosevelt, Jr., shared his father's concerns over the passing of the frontier and sought to preserve the "sturdy self-reliance, simplicity, and courage" it had bred. In an action that paralleled his father's creation of the Boone and Crockett Club in the late 1880s and the formation of the Buffalo Bill American Association, Roosevelt inspired a National Conference on Outdoor Recreation in 1924. The conference was addressed by President Calvin Coolidge, who lauded the benefits of life in the great outdoors. At the second national conference in 1926, future president Herbert Hoover addressed the audience on the need for a "return to the primitive life."[30]

With influential spokesmen such as Coolidge and Hoover and more eloquent spokesmen such as Emerson Hough and wilderness writer Aldo Leopold all stressing, to one degree or another, both the spiritual qualities of wilderness and the practical benefits of sensible resource management, the conservationist impulse retained its vitality in the 1920s.[31] That much was hardly surprising given the pervasiveness of the closed-frontier theme in that decade. In fact, Leopold drew heavily on Turner's frontier thesis in stressing the need for wilderness preservation. He wrote in the mid-1920s that "many of the attributes most distinctive of America and Americans [stem from] the impress of the wilderness and the life that accompanied it." With that much established, he asked rhetorically, "is it not a bit beside the point for us to be so solicitous about preserving [American] institutions without giving so much as a thought to preserving the environment which produced them and which may now be one of our effective means of keeping them alive?"[32]

While amateur social theorists such as Guy Emerson and Herbert Hoover gauged the vitality of the frontier spirit and novelists reminisced about the days of the open frontier, the frontier also became a theme in the writings of literary critics. Works such as Ralph L. Rusk's *The Literature of the Middle Western Frontier* (1925) and Lucy L. Hazard's *The Frontier in American Literature* (1927) gave attention to the role of the frontier as both a shaping force and a driving theme in American literature.[33]

Meanwhile, the role of the frontier became a dominant motif in the writings of American historians. John D. Hicks explained the agrarian movements of the late nineteenth century as a response to the closing of the frontier in the mid-1920s.[34] Inspired by Turner, Frederic Logan Paxson wrote his popular *History of the American Frontier, 1763-1893* (1924) and in 1929 delivered a series of lectures on the theme of the closing of the frontier.[35] Arthur M. Schlesinger paid special attention to the role of the frontier in American development in his *New Viewpoints in American History* (1922).[36] And Archer Butler Hulbert, a professor at Pomona College who had earlier worked with Turner as the archivist of the Harvard Commission on Western History, published his book *Frontiers: The Genius of American Nationality* (1929). Hulbert, like Emerson, Hoover, and others, expressed a keen optimism concerning the nation's frontierless future. The physical frontier might have passed, but luckily, Hulbert explained, "frontiers always breed frontiers." The frontier spirit was thriving as Americans pioneered the "intellectual, social, and political" frontiers of a new age.[37] Even as Turner's thesis started to come under attack in the 1920s from historians who downplayed the centrality of the frontier's role in American development, the significance of the frontier and the significance of its closing remained standard elements of American thought.[38]

The dominant strain in postwar American attitudes towards the frontier and the characteristic pioneer type was nostalgic and laudatory. For those such as Cather, Hough, and Rollins, the frontier age was a glorious epoch and its passing a saddening reality. For others such as Hoover and Emerson, nostalgia was mixed with a supreme confidence in the durability of the pioneer spirit, but there was an undercurrent in American thinking about the frontier in this period that was far from positive. A handful of writers, including Lewis Mumford, Waldo Frank, and Van Wyck Brooks, tore into the hallowed pioneer type with a vengeance.

The excessive individualism of the frontier age had been criticized in the prewar period by Croly in *The Promise of American Life*, and more forcefully by Walter Weyl in *The New Democracy*. Writing during the war, psychologist Alfred Booth Kuttner, in an essay in *The Dial* entitled "A Study of American Intolerance," echoed Weyl's harsh criticisms. Kuttner, a German-American, saw clearly the great danger and the unseemly consequences of "one hundred percent Americanism" during the war, and sought to explain how "a country which claims the highest democracy could at the same time be so crudely and often so savagely intolerant." The reason, he posited, was that the United States had never faced "the ultimate test of tolerance," which "does not come until people are compelled to live together in close and vital relations." The frontier experience, Kuttner explained, had provided Americans with the dangerous luxury of avoiding complex social relations. "The history of our Westward movement," he wrote, "is the history of people who moved on in order to be able to do what they pleased not only economically but socially and in religion. . . . Tolerance did not become an issue with us until the country had filled up, until the wave turned east again." It is not surprising that a nation made up predominantly of Anglo-Saxons who had never been forced to learn to live with each other experienced great difficulty and demonstrated extreme intolerance in trying to live with other people. Kuttner's brief but sweeping analysis, though not entirely free of racist overtones, did provide a unique explanation for "American" intolerance towards blacks, Asians, and southern and eastern European immigrants. After noting that all wars create a climate of intolerance, he concluded that the United States was fighting a "double war and a doubled intolerance." [39] Kuttner was relieved that the frontier had finally passed away, and he hoped that its deleterious spirit would dissipate in time.

Kuttner was a relatively obscure intellectual, but others of greater renown addressed the negative impact of the frontier in the postwar years. Unlike Turner and a hundred others who had stressed the admirable intuitive, pragmatic bent of the frontiersman, the nation's leading pragmatist and educational theorist, John Dewey, expressed no reverence for the intellectual qualities of the pioneering breed. In a commentary in the *New Republic* on William Jennings Bryan's campaign against evolution, Dewey attributed his subject's "obscurantism and intolerance" to the anti-intellectual bent in the frontier mind. The frontier, even after "it ceased to be a menace to orderly life," Dewey explained, "persisted as a limit beyond which it was dangerous and unrespectable for thought to travel." Bryan's anachronistic appeals, Dewey said, were symptomatic of the frontier forces "which are most powerful in holding down the intellectual level of American life." [40]

Novelist, social historian, and literary critic Waldo Frank dwelled at length on the harmful side effects of pioneering on the American psyche in his cultural history *Our America* (1919). Upending the traditional paeans to pioneer intuitiveness and practicality, Frank scathingly described a frontier age in which "virtues which leant themselves to material conquest and to endurance were extolled: virtues which called for inner peace or levied energy without a manifest material return were vices." The pioneer, Frank went on, "had no immediate need to consult either his social or his spiritual senses." The continent was finally settled and "the frontiers were clamped down," but unfortunately, "the rhythm of the pioneer ran on." The pioneer had been "immersed in a life of crass material endeavor" that had left him in a state of intellectual underdevelopment. "There is nothing more horrible," Frank said, "than a physically mature body moved by a childish mind."[41] America, he concluded, was a cultural wasteland and a haven of anti-intellectualism, but not a lost cause. Frank expressed a hope that the nation might finally exorcise its frontier spirit and "generate within [itself] the energy which is love of life"; exorcising the frontier spirit would make possible a new era of spiritual pioneering (one that would probably have horrified the Buffalo Bill American Association).

Frank expressed the same hope a decade later in *The Re-discovery of America* (1929). In this more abstract book he again lambasted the American pioneer type who so readily rejected European culture but created nothing to replace it with. Yet he looked forward to the time when America would transcend the atomistic pioneer individualism of the frontier age and become an "organic" society embracing aesthetic and spiritual values—the time when America would "re-discover" itself.[42] It is worth bearing in mind that the second of these works was also hopeful, even though it was separated from its predecessor by a decade of crass materialism and anti-intellectualism (as Frank saw things) that seemed to offer little promise for the fulfillment of its author's wishes. These "lost intellectuals" were hardly as washed up, disillusioned, and hopeless as a later generation of analysts would assume.[43]

The same hopeful tone was evident in the writings of the literary critic and cultural historian Van Wyck Brooks, who even earlier than Frank had lambasted the pioneer spirit. Brooks's *America's Coming of Age* (1915) laid bare the pioneer's rampant individualism and crass materialism, which had forestalled the formation of a high "collective spiritual life." Brooks linked the pioneer spirit with puritanism, arguing that the puritan contempt for human nature had unleashed man's acquisitive impulses and numbed his aesthetic senses.[44] But Brooks did express the hope in his essay "The Literary Life," in Harold Stearns's renowned collection *Civilization in the United States* (1922), that with the frontier gone the pioneer and puritan traditions would gradually wane. The present might be an age of reaction, but Brooks was optimistic that a higher level of consciousness, already becoming apparent in a few literary minds, would blossom in the future.[45] Stearns himself, in his essay on "The Intellectual Life" in the collection, lamented that Americans "still think in pioneer terms, whatever the material and economic facts of a day that has already outgrown their application." And, he went on, "the pioneer must of necessity hate the thinker . . . because the thinker is a liability to a community that can afford only assets." Stearns was actually a little kinder to the pioneer type than some of his fellow cultural critics, for he did at least argue that the pioneer's anti-intellectualism was a product of economic factors beyond that figure's control. Nevertheless, he deemed the shortcomings of American intellectual life a product of a pioneer mindset that was, unfortunately, still ominously present. Stearns did end on a positive note, however, expressing hope that "the shackles" of America's "spiritual prison" could be broken.[46]

Brooks's unflattering linkage of the puritan and the pioneer was repeated by a number of intellectuals in the period. Stearns's collection included an essay by musical composer Deems Taylor that attributed the technical and intellectual impotence of American compositions to "the pioneer," for whom "there was little room for art of any sort, and least for music," and "the Puritan," to whom "music, both for its own sake and as entertainment, was anathema."[47] Music critic Paul Rosenfeld commented in a similar vein that only "pioneering and puritanism and the republic of business" stood in the way of an American musical renaissance.[48] Social critic Henry L. Mencken also attacked the puritan strain in American culture, and though he did not often make direct mention of the pioneer, his scathing attacks on "the Anglo-Saxon" and the "husbandman," taken together, contain many of the elements present in Brooks's attack on the pioneer.[49]

The architectural critic and cultural analyst Lewis Mumford drew heavily on Brooks's ideas in formulating his critique of America's cultural underdevelopment.[50] In his 1924 work *Sticks and Stones: A Study of American Architecture and Civilization*, Mumford exploded the romantic images of the pioneer, replacing them with images of crass materialism and environmental destruction. Small wonder, then, that the country had not developed any high civilization when such low motives drove the nation's inhabitants.[51] But there was a healthy precedent for the future buried deep in the American past, Mumford argued in this next book, *The Golden Day* (1926). The pioneer was no less a villain in this work, but Mumford attempted to exonerate that popular target, the puritan, from responsibility as his cultural predecessor. The puritan, Mumford said, had sought an "inner grace" that was well complemented by the orderly, settled society that he tried to create. But the pioneer, with a wide-open continent before him, had "debased all the old values of a settled culture . . . [and] made the path of a dehumanized industrialism in America as smooth as a concrete road." If puritan society had been allowed to progress at a slow, orderly pace, a noteworthy culture would have developed. But the open frontier provided opportunity only for the evasion of social responsibility, "and the return to Nature led, ironically, to a denatured environment." "So much for an experience," Mumford remarked, "that failed either to absorb an old culture or create a new one!"[52] Yet he was confident that the frontierless future held great things in store for America. Mumford, his biographer tells us, viewed the New England towns of the puritan period as predecessors of "the garden cities he hoped to build in America, well-planned communities that had placed limits on their physical growth, and that had divided their land according to social need and function, not profit."[53] Again the point was that with the frontier closed and its influence fading, that bright future could be secured.

A similar argument was made in an article that appeared in the *Survey* in 1927 bearing the familiar title "America's Coming of Age." The author focused less on the nation's cultural development than on its likely role in world affairs now that the frontier age had passed. The pioneer's proclivity for spontaneous action without careful reflection, the essay stated, had been relatively harmless during the frontier period (aside from its effects on the Indians and the buffalo, the author noted), but now, in "a shrinking world filled with claims and clamors," the country would have to adopt a spirit of social responsibility. America would have to "come of age" if it was to bring to the world "some element of a larger and common humanity that will make war a crime . . . and the bullying of weaker nations the sign of a backward civilization." The passing of the frontier would make that possible.[54]

The work of these writers who breathed a sigh of relief at the passing of the frontier bears testimony to the pervasiveness of the closed-frontier theme in the period. Their ideas were an undercurrent, not the dominant tone, yet they would prove worthy precursors of the revolt against the frontier and the pioneer that developed more fully in the depression-ridden thirties. But concerns of a seemingly more pressing and practical nature than the supposed barrenness of American cultural life occupied the minds of a good many writers and thinkers in the postwar years. Would humankind even be able to subsist in the postfrontier world, let alone enjoy the fruits of high culture? That was a commonly asked question in the 1920s.

9. MALTHUS REVISITED

By the early 1920s Frederick Jackson Turner had formulated his "sectional thesis," but he continued throughout the decade to try to gauge the impact of the closing of the frontier and predict what lay ahead for the nation.[1] In "The Children of the Pioneers," which appeared in the *Yale Review* in 1926, Turner seemed fairly confident that the qualities of pioneers were being kept alive by succeeding generations. He did, however, express some concern that the qualities of individuality and originality might become victims of the standardization that marked the modern age—a course that would "be false to the spirit of the pioneer."[2]

But "frontier-related" matters far more pressing than the survival of the pioneer spirit concerned Turner in the 1920s. His chief worry was Malthusian in nature. With America's frontier gone and few uninhabited areas anywhere in the world awaiting the march of human settlement, Turner addressed the issue of the nation's and the world's future as the "pressure of population" pressed upon the "means of subsistence." That was a leading theme of the commencement address he delivered at Clark University in 1924. Noting first that the immigration into America was becoming virtually impossible to assimilate, Turner then suggested that perhaps as little as two percent of the nation's population owned three-fifths of the country's wealth—"food for reflection on the outcomes of the pioneer democracy that sought equality as well as opportunity."[3] But more significant than these unseemly developments were "the tendencies exhibited by the countries of the world, including the United States, towards overpopulation":

> It is the striking fact that at the end of the generation since 1890, when the Superintendent of the Census reported that the American frontier

112

line could no longer be traced, a whole group of careful and reputable scholars have attempted to demonstrate quantitatively that before the year 2000, so great is the increase of population and so rapid the exhaustion of resources and such the diminishing production of food relative to population, our present standards of life must be abandoned or the birth rate decreased if we are not to feel the pressure of want and even of universal famine and war.[4]

In his Clark University speech Turner did express the hope that humankind's intellectual capacity might be great enough to overcome these horrifying trends. But for all his optimism, much of the remainder of Turner's career would be marked by a fascination with the writings of the various Malthusian-minded biologists, geographers, and economists he discussed in the address.[5]

During the 1920s these "Malthusian Alarmists," as they were known at the time, voiced the ultimate expression of anxiety over the closing of the frontier.[6] Frontier anxiety no longer revolved solely around the future of grand concepts such as individualism and democracy. Attention was now also focused on a simpler, starker reality—the future subsistence of the human race in a closed-frontier world.

That such Malthusian concerns arose in the wake of the acknowledged loss of the frontier is hardly surprising. The land-to-man ratio had been an integral element of the frontier anxiety of earlier periods. William Graham Sumner, Josiah Strong, Achille Loria, and innumerable others had drawn attention to the changing land-to-man ratio in the late nineteenth century. It seems only logical that with the frontier ostensibly gone and the nation's arable land more fully settled, the issue would emerge again. The link between the closed frontier theme and Malthusian thinking was a natural one. Frontier anxiety and "Malthusian anxiety" went hand in hand; with the frontier declared gone, with the supply of uncultivated arable land rapidly diminishing and population steadily increasing, many wondered how the country would sustain its population in the future.

The surprising thing, perhaps, is that Malthusian concerns were raised so frequently in the 1920s, which were marked by agricultural depression resulting from overproduction. America's farmers were producing far more food than the nation could possibly consume, and world markets were glutted, too. In an age of acute agricultural overproduction, the great fear among much of the intellectual community was future underproduction. This seemingly misplaced fear during an era of general prosperity (though not for agricultural producers) was not unusual. The 1880s, for example, had on the whole been relatively good years economically, yet there was no shortage of predictions of gloom and doom in that period, many of them centering around the closing of the frontier. Intellectual anxiety is probably no less prevalent during good times than during bad times, but the Malthusian concerns of the 1920s seemed to be most directly a product of the Great War. The war prompted lengthy examinations of population and food supply in many countries,[7] and could even be viewed—as Malthus had viewed wars—as a check on population growth. In the United States, in the wake of the war, the adequacy of the world's food supply in the light of its rapidly increasing population became one of the pressing questions of the day. That historians have largely ignored this topic does nothing to diminish its significance.[8]

During the years immediately prior to the outbreak of World War I, Malthusian concerns were occasionally voiced, just as they had been from time to time in the late nineteenth century. Turner touched on the theme in his presidential address to the American Historical Association in 1910.[9] Walter Weyl espoused Malthusian strictures in various magazine articles and in The New Democracy (1912).[10] "The pioneer days are over . . . [and] the supply of cheap land is nearly exhausted" another writer announced in the Atlantic Monthly in 1912. The nation's laborers would have to return to the land in large numbers and engage in subsistence farming if the country's growing millions were to be sustained, the author added.[11] Similar predictions surfaced periodically over the next few years. In the teens a comparative handful of observers contended that the age of frontier abundance—marked by a low land-to-man ratio—was over and the country was "confronted by the law of diminishing returns."[12] Their prophecies parallel the occasional expressions of frontier anxiety in the 1870s that preceded the abundant frontier concerns of the 1880s and 1890s.

These Malthusian concerns, voiced periodically during the second decade of the twentieth century, became a dominant feature of the book and magazine literature of the 1920s. Malthusian Alarmism was also evident in the scholarly periodicals of the day. Marcel Aurousseau, a geographer at the Carnegie Institute, was at the forefront of the movement. In a paper in The Geographical Review in 1921 Aurousseau argued that the pressure of population on the means of subsistence was acute indeed. "We are heading toward the crisis," he proclaimed, "of not being able to provide food for our rapidly increasing numbers." The present generation, he said, was in no great danger, but the next generation was. Aurousseau insisted that people would have to return to the soil if they were to feed themselves. "[A] rural population based on agricultural and pastoral pursuits must be accepted as a fundamental element in world development," he said. Each family would support itself, there would be no surplus, and consequently "no urban population would be possible."[13] Commenting on Aurousseau's prediction, Frederick Jackson Turner noted, "the end could be like the beginning in U.S. history."[14]

That same year Oliver E. Baker, the senior agricultural economist in the Department of Agriculture, offered some similarly gloomy predictions on the topic. The rapid increase in the population of the United States had forced settlement into the poorer, semiarid lands of the trans-Mississippi West and "the leached lands of the South." "The waves of population," he said, "are beating against the barriers of adverse physical conditions all along the shore-line of settlement. . . . The United States is passing through, if, indeed, it has not already passed the most significant period in its history." With its lands now fully settled, the country could only maintain its present "standard of well-being" through careful intensive cultivation. And even if every inch of the land was intensively cultivated, diets would have to change—meat would become a luxury, and staple products like corn, vegetables, and alfalfa would have to be grown more extensively.[15]

Baker reemphasized the urgency of the problem in an article in *Geographical Review* in January 1923. The country was at a "turning point" in its development, Baker said. Arable land was a finite commodity in America, but the population knew no limits and was increasing at the rate of a million and a half a year. The country's population was destined to equal that of Europe, but the concomitant reality would be a "standard of living . . . much like that in Europe today." "Our nation," he concluded, "is probably near, possibly past, the crest of average income per capita; and every increment in population is likely to increase the complaint of the high cost of living."[16] America's postfrontier reality, then, would be a slow downward spiral inexorably leading the country back to the wretched conditions of its distant European past. Baker had predicted the end of Eden, and the metaphorical snake entering the garden was population growth. Like Baker, Raymond Pearl, head of the Department of Biometry and Vital Statistics at Johns

Hopkins University, concluded that "our children's children will have to face a standard of living much below that we enjoy."[17]

The population question, British economist John Maynard Keynes proclaimed in an introduction to one important book on the topic, "is going to be . . . the greatest of all social questions—a question which will arouse some of the deepest instincts and emotions of men, and about which feelings may run as passionately as in earlier struggles between religions."[18] Keynes's comments were not too far off the mark, either. In the United States a debate soon evolved around the question of the acuteness of the pressure of population on the means of subsistence. The debate had manifold ramifications: If the world was becoming overpopulated, then what was the "saturation point"—the level of optimum population—and when would it be reached? Should birth control be practiced to control population growth and ensure a decent standard of life? And if population was to be limited through birth control, would it not be best to restrict the productivity of the supposedly genetically inferior lower classes? Would it not make sense somehow to limit the fertility of the nonwhite races to prevent the Anglo-Saxon race from being overrun? Would the logical outcome of this population pressure be a massive war between developed continents for the food resources of less developed regions? Or might the future hold "a vast world struggle between higher civilizations with a low birth rate and lower civilizations with a high birth rate"?[19] Would (as renowned British geographer Halford J. Mackinder contended) Russia lead the Asian and Arabic peoples against the European coastal lowlands in a fight for foodstuffs and access to the sea?[20] Was the human race destined for a primal hand-to-mouth existence, or would wars, famines, and pestilences—Malthus's population controls—regulate population size? Or, in one of the brighter scenarios, would population regulate its size naturally in accordance with the planet's available resources?[21] All of these questions became common features of the debate.

On the question of the saturation point, though there was much concern with the world's future, many of those who addressed the theme focused primarily on the situation in the United States. One of the eminent figures engaged in the debate was the internationally renowned biologist Raymond Pearl. By the middle of the decade Pearl had rejected the gloomiest predictions of the Alarmists and had come to argue that population would level off whenever the pressure of population on the available resources became acute. Pearl experimented first with yeast cultures and vinegar fruit flies and developed logistic curves that demonstrated the leveling off of population in accordance with the availability of food resources. Pearl found that Algeria's population statistics fit his curves exactly. With the validity of his methods established, Pearl estimated that the United States would reach its optimum population level of 197 million in the year 2100 and would never grow larger.[22]

Don D. Lescohier, a professor of economics at the University of Wisconsin, put the saturation point at 300 million for the United States. Lescohier contended that it would not be "Pearl's Curves"—nature's answer to the pressure of population—but the ever-increasing intelligence of humankind that would safeguard a level of civilization befitting the twentieth century.[23] Lescohier explained in another essay, in the American Review, that as food became more scarce and prices rose, people would see the economic advantage in limiting their family size; human intelligence would be coupled with human ambition in limiting population growth.[24] Pearl and Lescohier were not alone in their hopeful predictions, but alarmism was more the order of the day than optimism.[25]

For many it was simply a question of when the country's saturation point would be reached, and a good deal of time was spent calculating how long food and mineral supplies would remain sufficient. While some predicted that a meager, peasant-like existence was the best the country could hope for in the postfrontier future, others predicted that a series of wars, plagues, and famines might ensure a decent level of existence, at least for those who escaped these ravages. Frederick Jackson Turner, who was an avid collector of writings on the population problem, wrote in 1923 that if people did not come to their senses and limit population growth, then perhaps the most desirable solution would be a "friendly comet" or a "chemist's bomb" bringing human existence to an abrupt end.[26] Turner vacillated in his thinking between a healthy skepticism regarding the Alarmists and a nagging fear that their predictions might ring true. And in his more pessimistic moments, a swift, Armageddon-like end seemed preferable to a future marked by peasantry.[27] Turner agonized over the dilemma and in the early 1920s delivered lectures on the "Strategy for a Saturated Earth" and "The Outcome of the Western Movement."[28] The lecture notes from his last teaching days at Harvard, in the spring semester of 1924, were filled with references to the writings of the Malthusian Alarmists and their more sober-minded opponents, and were marked by uncertainty on Turner's part.[29] As had been the case with his earlier efforts to address the problem of America's postfrontier future, Turner was unable to reach any firm solutions to the problem of "diminishing returns," though he did at one point allude to the feasibility of internationalizing the world's resources—a course that the World Agriculture Society also advocated in 1924.[30]

Some of those who addressed the problem offered solutions, too. The Harvard geographer Edward M. East, in his ominously entitled book *Mankind at the Crossroads* (1923), argued that America had reached the point of diminished returns and "by 1960 or 1980" would experience "a population pressure such as we of this age and generation have never imagined." East estimated that the saturation point for the United States would be a population of around 300 million. But if the rate of increase was not lessened, the country was likely to exceed that mark, and disastrous consequences would arise. There was, though, in East's reckoning, one sure way to take the pressure off the nation's dwindling food resources: "a severe permanent restriction on immigration." East contended that "any present cry for immigration can only be made by the fool, the hypocrite, or the ignorant." The United States was in a unique position, he said. It had, in little over a century, grown "from an unexploited wilderness" to a nation "approaching the saturation point" and experiencing "decreasing returns in agriculture."[31]

The problem was quite clear in East's thinking—the nation had entered the postfrontier age and needed to make the necessary adjustments. Mankind might be at the crossroads, but foremost in East's mind was making sure that the United States, with its comparative abundance, did not remain the destination for the transients of the world. The country, he said, had held to the strange belief that the "[Melting] Pot itself had a kind of mystical virtue, that it was built of the substance of the philosopher's stone and turned its contents into pure gold." "Such fairy-tales," he asserted, "are suited only to childhood, and the nation has passed its childhood." The Melting Pot had worked because the early immigrants, "even the earlier Jewish immigrants," came from the "best stocks." With good materials and an empty continent to work with, the process of assimilation and Americanization had been a relatively easy one, but this was no longer the case. Now it was the "lowest stocks" that were being poured into the melting pot, and "if dross is poured in," East charged, "dross it remains."[32]

East was hardly alone in linking the problem of population growth to the need for immigration restriction in the 1920s. The theme continued to be a prevalent one, just as it had been in the last decades of the nineteenth century. And, just as in those years, the closed-frontier theme often complemented the unabashedly racist arguments of the day. Madison Grant's enormously popular Nordic supremacist diatribe, *The Passing of the Great Race* (1916), appeared in revised editions in the early 1920s. Grant, like East, chided the nation's faith in its "Melting Pot." Grant displayed a heady enthusiasm for the country's pioneer heritage and extolled the virtues of the Nordic "Western frontiersman." But, Grant argued, the non-Nordic types were unassimilable and had to be denied entry to the country, and those tens of millions that already resided in the United States must be systematically exterminated through the application of eugenicist techniques—segregation and sterilization.[33] Raymond Pearl also prescribed sterilization and segregation as a partial cure for the nation's dilemma, but lamented that such procedures would be difficult to implement.[34] Cognizant of the fact that some regarded the science of eugenics as a rather unsophisticated justification for racism, one eugenicist writing in the *Yale Review* in 1921 declared, "don't call this Eugenics; call it scientific Americanization."[35] Whatever they were called, the racist urges of the postwar years were made more palatable when shrouded in a cloak of postfrontier Malthusian Alarmism.

Isaiah Bowman, director of the American Geographical Society of New York, addressed the immigration issue in the early years of the decade in a two-volume work, *The New World: Problems in Political Geography.* Bowman declared that the era of diminishing returns had been reached with the completion of the settlement of the public domain and commended the Emergency Immigration Act of 1921 for addressing the problem directly. The legislation, Bowman said, was doing a good job of keeping inferior and less assimilable southern and eastern European elements out of the country. Consequently the country's democratic institutions would prevail and a healthy land-to-man ratio would be preserved.[36]

It is difficult to determine exactly the effect that this postfrontier Malthusian Alarmism had on the shaping of immigration policy in the early 1920s. Racism was certainly the prime motivating force behind this legislation, but the congressional debates often featured a mixture of Malthusian Alarmism and simple racism. If the population of the United States were destined by the end of the century to number in excess of 200 million, then what possible justification could there be for allowing immigrants to continue to pour in and exacerbate the population problem, especially when they were the "dullest and dumbest people in Europe"?[37] Michigan representative Earl C. Michener, speaking in the House in April 1924, expressed his sympathy for the people of Europe who sought the asylum of America, but added: "Water seeks its level, and without a dam at the border the overflow will inundate us and the time will soon be when the salient features of our government will be obliterated and when we will be more foreign than American. . . . The early pioneers, who with the ax in the forest and the plow in the prairie transformed the great American wilderness into this modern Garden of Eden, were men from Northern Europe." But the inferior new immigrant elements were less assimilable and the country was suffering from "national indigestion."[38]

Among the dissenting voices was that of Oliver E. Baker, who was more a Malthusian Alarmist than a racist. For Baker, it was simple population growth that threatened the Garden of Eden, not the quality of the incoming immigrants. And for Louis I. Dublin, president of the American Statistical Association and editor of a collection of essays on *Population Problems in the United States and Canada* (1926), the efforts of those like Michener and Grant to shroud their nativism in a cloak of science and statistics were reprehensible. This same "exaggerated nationalism," Dublin charged, had given rise to both the new immigration policy and the Ku Klux Klan. Population problems must be addressed with a higher level of detachment and sophistication, he said.[39]

Unfortunately Dublin's call was rarely answered in the 1920s, and racism and Malthusian Alarmism together proved a more common mix than detachment and sophistication. Edward M. East, for example, lectured in 1925 on "The Biology of the Immigration Question" before a round table on "Agriculture and Population Increase" at Williams College, Massachusetts. Responding to a paper by the Italian fascist Count Antonio Cippico, which demanded outlets for his country's surplus population, East created quite a stir when he insisted that birth control was the only rational solution to that country's dilemma. If the United States continued to offer refuge to "the dregs" of Italy, then that country would continue to reproduce at an alarming rate.[40]

The same argument was made by the sociologist Edward Allsworth Ross in his book *Standing Room Only* (1927). Ross concentrated less on the southern and eastern European immigrants than on the "Asiatic masses [who] breed without reflection or forethought, imagining virtue and profit in multitude." Ross expressed extreme relief that the United States had reversed its traditional immigration policy. "Another liberal half-century," he said, "and the American people would have become as motley as the dwellers in the Nile Valley today. The economic, cultural, and social elevation of the common man—which is likely to be America's best gift to humanity—would have been aborted." Simply put, the lack of immigration restrictions would encourage the so-called lower races to reproduce at an alarming rate, because the excess could be siphoned off into less heavily populated regions like the United States. If this phenomenon were allowed to continue, there would be "standing room only" in the world. Thus the United States, by restricting immigration, was doing the world a favor without the world knowing or appreciating it.[41]

By the last years of the decade the clamor over immigration restriction had subsided, partly because the restrictionists had secured and defended the legislation they desired, and their opponents knew it would not soon be overturned. Malthusian fears subsided, too, partly because statistics clearly demonstrated that the birthrates in Europe and America were declining, partly because overproduction was becoming an obvious reality in America,[42] and partly, it ought to be added, because a restrictive immigration policy had been secured. Malthusian fears—which in the United States were largely centered around the notion of America as a frontierless nation incapable of increasing significantly its agricultural capacity—had played an important role in shaping major public policy debates. As the country began to slip into a deep economic depression—in part because of the problem of overproduction—those same Malthusian fears about the future were displaced by the more immediate concerns of the present. But if Malthusian Alarmism became redundant in the depression years, the closed-frontier theme certainly did not. In fact, during the New Deal years this theme was as central an element of social, cultural, and political thought as it had been during any other period, including the 1890s.

10. THE NEW DEAL FRONTIER

In May 1931 an essay by Charles Morrow Wilson entitled "The Surviving American Frontier" appeared in the journal *Current History*. Wilson commented favorably on the qualities—rigor, virility, spontaneous democracy—traditionally associated with the frontier. There was a certain validity to these characterizations, Wilson said, but the accompanying popular assumption "that the age of frontiers is passed is decidedly at variance with fact." "The essential qualities of frontier life are little changed," he argued, and went on to describe the hardships endured by the nation's contemporary pioneers in the "Southern Highlands"—Appalachia and the Ozark Hills of Missouri, Arkansas, and Oklahoma.[1] In viewing Appalachia as a residual frontier, it seems that Wilson was confusing backwoods poverty with the idealized frontier simplicity of an earlier age. If he had told the inhabitants of the southern highlands what he told his readership in the essay—that their poverty and despair were benign attributes that heightened their simple democratic virtuousness—he might have experienced a kind of frontier justice similar to that of earlier days.

Wilson was not alone in pointing to the significance of America's residual frontiers. Another writer claimed that the nation's wilderness areas were only half settled and were growing in size as farmers fled to the city. The author pointed to residual frontiers in Pennsylvania, northern New York, in the South's coastal plain from Virginia to Georgia, in New England, and around the Great Lakes—even in New Jersey, where wildcats were being hunted once more. In fact Wilson listed wild frontiers in just about every state in the nation. America, it seems, was vastly underpopulated; indeed, settlers had been dropped into the wilderness "like a handful of seed thrown from a mountain top," and were simply unable to stem the counterattack of an "unconquered frontier."[2] Johns Hopkins geographer Isaiah Bowman, in his study *The Pioneer Fringe* (1931), argued that frontier areas existed in parts of the United States—and all over the world, for that matter. "The attack upon the conquerable land continues on a wide front," Bowman argued, and "tens of thousands of men of varied breeds still seek the frontier zone of every continent." If all the existing frontier lands of the world were gathered together they would rival the United States in size, he said. Millions already resided in these frontiers, and millions more could be accommodated. These lands were "not merely crumbs for the poor man." Hard work—of the traditional pioneering sort—would be required for settling them, but they were potentially profitable tracts of land. Bowman's thesis, particularly as it was outlined in an article on Montana's remaining frontier in the *American Geographical Review* earlier that year, irritated Frederick Jackson Turner. Bowman had implied that Turner was mistaken in assuming the frontier had closed in 1890, and it took an interesting exchange of letters between the two (which demonstrates Turner's annoyance at having to defend a paper that was nearly forty years old) to calm the waters.[3] Bowman's thesis was quite interesting, and his study was broad in scope and exhaustive in detail. Similar commentaries on the continued existence of the physical frontier appeared from time to time in the thirties (though most dealt only with the United States), but they were all, in a sense, anomalies.[4] Though Turner's thesis was almost four decades old and the frontier theme in American thought was more than a century older, the question of the presence of a landed frontier was still generating debate. For the vast majority of observers the physical frontier was a thing of the past, but these statements of faith in the survival of the physical frontier neatly parallel one of the key intellectual themes of the 1930s.

Although the Malthusian Alarmism of the 1920s had subsided, the onset of the Great Depression was a clear indication for some that the era of diminished returns had arrived. The nation's economy, it was charged, had matured during the postfrontier age, but now the inevitable consequences of the frontier's closing were being felt.[5] If the great frontier safety-valve was now gone, then the government would have to step in and compensate for its loss, or so New Deal liberals argued. For conservative-minded thinkers, such as arch-individualist Herbert Hoover, the frontier could never close so long as its spirit survived, and a good dose of healthy individualism would see the country through this latest economic setback just as it supposedly had during earlier trying times. In the political arena, the "frontier debate" of the depression years had little to do directly with whether or not the genuine "Leatherstocking types"—which so occupied Charles Morrow

Wilson—still existed, but it focused on the question of the existence of the frontier and its potency as a safety valve. And many conservative-minded intellectuals were as adamant in their defense of the continued existence of pioneer qualities as Wilson and a few others were in their insistence that the pioneer environment—the physical frontier—was alive and well. Furthermore, in the literary arena the themes of the closing of the frontier and the passing of the frontier type received perhaps their fullest expression in the 1930s.

In the mid-1920s Frederick Jackson Turner had written of the achievements of the "Children of the Pioneers," hoping that pioneer qualities might survive in the absence of the environment that had fostered them. A lesser-known historian remarked gloomily in 1932, "we have lost the individual self-reliance of our grandfathers, who knew how to do things for themselves. . . . [and] our society has been evolving in such a way that it has been producing fewer and fewer of the old pioneering class."[6] John Steinbeck adopted a more neutral tone, but nonetheless gave the theme of the end of pioneering its most poignant treatment in his story "The Leader of the People" (1938). In this story Steinbeck addressed the psychological effects of the closing of the frontier on Grandpa Tifflin, who had led the settlers across the plains and the mountains to California. The old man is reduced to spending his last days retelling the story of his pioneering exploits. His son, Carl, has no time for the old man's reminiscences, but his grandson, Jody, listens eagerly and expresses the hope that someday he might lead the people in similar endeavors. But Grandpa smiles ruefully at Jody's suggestion and tells him that the "westering" process is over and "There's no place to go. There's the ocean to stop you. There's a line of old men along the shore hating the ocean because it stopped them." Maybe the ocean doesn't have to be the end of it all, Jody replies, suggesting that he might lead the people across the sea to new frontiers. But Grandpa reminds him again that "there is no place to go. . . . Every place is taken." And "that's not the worst," he adds; the saddest part is that "westering has died out of the people. Westering isn't a hunger any more. It's all gone."[7] The old man has no place and no purpose in postfrontier America.

The closing of the frontier and the destruction of the myth of the garden were central elements in Steinbeck's work in the 1930s. In *To a God Unknown* (1933) he adopted his home locale—the fertile valleys of northern California—as the setting in which Joseph Wayne unsuccessfully seeks to fulfill the promise of the garden myth. The notion of an Arcadian paradise was further dismantled in the harrowing collection of tales in the ironically titled *The Pastures of Heaven* (1932).[8] The sturdy, independent yeoman farmer—a central element in America's agrarian mythology—was replaced in *In Dubious Battle* (1936) by those elements most antithetical to the myth— large landholders and oppressed workers. In *Of Mice and Men* (1937), Stein- beck traced the destruction of George and Lennie's dream of carving out a little place of their own and achieving independent yeoman status. In his finest and most successful work, *The Grapes of Wrath* (1939), Steinbeck showed that contrary to Grandpa Tifflin's lamentations, the hunger for westering still remained and the garden myth was still a potent force, as ex- pressed most poignantly by Grandpa Joad, who swears that when he gets to the promised land he will "get a whole big bunch a grapes . . . an' . . . squash 'em on my face an' let 'em run offen my chin."[9] The promise of the frontier— the California Eden—was still alive for the Joads and for tens of thousands of families like them who were forced off the Great Plains by the depression and the dustbowl of the 1930s. But they discovered that the frontier had lost its transience and the promised Eden was more akin to a hell on earth.

The solution to the dilemma of the closed frontier that Steinbeck offered in *The Grapes of Wrath* was government intervention. Numerous references to the inhumanity of the corporations (which are viewed as a postfrontier phenomenon) are scattered throughout the book, and the only place of ref- uge for the migrant workers is the Weedpatch government camp. It seems that for Steinbeck, who was a frequent visitor to the migrant labor camps set up by the Roosevelt administration, government assistance and a healthy collective democratic spirit were the only things that might offset the devastating effects of the passing of the frontier.[10]

The poet Archibald MacLeish, too, placed heavy emphasis on the closing of the frontier and the concomitant rise of corporate power.[11] In his moving poem "The Land of the Free," which was accompanied by the photographs of Dorothea Lange, Arthur Rothstein, and Walker Evans, among others (all under the auspices of the New Deal's Farm Security Administration), Mac- Leish pointed to the falseness of the assumption that the frontier's benefits would last indefinitely. "There was always some place else a man could head for," he says. "We looked west from a rise and we saw forever. . . ." [but] Now that the land's behind us we got wondering/ We wonder if the liberty was land and the/ Land's gone: The liberty's back of us."

MacLeish explained that the security the frontier had offered was gone. The time had passed when a settler on a "quarter section of free land" could "look any goddam sonofabitch in the eye and tell him to head for hell at the next turn-off."

> To tell the sonofbitches where to head
> You need your heel-hold on a country steady
> You need a continent against your feet.

Now that security no longer existed, the dust bowl had blown away the top-soil and the land was no longer free. The reader is reminded of the share-croppers at the beginning of *The Grapes of Wrath* who are powerless against the land company that evicts them from the land, and anguished and frustrated because there is no individual who can be held accountable. MacLeish wondered "if the liberty is done," if "the dreaming is finished," and (like Steinbeck) "if there's a liberty a man can mean that's Men—not land. We wonder. We don't know, we're asking," he painfully concluded.[12]

Another tremendously moving book of photographs with accompanying commentary by Dorothea Lange and Paul Schuster Taylor, entitled *An American Exodus* (1939), would have provided the perfect visual accompaniment for *The Grapes of Wrath*, which appeared the same year. And the authors' message was the same, too. "For three centuries an ever-receding western frontier has drawn white men like a magnet," the authors stated. And unfortunately, "the tradition still draws distressed, dislodged, determined Americans to our last West, hard against the waters of the Pacific." But the last West, the authors instructed, was gone, and the "opportunity to obtain intermittent employment in a disorganized labor market—no experience required—is our new frontier, our new West."[13]

Although both Steinbeck and MacLeish were enamored of the myths of the West, they argued against their perpetuation like Lange and Taylor. They were joined in this by scores of writers and thinkers in the 1930s. Typical of this genre was an article in the *North American Review* in 1931 by Carey McWilliams. McWilliams criticized the historical and literary writing on the West that had appeared since 1900, calling it a "post mortem on the frontier" and "a literature of rediscovery." He charged that it was hard "to forgive those elaborate and unnecessary obfuscations of the rediscoverer, who sits in a swivel chair and enjoys the vicarious thrill of being an imaginary frontiersmen." "Out of this misty and mythological mood," he went on, "has been born the inordinate modern day enthusiasm for the frontier and the frontiersman."[14] The frontier, McWilliams later asserted in his classic account of migratory farm labor in California, *Factories in the Fields*

(1939), "became useless long before it quit functioning." Now it was time to bury the heroic images of the homesteader and look instead at the wheat and cattle barons and the modern-day land companies and agribusinesses that forced the laborer into a life of deprivation and servitude.[15]

This change in outlook toward the frontier tradition was evident in the historical writing of the 1930s. Attacks on Turner's frontier thesis began appearing in the 1920s and by the 1930s constituted the dominant strain in writing on the West and the frontier.[16] Popular restatements of the frontier thesis did appear in the thirties, including Robert E. Riegel's *America Moves West* (1930) and Dan Elbert Clark's *The West in American History* (1937), but the transition from neo-Turnerian to anti-Turnerian was well under way by this time. The Turner thesis came under attack for various reasons, among them Turner's hazy definition of the frontier itself and the questionable effectiveness of the safety valve. But the most cutting criticism centered around Turner's evaluation of the virtues of rugged individualism—qualities that now seemed inapplicable to the conditions of the postfrontier era. In an age when historians adopted more firmly a "presentist" perspective in an effort to make their writings serve a social purpose, the unrestrained individualism of the frontier era came to be viewed as a malevolent aspect of the nation's development, just as it had been during the Progressive era.[17] The widely read historian Charles A. Beard, for example, attacked "The Myth of Rugged Individualism" in an article in *Harper's Magazine* in 1931. Beard argued that "the individualist creed of everybody for himself and the devil take the hindmost is principally responsible for the distress in which Western civilization finds itself." He pointed to the need for a radical modification of the philosophy of rugged individualism to meet the needs of an age that required a more "cooperative" ethos. Beard, whose primary emphasis was on the struggle between capital and labor, made no allusions to the closed frontier theme in his essay, but there was no shortage of historians who did.[18]

New York University professor Henry Steele Commager bade a fond "Farewell to Laissez-Faire" in *Current History* in August 1933. He argued that the legislation of the First Hundred Days (begun only a few months earlier) marked a healthy "repudiation of obsolete shibboleths of individualism and laissez-faire and a full throated assertion of the right and purpose of democratic society to readjust its legal machinery to the demands of a new order. . . . Laissez-faire, despite its foreign accent, was no importation. It was born of the American wilderness and of the boundless resources of the American continent." The philosophy had been a sound one for America in the late eighteenth and early nineteenth centuries, when there was enough land and resources "to make all men independent." But then, with "the principle of non-interference . . . firmly established":

> Like an invading horde Americans surged across the continent, reaping where they had not sowed, destroying where they had not created, dissipating the resources of nature that were meant for future generations. . . . In the name of individualism and enterprise Americans had used up those fabulous stores of wealth that were to be the foundation of a new society.[19]

The old pioneers of the open frontier, Commager explained, were the natural ancestors of the businessmen of the postfrontier age. These men had been objects of adulation in the 1920s when the Republican administrations had lent full support to the creeds of laissez-faire and rugged individualism. But the depression had "shattered . . . the temple of prosperity . . . and the religion of individualism which it symbolized." Commager was relieved by the New Deal's abandonment of laissez-faire, which could only be destructive in the postfrontier era, and hoped that repudiation would be upheld in the courts.[20]

The popular amateur historian and columnist James Truslow Adams made similar observations in a lead article in the *New York Times Sunday Magazine* in March 1934. Adams directed his thoughts at "those who profess the greatest fear lest the New Deal may destroy our rugged individualism." One quality that was conspicuously absent from this revered "rugged individualism," Adams said (echoing the thinking of Waldo Frank, Lewis Mumford, Van Wyck Brooks, and others), was originality. Americans, he charged, had been "marvelously ingenious in utilizing the ideas of others," but low on ideas of their own. Furthermore, Adams argued quite subtly, the lauded "self-reliance" of the pioneers did not in fact constitute a very accurate mirror of reality. These unrestrainable individualists were (as some historians have subsequently noted) not too proud to ask for government assistance when it served their interests. But the doctrine of rugged individualism had "gradually emerged as a combination of a sentimental legend of the self-reliance of the farmer and the frontiersman, with the calculated policy of ruthless exploiters of big and little business enterprises." This doctrine "demanded the least possible interference by government" and came to be linked with the self-reliance of the frontier, which might be ruined by paternalism.[21]

The demands of the present, Adams concluded, were different from those of the frontier past when Jefferson had called for only minimal restraints upon the lives of individuals. Yet even in the infinitely more complex present, totalitarian controls were hardly necessary; rather, individualism might ascend to higher levels "by the exercise of self-control, cooperation and social intelligence." Adams did not expect the New Deal to bring about a revolution in American life, but if it succeeded in making the individual more socially responsible, it would help dismantle the mythological constructs that had been reinforced by the Republican administrations of the 1920s and thereby achieve a success of no small proportions.[22]

That much of American history in the 1930s was "present-minded" should hardly come as a surprise, for present-mindedness has rarely been absent from historical writing in America. That the concerns of historians were so clearly dictated by the realities of the present in that decade should come as no great revelation either; periods of crisis have as marked an effect on historians as they do on any other social commentators. It is interesting, however, that the historical concerns of the era were so clearly paralleled by the political concerns. The frontier theme played as obvious a role in the political thought of the depression decade as it did in the historical discourse, even if subsequent generations of historians have been slow to understand that reality.

Curtis Nettles, a student of Turner's, focused on the relationship between the passing of the frontier and the rise of the New Deal in an article in the *Wisconsin Magazine of History* in March 1934. "One striking view of the engineers of the new deal," he said, "is their perception of the passing of the economic stimulus of the frontier." Now that the frontier no longer existed, something had to be put in its place. Ruthless competition would have to give way to an ordered economic society, and the New Dealers seemed to realize as much. In decidedly Turnerian fashion, Nettles argued the more questionable thesis that those New Dealers who advocated a new frontier of governmental intervention to replace the old frontier of free land tended to come from western states, "where the pioneer ideals of democracy and opportunity still enjoy a robust life."[23] But if the New Deal was not a product of the frontier itself, Nettles was on solid ground when he argued that it was heavily influenced by the recognition of the frontier's passing. And, in fact, the most influential and extensive commentary by a historian on the closed-frontier theme in the thirties came in direct response to the Supreme

Court's decision in January 1936 on the unconstitutionality of the the New Deal's Agricultural Adjustment Administration.

Walter Prescott Webb's book *Divided We Stand: The Crisis of a Frontierless Democracy* (the title was actually chosen by the publisher) appeared in November 1937 after a "publishing crisis" of no small proportions. Though it sold poorly, copies of the book reached Roosevelt and various congressmen, and the president utilized some of the book's ideas in a nationally aired radio speech the following January.[24] Making use of the book's main themes (particularly its virulent antimonopolism) must have been an easy task. *Divided We Stand* was as present-minded a piece of historical writing as any; in fact, in many ways it was less history than contemporary political observation—of the most polemical kind. Webb argued that the North dominated economically both the South and the West. The vast majority of the nation's banks and corporations, insurance firms, and media outlets were centered in the North, along with the federal government. Northern industrial interests, in close collusion with the Republican Party, had their regional neighbors locked in a corporate stranglehold and were bleeding them dry. And this dangerous situation, Webb charged, had unfolded since the closing of the frontier in 1890.

According to Webb, historians had been quick to note that the frontier had been a dominant force up to 1890, but had been slow to realize that "the *absence* of the frontier has been just as dominant since 1890."[25] He was underestimating the prevalence of the closed-frontier theme in American thought since 1890; others, of course, had pointed to the emergence of corporate America in the wake of the frontier's passing. But Webb's argument was more forceful and direct than any others before it. His earlier masterpiece, *The Great Plains* (1931), had focused squarely on the regional distinctiveness of the West, treating it as a "place" rather than a "process"—a stage in the advance of the frontier. [26] Though Webb never downplayed the West's distinctiveness, in *Divided We Stand* he treated its development (or better, underdevelopment) within the broader context of the nation's frontier past. The last of the country's regions to be developed, the West had become, predictably, a colonial dependent of the well-developed North. Webb concurred with previous generations of American "exceptionalists" that the frontier process had made the nation distinct, and that its termination was grave cause for concern. Historians, he said, had either "claimed too much for the frontier as a cause for what is considered American," or they were left with the difficult task of "telling us how we can preserve the frontier virtues of individualism, self-reliance, and other virtues essential to democracy when there is no frontier." He then went on to insist that historians had not claimed too much for the frontier, but that the time had come to "recognize it as a past fact, and no longer a positive factor in American growth"—to recognize the full seriousness of its absence. Historians had for too long explored "Turner's Peak," Webb said, and were now obligated to "go into the valley on the near side of the peak"—the postfrontier present—and examine it just as thoroughly.[27]

Webb's focus on the frontier virtues of individualism and self-reliance seemed at first to echo that of conservatives who sought to protect such qualities from the stifling influence of government regulation. But Webb did have major misgivings about the viability of unrestrained individualism in a postfrontier environment. Businessmen might complain about the infringements on their freedom, but Webb argued that if "business enslaves men, then men must unite to limit business in order that they may regain some measure of freedom." If laissez-faire was passing away, or being legislated out of existence by the government, it was only because the law was "making general what business practise [had] already made actual." In short, business had "abandoned the principle of laissez-faire for that of monopoly," and the government was abandoning the principle, too, "in behalf of the people." Webb concluded that "Democracy of the frontier type must give way in both cases."[28]

After discussing the change in America's immigration laws in the context of the closing of the frontier, Webb discussed the opportunities afforded the nation's inhabitants by the western safety valve. The need for substantive government intervention during the frontier era had been minimal. However, the task of democratic government in the postfrontier era—in the absence of the safety valve—Webb said, was "one of providing conditions under which a considerable majority of the people may be fairly prosperous." Those who objected to the government's efforts to alleviate the depression on the grounds that democratic principles were being abandoned were thoroughly mistaken. The government had simply taken over the task that the frontier had once performed; it was administering aid and regulating big business in the public interest instead of giving away individual homesteads.[29] And the Supreme Court was reacting to the New Deal government's necessary assumption of responsibility by declaring its agencies, particularly the National Recovery Administration and the Agricultural Adjustment Administration, unconstitutional.

Webb's book was most certainly a "tract for the times."[30] It was a provocative commentary on the centrality of the issue of the closed frontier to the sociopolitical present. And considering the high respect afforded intellectuals by the Roosevelt administration, it was hardly surprising that the closed-frontier theme so prevalent in the intellectual climate of the era entered into the political discourse of the day.

The onset of the Great Depression marked a definite watershed, not just in the country's economic fortunes, but in the minds of the public. "There was," as one historian remarked, "an acute historical awareness on the part of contemporary observers [that they had] . . . reached a turning point in their lives and in the evolution of the country," that one era had closed and another had begun.[31] In October 1930, a year after the stock market crash, a dialogue in the *Forum* between four prominent intellectuals—historian James Truslow Adams, literary critic Henry Seidel Canby, economist and social planner Stuart Chase, and author and dramatist Howard Mumford Jones—focused on the magnitude of the change. The discussion began with some reflections on the importance of the closing of the frontier in 1890, and Adams charged that the effects of its closing were only now beginning to be felt. The automobile industry and big business booms precipitated by the war had delayed the inevitable for a time, but now the nation was faced with the stark realities of the postfrontier age. Canby agreed that different economic habits from those developed during the pioneering era were sorely needed.[32]

The closed frontier-theme made an appearance in the political arena in January of the following year when newly inaugurated governor of Wisconsin, Philip La Follette, presented his program for a controlled state economy to the legislature. La Follette prefaced his plan with a summary of the Turner thesis, arguing that increased government intervention was necessary to replace the vanished frontier. To compensate for the loss he declared that "we must find our freedom and make our opportunity through wise and courageous readjustments of the political and economic order of State and Nation to the changed needs and changed conditions of our time."[33]

In September 1932, Franklin Delano Roosevelt made the theme the central element of his famous "Commonwealth Club" campaign address in San Francisco. The frontier theme was so much a part of the sociopolitical discourse of the day that it would have been surprising had Roosevelt not utilized it. It is worth mentioning, however, that almost thirty years before, as a Harvard undergraduate, Roosevelt had been enrolled in Turner's course on "The Development of the West," which addressed at some length the question of what was to be done in the absence of the frontier.[34] Pointing, in his speech, to the period of expansion in the nineteenth century and the socio-economic relations it had fostered, Roosevelt remarked:

> As long as we had free land; as long as our population was growing by leaps and bounds; as long as our industrial plants were insufficient to supply our needs, society chose to give the ambitious man free play and unlimited reward provided only that he produced the economic plant so much desired. . . . In retrospect we can now see that the turn of the tide came with the turn of the century. We were reaching our last frontier; there was no more free land and our industrial combinations had become great uncontrolled and irresponsible units of power within the state.[35]

The result of all this, Roosevelt noted, was that "equality of opportunity as we have known it no longer exists" because "Our last frontier has long since been reached and there is practically no more free land." He further explained, "There is no safety valve in the form of a western prairie to which those thrown out of work by the Eastern economic machines can go for a new start." In the postfrontier age the country had "steered a steady course toward economic oligarchy," and now a "re-appraisal of values" was desperately needed. Unrestrained individualism would have to be tempered, and the government would have to play a wider role in ensuring "everyone an avenue to possess himself of a portion of that plenty sufficient for his needs, through his own work."[36]

Stuart Chase's A New Deal (1932) was published around the same time as Roosevelt's "Commonwealth Club" speech.[37] Chase reminded his readers of the statesman Albert Gallatin's century-old prophecy: Gallatin had marvelled at the tremendous material benefits that the United States enjoyed, but warned that they would last only "so long as the cheapness of unimproved land shall offer a certain employment to labor." The prophesied end had arrived, Chase asserted. And what was worse, the legacy of the open frontier had hampered the nation's development. "The pioneer," Chase argued, "while a bold fellow with axe and gun was a timorous fellow when it came to thinking about economic difficulties." Rather than get to the roots of the economic malaise that confronted him, the pioneer hitched up a covered wagon and escaped responsibility. But he could no longer avoid those responsibilities, because "the Utopia shut up shop forty years ago. The covered wagon reached the Pacific long since." "The realization that our future is not boundless," be observed, "is only now thrusting home." There was no longer any escape; economic battles would now have to be fought at home. The old pioneer psychology had little time for government, but the new society that Chase envisioned would have to find a place for it.[38]

What was needed, according to Chase and other commentators, such as *New Republic* editor George Soule and historian Charles Beard, was a carefully planned and regulated society. One group, led by the civil engineer Howard Scott and influenced by Thorstein Veblen's *The Engineers and the Price System* (1921), went so far as to propose the establishment of a "technocracy" run by a "directorate" of economic experts.[39] These social planners rejected capitalism altogether (though like Chase, many wished to work within the framework of representative democracy). The New Dealers, on the other hand, proposed a more moderate course, choosing to regulate the excesses of frontier individualism but to work within the capitalist framework.[40]

Roosevelt reiterated the closed-frontier argument in his book *Looking Forward*, which first appeared in March 1933 as the "First New Deal" got under way, and went through three subsequent printings that month. He looked back on the days of the open frontier, "the day of the individual against the system, the day in which individualism was made the great watchword in American life." In that era "starvation and dislocation were practically impossible," and "at the very worst there was always the possibility of climbing into a covered wagon and moving West." When a depression came it was easily alleviated by the opening of a new section of land in the West. But with the end of the frontier such simple solutions to economic distress were gone forever.[41] Roosevelt stressed the need for economic planning to regulate the power of the corporations. The wider public interest would have to take precedence over the interests of corporate America; the interests of the consumer would have to be elevated above those of the producer if "a more equitable distribution of the national income" was to be secured. Roosevelt was arguing (although he did not say it directly) that with the physical frontier gone the government would have to provide a new safety valve. Hugh Johnson, head of the National Recovery Administration (NRA), made the point explicitly in a speech in Chicago in September 1933. The open lands of the West had provided an outlet for the downtrodden during past depressions, he said, but now that the outlet was gone, the NRA would have to take over its function.[42]

Rexford G. Tugwell, Roosevelt's assistant secretary of agriculture, played up the closed-frontier theme in a lead article in the *New York Times Sunday Magazine* in July 1933. The article was designed to give the public an idea "of the basic philosophy of the experiment going on in Washington."

Tugwell presented that philosophy quite plainly. There could be no turning back to "the splendid simplicity of our log-cabin and town-meeting era." The imagined pleasantries of the past and the unattainable utopian visions of the future had to be exorcized from the American mind. "The reckless individualistic expansion of the nineteenth century is a closed era," Tugwell said. "We have come to the end of a prodigal childhood." The age of unrestrained individualism had created an unstable economic structure that had come crashing down.[43] A few months later, in December 1933, Secretary of the Interior Harold Ickes made the same point in an article in the *Saturday Evening Post*. "We have reached the end of the pioneering period of go ahead and take," he said, and "we are in the age of planning for the best of everything for all."[44] New York Mayor Fiorello La Guardia reiterated the argument in a front-page article in the *New York Times* the following month. The country had passed through previous crises, La Guardia said, "because of the natural vigor of a growing country," but "these days are done," and "we have no more frontiers now." There would have to be "unselfish co-operation" to offset that loss. La Guardia pleaded for the continuation of the Civil Works program and for a system of national unemployment insurance. The safety valve of free land had acted as a kind of welfare state; now an officially mandated welfare state would have to take its place.[45]

Secretary of Agriculture Henry A. Wallace provided the fullest treatment of the theme by a New Dealer in his book *New Frontiers*, which appeared in 1934. America, Wallace declared, was caught between two worlds. On the one side there was the era of the open frontier, and on the other was the postfrontier age, in which the reckless individualistic values of the earlier age could only be harmful. Unfortunately, those frontier values were still being heralded after the frontier had closed. "We educated our children," he said, "among them, millions of unemployed young—in the belief that the United States was still a pioneer country where . . . rugged individualistic values . . . would inevitably bring success." But the age of laissez-faire was over, and a new frontier of socially responsible individualism had to replace it. In exultant tones Wallace declared: "What we approach is not a new continent but a new state of heart and mind resulting in new standards of accomplishment. We must invent, build and put to work new social machinery. This machinery will carry out the Sermon on the Mount as well as the present social machinery carries out and intensifies the law of the jungle."[46] The New Deal, Wallace confidently predicted, could, by "working within the capitalist order," secure a "New Frontier" marked by the social and civic responsibility of the individual. Individual success could still be achieved, but within a community framework. "A truly modern community feeling" would be the end result of this truly elevated individualism.[47]

In a book published that same year entitled *The New Democracy*, Ickes repeated the calls for curbing laissez-faire and developing rational government planning to serve the common good. It was only natural that the emphasis was placed on productive activity during the "pioneer stages of our development," but now that they were over, the interests of the consumer had to be made paramount, he said.[48] Rexford Tugwell reiterated the same theme in *The Battle for Democracy* (1935). During the open frontier era, he said, "unrestricted competition may have been a useful economic creed. . . . Nature offered sufficient resistance to the ill-equipped producer to keep the market undersupplied." In that era the problem of overproduction did not exist and "the ruthless creed of free competition was appropriate enough to the task of conquering the continent. . . . Competition was assumed to be an inherent part of democracy. Indeed competition and democracy came to be thought of as one and the same value." But circumstances had changed, Tugwell insisted, and "sooner or later a people, in a new country, must bow to limits, stop grabbing and grow up. . . . Now we must settle down, put our lands in order, rid our hearts and minds of the barbaric notion that unlimited economic conflict leads somehow to universal balance and plenty, and learn to live together as a civilized people should." In no other land, he added, had "individual enterprise and freebooter initiative ever [been] carried to such a pitch" as in America during the century prior to the advent of the New Deal, but now that era was over. Democracy and competition were separable and would have to be separated if the "New Democracy" was to be achieved.[49]

Conservative critics of the New Deal answered the closed-frontier rationale for government regulation and increased cooperation with a frontier argument of their own. In New York's Madison Square Garden, in October 1932 (a little more than a month after Roosevelt had delivered his "Commonwealth Club" speech), Herbert Hoover addressed his opponents' arguments in the most direct fashion. Hoover quoted F.D.R.'s pronouncements on the closing of the frontier safety valve and his recommendation that Americans stop discovering resources and producing more goods and start administering the resources in hand wisely. Hoover argued that the Democrats' explanations for the depression and their big-government-centered plans to alleviate it demonstrated a lack of faith in capitalism and in America itself:

I do challenge the whole idea that we have ended the advance of America, that this country has reached the zenith of its power, the height of its development. That is the counsel of despair for the future of America. That is not the spirit by which we shall emerge from this depression. That is not the spirit that made this country. If it is true, every American must abandon the road of countless progress and unlimited opportunity. I deny that the promise of American life has been fulfilled, for that means we have begun the decline and fall. No nation can cease to move forward without degeneration of spirit.[50]

Hoover was not speaking of the same "promise of American life" that Herbert Croly had hoped would be fulfilled. In fact, he was once more lauding that same pioneer spirit that Croly, Weyl, and other Progressives, along with a generation of New Deal Progressives, were so suspicious of.

Hoover elaborated on his thesis, reiterating the open frontier argument he had propounded in the 1920s, in his book *The Challenge to Liberty* (1934). It was ironic that the Book of the Month Club chose to offer the book as a joint selection along with Henry Wallace's *New Frontiers*, much to Hoover's annoyance, since it would be difficult to imagine two more diametrically opposed treatises on the closed-frontier theme.[51] In the book Hoover objected vehemently to the notion that the closing of the physical frontier rendered rugged individualism dangerous or obsolete:

A declared part of the philosophy of those who object to the American system is the notion that America has reached the end of the road of economic development—the end of the road of progress. We have been told that our industrial plant is built, that our last frontier has long since been reached, and that our task is now not discovery or necessarily the production of more goods, but the sober, less dramatic business of administering the resources and plants already in hand.[52]

What better way of destroying "liberty," Hoover went on, than to deny the spirit of individualism a climate in which to breathe? The closed-frontier argument was absurd, he argued, because there were still many frontiers to conquer: "There are vast continents awaiting us of thought, of research, of discovery, of industry, of human relations, potentially more prolific of human comfort than even the Boundless West." But these new frontiers could only be "conquered and applied to human service by sustaining free men, free in spirit, free to enterprise, for such men alone discover the new continents of science and social thought and push back their frontiers." Castigating the New Deal order Hoover added that "Free men pioneer and achieve in these regions; regimented men under bureaucratic dictation march listlessly, without confidence and hope."[53] Hoover was horrified, he declared in a Constitution Day speech the following year, that the devastating effects of the depression were leading men to "surrender their freedom for false promises of economic security. Whether it be Fascist Italy, Nazi Germany, Communist Russia, or their lesser followers, the result is the same. Everyday they repudiate every principle of the bill of rights." The citizen, he argued, was being "submerged in the state."[54]

Kansas governor and 1936 Republican presidential candidate Alfred M. Landon voiced the same objections to the closed-frontier argument and its stifling effects on individualism in his campaign book *America at the Crossroads* (1936). "We are told," he said, "that we got out of previous depressions because of the natural growth of the country and the westward expansion of the frontier. We are warned that we are at the end of the era of expansion and must face a new situation." Much the same thing had been said during the depression of the 1890s, Landon maintained (and he was right), but since then new frontiers had been discovered, and "men with courage and imagination" were needed to develop them. The Republican Party hoped to carry out the task, he said, but its work would be hard because of "the social and economic experiments introduced in the last three years by the national administration."[55] The same argument was made by dozens of conservatives in the mid-1930s.[56]

Meanwhile, New Deal liberals continued to utilize the closed-frontier theme when the Supreme Court began to declare some of the New Deal measures unconstitutional in 1935 and 1936. Speaking to the House in January 1936, Representative Roy E. Ayers of Montana discussed the role of the open frontier and the benefits it had afforded in times long past. The Agricultural Adjustment Administration, he said, was one of the "New Frontiers" of government intervention that had played a role in offsetting that loss, but the Court had struck it down.[57] And of course, the following year an angry Walter Prescott Webb said the same thing at much greater length in *Divided We Stand*.

Speaking before Congress in April, Governor George Earle of Pennsylvania made remarks similar to those of Ayers, this time in response to the Court's decision against the National Recovery Administration. Earle spoke of the expansion across the frontier and the concomitant growth of the corporate machine. "With its pioneer work ended [the machine] became a

Frankenstein monster that turned to destroy us," he said. The country needed to control the machine before it was destroyed by it, and the NRA had begun the job of doing just that, "but the Supreme Court shut it down and left nothing to replace it."[58] Alabama Senator Hugo L. Black utilized the closed-frontier theme in July 1937 when he endorsed the proposed federal minimum wage and maximum hour legislation. "Having conquered and overcome our geographic frontiers," he argued, "we must extend the frontiers of social progress." A few months later in the House, New York representative James M. Mead echoed the call for "expansion of our social frontiers" to offset the absence of the landed one. Works Progress Administration head Harry Hopkins employed the same theme in 1938 to defend his organization against charges that it was being used as a political machine.[59]

It was not only New Deal liberals and their conservative opponents who drew on the closed-frontier theme during these years. Wisconsin's progressive Republican Governor Philip La Follette utilized the theme when he turned against the New Deal in 1938 and launched a new third party, the National Progressives of America. Speaking in June to the Vermont Young Republicans, La Follette announced that "the old Western frontier is gone" and that old fashioned capitalism was obsolete; "the days of Hoover, Coolidge, and Harding are over." In a strange hybridization of New Deal and conservative frontier arguments, he argued that the era of "horizontal development" was over and the era of "vertical development" must begin. New frontiers of "increased production had to be opened up" to secure a decent standard of life for that one-third of the population that was "ill-fed, ill-clothed, and ill-housed." It was necessary to "blaze a new trail," because all the presently existing socioeconomic systems—"communism, fascism, socialism, and old-fashioned capitalism"—were unacceptable. The vague system La Follette proposed was one in which the country would be able to act collectively, but at the same time preserve individual initiative, thus "preventing any developments like those in Germany, Italy, and Russia."[60]

Those on the far left of the political spectrum claimed that the capitalist system, in the absence of the frontier, had reached its limits and was on the very verge of destruction. Lewis Corey presented this thesis in *The Decline of American Capitalism* (1934). Corey, who under the pseudonym Louis Fraina had helped found the American Communist Party in 1919, argued that the "expansion of the frontier" had ensured the growth of capitalism in America, and the industrial boom of the 1920s had sustained its growth. Furthermore, Corey added, "Turner and his successors were not satisfied to consider the influence of the frontier as temporary and past, but projected it into the future as a 'spirit' still animating American life." But the frontier was gone, and the nation would have to come to terms with the existence of "monopoly capitalism . . . class stratification, economic decline, and crisis."[61] Marxist social analyst Anna Rochester argued similarly in her book *Rulers of America* (1936) that the open frontier had afforded capitalism the room to expand. The inherent contradictions of the capitalist system had been temporarily postponed by the existence of a vast public domain that had guaranteed a degree of social fluidity and had delayed the country's passage into the last stage of capitalism—imperialism. But now the system had reached that final stage.[62]

The closed-frontier theme played an integral part in the arguments of numerous other leftist thinkers in the thirties,[63] and there were even a few on the extreme right of the ideological spectrum who drew on it. Most notorious was "America's dissident fascist," Lawrence Dennis.[64] In *Is Capitalism Doomed?* (1932), Dennis stated that "the businessman in America has been our chief inspired believer [but] his faith has belonged to a frontier era which has passed." The "American business faith" prospered while the frontier provided for economic expansion, but now could no longer do so. He explained that although the frontier had closed in the late nineteenth century, the war had "staged . . . a return engagement of the frontier era." But then "the crash of 1929 rang down the curtain on what will probably be the last return engagement of this popular drama."[65] In his belief that capitalism in the postfrontier age was doomed, Dennis was joined by many thinkers on the left and even (in their more pessimistic moments) by conservative critics of the New Deal, who charged that it was killing the pioneer spirit of the country. The New Dealers, in response, argued that they sought to preserve capitalism by curbing its excesses and stressing, in various degrees, the value of a cooperative ethic for the new era. And this spectrum of views on the theme of cooperation was mirrored in one response in the 1930s to the closing of the frontier, a reinvigorated "back-to-the-land" movement.

Although it was an ironic response, at least on one level, to the purported disappearance of the frontier, the back-to-the-land movement of the thirties was in some ways a natural one. From the late nineteenth century on, frontier anxiety had fostered in many a desire to return to the simpler life of an earlier age, and as concern over the arrival of the "machine age" heightened so did arcadian longings. One of the most renowned responses to the accelerating urbanization, industrialization, and collectivization of the era was the collection of essays by the Southern Agrarians, *I'll Take My Stand: The South and the Agrarian Tradition* (1930). The group, which included John Crowe Ransom, Robert Penn Warren, Allen Tate, Herman Clarence Nixon, and Donald Davidson, lauded the leisurely rural culture of the Old South, contrasting its benefits with the perils of state planning. During the decade they attacked the centralizing tendencies of the New Deal and opposed the regional planning efforts of the Tennessee Valley Authority, which, they argued, threatened to destroy the distinctiveness of the South.[66]

But there was one motif in New Deal thought that was not so very far removed from the agrarian outlook of those Southern writers. For all the talk of new frontiers of cooperation and government planning to offset the loss of the physical frontier, there was a vein of Jeffersonian agrarianism running through the thought of some New Dealers. In 1931 Roosevelt, then governor of New York, stressed the improvements in rural living and the possibility of offering the urban unemployed "a few acres in the country and a little money and tools to put in small food crops."[67] The following year New York's state relief agency (the Temporary Emergency Relief Administration) placed 244 families on subsistence farms, paid their rent, and provided them with basic necessities. Numerous other applicants had to be turned down by the agency.[68] By January 1933, Roosevelt was proposing subsistence farming to the urban unemployed on the national level and praising the Boy Scout movement for fitting city boys for country living.[69] A few months later he was speaking to the Future Farmers of America about the benefits of rural life. The odds of becoming millionaires as farmers were very slim, he said, "but you will be doing something more important than becoming millionaires. You will be building up for future generations the soundest kind of American life and will." More and more urbanites, Roosevelt concluded, would see the advantages of rural life.[70] By that summer the Subsistence Homesteads Program was born and twenty-five million dollars was allocated to Harold Ickes to run it.[71] Less than two years later, the New Deal's Division of Rural Rehabilitation of the Federal Emergency Relief Administration financed the establishment of a two-hundred-farm project in America's "last frontier," Alaska. The Matanuska Colony, though it made slow progress in the beginning and was nothing more than a minor New Deal program, became the subject of massive media coverage that generally played up the frontier theme, treating the settlers as the latest examples of the nation's long pioneering tradition.[72]

While Jeffersonian impulses underlay the initiation of the Subsistence

Homesteads Program, under the directorship of Milburn L. Wilson it began to take on a cooperative ethos more in line with the closed-frontier theorizing that characterized New Deal philosophy. Wilson described the program as a retreat from a highly individualistic and competitive society to a simpler, more socially-minded existence. The "subsistence homesteads community can well serve as a cradle for a new growth of the co-operative attitude," he said.[73] Wilson's philosophy was shared, in some degree at least, by the decentralist planner Ralph Borsodi, who throughout the decade advocated the creation of agrarian communities. Borsodi's unabashed elitism ensured that the communities he envisioned would be small ones; he directed his message only at those whom he labeled the "quality-minded," who accounted for only about one percent of the population. His most publicized effort to implement his ideas was the Liberty Homestead project in Dayton, Ohio, which in October 1933 received the very first loan from the Division of Subsistence Homesteads. Unfortunately, the "quality-minded" cooperative homesteaders of Dayton did not get along very well amongst themselves or with the people of Dayton, and the project ended up in failure.[74] Meanwhile, others advocated subsistence farming on an individual or family basis and produced guidebooks for small farming.[75] And these last efforts were the only ones with any appeal for conservative critics of the New Deal, who naturally objected to the cooperative bent of the Subsistence Homestead Program.

The Taylor Grazing Act of 1934 signaled an end to homesteading on an individual basis (in a sense marking a final symbolic end to the frontier), yet the Roosevelt administration continued to promote the virtues of rural life and promote the establishment of new rural communities. In a sense it was a fitting reflection of the philosophy behind the New Deal—the age of pioneering was over and the individual homesteader was unable to make it alone, but with government assistance and a stronger community ethic a higher individualism could be secured.

The closed-frontier theme was a pervasive element in the social and political thought of the 1930s. The political debates of the decade often revolved around the theme because it crystallized perfectly the underlying concern of the era—the relationship between the individual and the community, and the government's role in securing it. With the onset of World War II and the subsequent end of the depression, the frontier debate subsided. Yet even in the postwar era the frontier theme did not lose its potency altogether, because its underlying concern over the limits of individualism has never been far from the center of American thought.

EPILOGUE:
THE ENDURING FRONTIER

The very immediate concerns that were voiced over the closing of the frontier in the period from the late nineteenth century through the New Deal are no longer with us today and have not been an important strain in intellectual thought in America since the end of the depression. However, the potency of the frontier theme has not dissipated altogether. In fact, for all the anxiety over the closing of the frontier in that earlier period, it is quite feasible to argue, on one level at least, that the frontier never closed. Free or cheap land became a scarcer commodity in the last decades of the nineteenth century, but after the frontier officially "closed" in 1890, homesteading continued. More homesteads were settled in the first few decades of the twentieth century than in the whole of the nineteenth century. It was harder to farm in the semiarid western plains, but the practice of homesteading had never been an easy one. New farming techniques, such as dry farming and irrigation, perhaps created a new frontier out of that region in the early decades of the present century, and even after the practice of giving out homesteads came to an official end with the Taylor Grazing Act of 1934, the center of population continued to move westward. And there was always Alaska. That vast state remains a frontier of sorts today and is still hailed as such on Alaskan license plates. No one expects a homestead today, but the prospect of a high-paying job and a warm climate (not in Alaska, to be sure) are incentive enough to convince large numbers of Americans to make the "trek" westward. The west still retains a certain charm, and a trip out West in a supercharged covered wagon is still an attraction to many.

The environmental concerns of the present are not so far removed from the frontier concerns of times past. The worries of conservationists in the late nineteenth and early twentieth centuries over forest depletion are with us again today as we ponder the alarming ramifications of the destruction of the Brazilian rain forest and question the practices of lumber companies at home. Even the ghost of Malthus has returned once more to haunt us in the 1980s and 1990s on both a world and a national level. Population growth is a serious concern today, just as it was for some in the 1920s, and the vigilantes who patrol the Mexican border today to keep out "undesirables," hold up wage levels, and hold down population growth are not so different from the immigration restrictionists of that earlier age. Furthermore, as long as immigrants continue to come to the United States, the country as a whole remains a frontier of sorts, at least if we use the term as a metaphor for promise and improvement.

The closed-frontier theme, though never again expressed with John Steinbeck's immediacy and poignancy, has remained an important element in American literature since the 1930s, most obviously in the epic western dramas of A. B. Guthrie, Jr.: *The Big Sky* (1947) and *The Way West* (1949). It is present, too, in Jack Kerouac's *On the Road* (1957), with its main protagonists (Sal Paradise and Dean Moriarty) racing across the continent in search of the Promised Land, only to find that the Wild West has been civilized, suburbanized, and commercialized. When he reaches California, Sal (Kerouac) proclaims, "Here I was at the end of America—no more land—and now there was nowhere to go but back."[1] Sal reminds the reader of Steinbeck's Jody Tifflin, in "The Leader of the People," as he is awakened to the fact that the frontier is gone. The tradition is also very much alive in the novels of Larry McMurtry, especially *Lonesome Dove* (1985) and *Buffalo Girls* (1990), as the characters try unsuccessfully to come to grips with the passing of the Old West.

The Cowboy Artists of America still meet once a year on a western ranch to find new inspiration, and their fascination with the Old West, though particularly acute, mirrors a much wider public interest.[2] The public's continuing fascination with the West is evident in the success of recent movies, such as *Young Guns* and its unimaginatively entitled sequel, *Young Guns II*, and in the concluding installment of the time-travel trilogy *Back to the Future III* (which is set in the Wild West). Current television series such as *The Young Riders* and recent mini-series such as *Lonesome Dove* and *Son of the Morning Star* (about General Custer) also attest to the salability of the theme. The myths of the West and its heroic settlement have recently come under fire in Kevin Costner's tremendously successful movie *Dances with Wolves*, which has heightened media coverage of the New Western History.

It is interesting to note that the movie starts with the main protagonist proclaiming that he wants to see the frontier before it's gone.

The call for "New Frontiers" has not dissipated completely in recent American history. President Roosevelt, in a 1944 letter to Vannevar Bush, the director of the Wartime Office of Scientific Research and Development, wrote that "new frontiers of the mind are before us, and if they are pioneered with the same vision, boldness, and drive with which we have waged this war we can create a fuller and more fruitful employment and a fuller and more fruitful life." Bush found in FDR's letter the inspiration for the title of his report to the president the following year, *Science: The Endless Frontier*, which helped secure a large federal subsidy for research in the natural sciences.[3]

More famous, but in the same vein, was President Kennedy's call for a "New Frontier" in 1960. The country, Kennedy suggested, could reach new heights, achieve new greatness, and did not have to settle for "Eisenhower moderation." Republican Ronald Reagan and Democrat Edward Kennedy both drew on the theme at their respective nominating conventions in 1980, and Reagan went on to laud the benefits of rugged pioneer individualism throughout his two terms.[4] Accepting his party's nomination for the presidency at the 1988 Democratic Convention, Michael Dukakis spoke of the "next American frontier." The current ideological debate in the political sphere is reminiscent of that of the 1930s—liberal Democrats continue to call for new frontiers of government intervention, and conservative Republicans continue to stress the benefits of rugged individualism and call for new frontiers of business enterprise and government deregulation.

Yet the term "frontier" has become something of a cliché in the half century or so since the end of the New Deal. Frontier has become a metaphor for promise, progress, and ingenuity; some would argue that it was never any more than that anyway, and was a cruel metaphor to boot. While the term has been invoked frequently in the last fifty years, it is unlikely that it has ever been invoked with the urgency that marked its use in the previous half century. The word "frontier" is a widely used cliché today whereas the question of the frontier's absence at the end of the nineteenth century helped define the parameters of important public policy debates and shape the broader cultural milieu of the age.

The frontier metaphor survives as a lasting vestige, or perhaps a painful reminder of the past, depending upon one's ideological orientation. And the frontier theme seems unlikely to disappear completely from the American scene in the near future. Whether the frontier itself was a beneficent factor—the bulwark of democracy and individualism and a safety valve for the discontented—or a symbol of the nation's most malevolent tendencies (as the new generation of western historians would argue), the myth of the frontier has remained an integral part of the national culture. And while it is one thing to deny the significance of the frontier itself, it is quite another to deny the importance of the frontier concept and the role it has played in the nation's development. Whether it be land policy, immigration restriction and expansionism in the late nineteenth century, Malthusian Alarmism and the reemergence of immigration restriction in the 1920s, or the New Deal debates of the 1930s, concern over the closing of the frontier played a central role, and it did so because the broader frontier mythology was such a pervasive force.

The historiographical debate that developed around Frederick Jackson Turner's essay "The Significance of the Frontier in American History"—and still rages today as the New Western Historians continue to exorcize the ghost of Turner—has perhaps obscured the real significance that the notion of the closing of the frontier held for generations of Americans. It is important to listen to voices of people from the past, because their beliefs, often translated into action, played a crucial role in the nation's development. And whether one approves of the course the nation has taken or not, to deny the significance of those voices is to write our own history and not theirs. As Turner and others wrote, and "newer" western historians are once more proving, each generation rewrites the past; indeed, it is obligated to do so. But as we bring the concerns of the present to bear on the past, we would be wise to not forget the concerns of the past as they bear on the present. Whether they are the concerns of heretofore under-studied minority groups, or of intellectuals whose anxiety helped define public policy, they demand our attention. The mythology that surrounded the frontier and the "frontier anxiety" that sprang from it helped shape the climate of the past for many Americans. Frontier anxiety as such—once a very real and immediate concern—may no longer exist, but the frontier mythology it spawned, the "frontier heritage of the mind," is still with us today and probably will be for generations to come.

NOTES

PREFACE

1. Patricia Nelson Limerick, *The Legacy of Conquest: The Unbroken Past of the American West* (New York: W. W. Norton, 1987); Donald Worster, *Rivers of Empire: Water, Aridity, and the Growth of the American West* (New York: Pantheon Books, 1985). The most recent major work in the field is Richard White, *"It's Your Misfortune and None of My Own": A New History of the American West* (Norman: University of Oklahoma Press, 1991). The most recent collection of writings about the new revisionist approach is Patricia Nelson Limerick, Clyde A. Milner II, and Charles E. Rankin, eds., *Trails: Toward a New Western History* (Lawrence: University Press of Kansas, 1991). A good sampling of writings by revisionist-minded historians can also be found in Clyde A. Milner II, ed., *Major Problems in the History of the American West* (Lexington, Mass.: D. C. Heath, 1989).

2. This characteristic of the New Western History is most apparent in Limerick's *The Legacy of Conquest* and William Cronon's article "Revisiting the Vanishing Frontier: The Legacy of Frederick Jackson Turner," *Western Historical Quarterly* 18 (April 1987): 157–76.

3. Martin Ridge provides coverage of the theme of American exceptionalism in several articles: "Ray Allen Billington, Western History, and American Exceptionalism," *Pacific Historical Review* 56 (November 1987): 495–511; "Frederick Jackson Turner and His Ghost," in Martin Ridge, Elizabeth A. H. John, Alvin M. Josephy, Jr., Howard Lamar, Kevin Starr, and George Miles, *Writing the History of the American West* (Worcester, Mass.: American Antiquarian Society, 1991), 65–76, especially 68; and "The American West: From Frontier to Region," *New Mexico Historical Review* 64 (April 1989): 125–41. Also worth mentioning is Donald K. Pickens's "Westward Expansion and the End of American Exceptionalism: Sumner, Turner, and Webb," *Western Historical Quarterly* 14 (October 1981): 409–18. Apologies to Pickens for my use of his phrase "the end of American exceptionalism." Interesting, too, in this context are Ian Tyrrell, "American Exceptionalism in an Age of International History," *American Historical Review* 96 (October 1991): 1033–55, and Michael McGerr, "The Price of the New Transnational History," ibid.: 1056–67.

4. Miriam Horn, "How the West Was Really Won," *U.S. News and World Report*, 21 May 1990, 56–65; Larry McMurtry, "Westward Ho Hum: What the New Historians Have Done to the Old West," *New Republic*, 9 October 1990, 32–38. See also "Rewriting the West," *USA Today*, 7 December 1990), D, 1–2. Also worth noting is Richard Bern-

stein, "Ideas and Trends: Among Historians the Old Frontier Is Turning Nastier with Each Revision," *New York Times*, 17 December 1989, E, 4–6.

5. There are some very notable exceptions to this tendency to overlook the theme of concern over the closing of the frontier: First, the late Robert Athearn's excellent book, *The Mythic West in Twentieth-Century America* (Lawrence: University Press of Kansas, 1986). Athearn's work, while it has proven an invaluable source of background information for this study, focuses more on western responses to the closing of the frontier in the twentieth century, while the current work deals more with the connection between frontier anxiety and larger public issues such as immigration and foreign policy. G. Edward White's *The Eastern Establishment and the Western Experience: The West of Frederic Remington, Theodore Roosevelt, and Owen Wister* (New Haven, Conn.: Yale University Press, 1968) was also a vital source of information on the frontier concerns of the late nineteenth century. Henry Nash Smith's *Virgin Land: The American West as Symbol and Myth* (Cambridge, Mass.: Harvard University Press, 1970) may be the work that influenced this study most. Smith provided a wealth of information on the role of the frontier, and the concern over its future disappearance, in American thought in the period before Turner. Finally, mention must be made of Gerald Nash's masterly new historiographical work *Creating the West: Historical Interpretations, 1890–1990* (Albuquerque: University of New Mexico Press, 1991). Nash, in his opening chapter, "The West as Frontier, 1890–1945," 3–48, provides such excellent discussion of so much of what I cover in this study that its appearance while I worked on the last draft of this manuscript proved both heartening and disheartening. In the last analysis, though, Nash's recent writing on the closed-frontier theme served to reassure me that I had been laboring on a topic of no small importance and had been using many of the best examples of "frontier anxiety."

CHAPTER 1. EDEN UNMARRED

1. See, for example, Lee Benson's *Turner and Beard: American Historical Writing Reconsidered* (New York: Free Press, 1960) and "The Historical Background of Turner's Frontier Essay," *Agricultural History* 25 (April 1951): 59–82; Ray A. Billington's *America's Frontier Heritage* (New York: Holt, Rinehart and Winston, 1966), *The Genesis of the Frontier Thesis: A Study in Historical Creativity* (San Marino, Calif.: Huntington Library, 1971), and *Frederick Jackson Turner: Historian, Scholar, Teacher* (New York: Oxford University Press, 1973); and Fulmer Mood's "The Development of Frederick Jackson Turner as a Historical Thinker," *Publications of the Colonial Society of Massachusetts* 34 (Transactions 1937–1942): 283–352. On the other hand, Billington's essay "Frederick Jackson Turner and the Closing of the Frontier," in Roger Daniels, ed., *Essays in Western History in Honor of Professor T. A. Larson* (Laramie: University of Wyoming Publications, 1971), and his *Land of Savagery, Land of Promise: The European Image of the American Frontier in the Nineteenth Century* (New York: W. W. Norton, 1981) concentrate more on placing Turner's "frontier anxiety" in historical context than on reconstructing that context around Turner. Excellent short summaries of these works and hundreds of others relating to Turner can be found in Vernon E. Mattson and William E. Marion, comps., *Frederick Jackson Turner: A Reference Guide* (Boston: G. K. Hall, 1985).

2. Characteristic of this approach are Benson's appraisal of Achille Loria in *Turner and Beard*; Wirt A. Cate's "Lamar and the Frontier Hypothesis," *Journal of Southern History* 1 (February 1935): 497–501; and Edith H. Parker's "William Graham Sumner and the Frontier," *Southwest Review* 44 (Autumn 1956): 357–65. See also Fulmer Mood's "The Concept of the Frontier, 1871–1898: Comments on a Select List of Source Documents," *Agricultural History* 19 (January 1945): 24–30, and "A British Statistician of 1854 Analyzes the Westward Movement in the United States," *Agricultural History* 19 (July 1945): 142–51.

3. Turner's dated and marginally notated books and his voluminous notecard collection leave little doubt that his conception of the thesis was a long and toilsome process. Billington's *The Genesis of the Frontier Thesis* is the best account of that process.

4. William Cronon, "Revisiting the Vanishing Frontier: The Legacy of Frederick Jackson Turner," *Western Historical Quarterly* 18 (April 1987): 157-76, 172. Patricia Nelson Limerick's *The Legacy of Conquest: The Unbroken Past of the American West* (New York: W. W. Norton, 1987) is of course, among many other things, a reaction to the notion that a sharp break— the closing of the frontier—has occurred in American western history.

5. It is particularly interesting that concern over the closing of the frontier should become a significant phenomenon in the 1880s, which were among the most prosperous years of the nineteenth century. This suggests that purely economic indices cannot give a full indication of the underlying tensions that mark certain periods. It is worth noting, too, that the decade of the 1870s (or at least the period from 1873 to 1878) was one of serious depression in the United States. (On this point see Herbert G. Gutman, "Social and Economic Structure and Depression in American Labor in 1873 and 1874" [Ph.D. dissertation; University of Wisconsin, 1959]). Nevertheless, the link between real economic hardship and the recession of the frontier was less readily made in those years. For a fascinating insight into the economic realities of this period from a world perspective, see Walter Nugent's recent article, "Frontier and Empires in the Late-Nineteenth Century," *Western Historical Quarterly* 20 (November 1989): 393-408.

6. See, for example, Henry S. Commager, "The Watershed of the Nineties," in *The American Mind: An Interpretation of American Character and Thought since the 1880s* (New Haven, Conn.: Yale University Press, 1950): 41-54; and Richard Hofstadter, who talks of "the Psychic Crisis of the 1890s" in his "Manifest Destiny and the Philippines," in Daniel Aaron, ed., *America in Crisis* (New York: Alfred A. Knopf, 1952), 172-200. Both of these viewpoints are discussed in Marcus Cunliffe's "American Watersheds," *American Quarterly* 13 (Winter 1961): 480-94.

7. Gerald Nash questions the accuracy of the prophetic announcement made by Robert P. Porter, superintendent of the Eleventh Census, in "The Census of 1890 and the Closing of the Frontier," *Pacific Northwest Quarterly* 71 (July 1980): 98-100.

8. See Henry Nash Smith's classic study, *Virgin Land: The American West as Symbol and Myth* (Cambridge, Mass.: Harvard University Press, 1978), 123-32; David Noble's excellent chapter on "The Crisis of 1890" in his *The Progressive Mind, 1890-1917* (Minneapolis, Minn.: Burgess, 1981), 1-22; J. G. A. Pocock's chapter, "The Americanization of Virtue: Corruption, Constitution, and Frontier," in his *The Machiavellian Moment: Florentine Political Thought and the Atlantic Republican Tradition* (Princeton, N.J.: Princeton University Press, 1975), 506-52; and Peter S. Onuf, "Liberty Development and Union: Visions of the West in the 1780s," *William and Mary Quarterly* 43 (April 1896): 179-213.

9. Benjamin Franklin, "The Internal State of America, Being a True Description of the Interest and Policy of That Vast Continent," in Albert K. Smythe, ed., *The Writings of Benjamin Franklin*, 10 vols. (New York: Macmillan, 1907), 10: 1789-1790: 117-118. For an excellent account of Franklin's thoughts on the topic of the West and American democracy see James H. Hutson, "Benjamin Franklin and the West," *Western Historical Quarterly* 4 (October 1973): 425-34. Hutson's article points to Franklin's faith in the democratic character of the frontier and to his fear that a large urban proletariat would be fatal to democracy.

10. Hector St. John de Crèvecoeur, *Letters from an American Farmer* (New York: Fox, Duffield, 1904), 41, 43-44, and 61. Smith examines the popular response to this book in *Virgin Land*, 126.

11. For a more detailed discussion of Thomas Jefferson's views on the subject see Smith, *Virgin Land*, 123-32. For the Jefferson quotation see Gilbert Chinard, *Thomas Jefferson: The Apostle of Americanism* (Boston: Little, Brown, 1929), 80-82; James C. Malin, *The Contriving Brain*

and the *Skillful Hand in the United States* (Ann Arbor, Mich.: Edwards Brothers, 1955); and H. A. Washington, ed., *The Writings of Thomas Jefferson*, 2 vols. (Washington, D.C., 1854), 2: 332.

12. Georg W. F. Hegel, *Lectures on the Philosophy of History* (New York: Colonial Press, 1900), 85–87. The lectures were first delivered in 1822–1823 and first published, in German, in 1837. The first English edition was published in London in 1852. Hegel's commentary on America's landed frontier is the subject of an article by W. Stull Holt, "Hegel, the Turner Hypothesis, and the Safety-Valve Theory," *Agricultural History* 22 (July 1948): 175–76.

13. Alexis de Tocqueville, *Democracy in America*, Henry Reeve text as revised by Francis Bowen, ed. Phillips Bradley, 2 vols. (New York: Macmillan, 1945), 1: 291.

14. *Quarterly Review* 30 (October 1823): 25–28.

15. Ibid. 46 (January 1832): 583–85, quoted in G. D. Lillibridge, *Beacon of Freedom: The Impact of American Democracy upon Great Britain, 1830–1870* (Philadelphia: University of Pennsylvania Press, 1955), 93.

16. See Stephen Tatum, "A Picture Gallery Unrivalled of Its Kind: *Blackwood's* American Frontier and the Idea of American Democracy," *Western Historical Quarterly* 14 (January 1983): 29–48, 29.

17. Arnout O'Donnell, "Democracy in America," *Blackwood's Magazine* 37 (September 1835): 399–400, quoted in Tatum, "A Picture Gallery Unrivalled," 40.

18. Archibald Alison, "Whither Are We Tending?" *Blackwood's Magazine* 37 (September 1835): 399–400, quoted in ibid., 40.

19. "Lord Macaulay on American Institutions," *Harper's New Monthly Magazine* 54 (February 1877): 460, quoted in Warren French, "Death of the Dream" (unpublished seminar paper for Walter Prescott Webb, University of Texas, Austin, c. 1953), 9; also quoted and discussed in William M. Tuttle, Jr., "Forerunners of Frederick Jackson Turner: Nineteenth-Century British Conservatives and the Frontier Thesis," *Agricultural History* 41 (July 1967): 219–27, 223–24. The *Harper's* piece is a reprint of Macaulay's letter to Henry S. Randall dated 23 May 1857.

20. Thomas Carlyle, "The Present Time," in *Latter-Day Pamphlets* (London: Chapman and Hall, 1850), 17–18, quoted in French, "Death of the Dream," 7–8.

21. *Blackwood's Magazine* 34 (September 1833): 292, quoted in Tuttle, "Forerunners of Frederick Jackson Turner," 223.

22. The proslavery intellectual Thomas Dew, writing in 1836, was perhaps the first southerner to express these sentiments.

23. George Fitzhugh, "Sociology for the South," in Harvey Wish, ed., *Antebellum: Writings of George Fitzhugh and Hinton Rowan Helper on Slavery* (New York: Capricorn Books, 1960), 22; and Fitzhugh, *Cannibals All! (Or Slaves without Masters)* (Cambridge, Mass.: Harvard University Press, 1960), 60.

24. Horace Greeley had begun to encourage westward emigration as early as 1837. See Roy M. Robbins, "Horace Greeley: Land Reform and Unemployment, 1837–1862," *Agricultural History* 7 (January 1933): 19.

25. James D. Richardson, ed., *A Compilation of Messages and Papers of the Presidents*, 8 vols. (Washington, D.C.: Bureau of National Literature and Art, 1910), 6: 57–58. See also Roy M. Robbins, "The Public Domain in the Era of Exploitation, 1863–1901," *Agricultural History* 13 (April 1939): 97–108, 98.

26. Gilbert C. Fite provides a useful summary of the historiographical debate on the effectiveness of the Homestead Act in "The American West of Farmers and Stockmen," in Michael P. Malone, ed., *Historians and the American West* (Lincoln: University of Nebraska Press, 1983), 209–23. William F. Deverell's excellent article, "To Loosen the Safety Valve: Eastern Workers and Western Lands," *Western Historical Quarterly* 19 (August 1988): 269–85, is the most recent discussion of the operation of the act.

27. E. L. Godkin, "Aristocratic Opinions of Democracy," *North American Review*

100 (January 1865): 194–232; the quotation is from the reprint in *Problems of American Democracy: Political and Economic Essays by Edwin Lawrence Godkin* (Cambridge, Mass.: Harvard University Press, Belknap Press, 1966), 1–67, 30.

28. Charles H. Pearson, "The Land Question in the United States," *Contemporary Review* 9 (November 1868): 342–56, 346–47.

29. Ibid., 347.

30. Ibid., 347–48, 354.

31. See Charles A. Barker, *Henry George* (New York: Oxford University Press, 1955), 143; Horace Greeley, "Advice to American Farmers," in James Parton, *Life of Horace Greeley* (Boston: Fields, Osgood, 1869), 595–96; and Roy M. Robbins, "Horace Greeley: Land Reform and Unemployment," 18.

32. Henry George, *Our Land and Land Policy, National and State* (New York: Doubleday Page, 1904), 11.

33. Nordhoff, *The Communist Societies of the United States: From Personal Visit and Observation* (New York: Hilary House, 1961), 12. Nordhoff had touched on the notion of the frontier as a "psychological safety valve." For a further discussion of this theme see Ellen von Nardroff, "The American Frontier as a Safety-Valve: The Life, Death, Reincarnation, and Justification of a Theory," *Agricultural History* 36 (July 1962): 123–42; Lewis O. Saum, "Pat Donan's West and the End of the Age of Hate," *Pacific Northwest Quarterly* 60 (April 1969): 66–76; and Billington, *America's Frontier Heritage*, 37–38. Lee Benson argues against this notion in his article "The Historian as Myth-maker: Turner and the Closed Frontier," in David M. Ellis, ed., *The Frontier in American Development: Essays in Honor of Paul Wallace Gates* (Ithaca, N.Y.: Cornell University Press, 1969), 3–19.

34. The Hazen-Custer debate is the topic of Edgar I. Stewart's *Penny-an-Acre Empire in the West* (Norman: University of Oklahoma Press, 1968). "Our Barren Lands" is reprinted in that work, 139–83. Hazen's findings were also commented upon at some length by the English author William Hepworth Dixon in *White Conquest*, 2 vols. (London: Chatto and Windus, 1876), 2: 363–65.

35. Hazen, "The Great Middle Region of the United States," *North American Review* 120 (January 1875): 1–36, 22; reprinted in Stewart, *Penny-an-Acre Empire*, 185–216.

36. Powell, *Report on the Lands of the Arid Region of the United States*, edited by Wallace Stegner (Cambridge, Mass.: Harvard University Press, 1962), xi.

37. Powell, *Report of Explorations in 1873 of the Colorado River of the West and Its Tributaries, under the Direction of the Smithsonian Institution* (Washington, D.C.: Government Printing Office, 1874), 10, 14, 143–45, 171.

38. The propagators of the myth that rain followed the plow are discussed in David M. Emmons, *Garden in the Grasslands: Boomer Literature of the Central Great Plains* (Lincoln: University of Nebraska Press, 1971), 128–61. Particularly interesting examples are the massive volumes of Ferdinand V. Hayden, *The Great West: Its Attractions and Resources* (Philadelphia: Franklin Publishing, 1880); and Linus P. Brockett, *Our Western Empire; or The New West Beyond the Mississippi* (Philadelphia: Bradley, Garretson, 1882).

CHAPTER 2. PROPHECIES OF GLOOM AND
DOOM: THE ANXIOUS EIGHTIES

1. This codification by Alexander T. Britton spanned almost 1600 pages in three volumes. See Paul W. Gates's introduction to the 1884 edition of Thomas Donaldson's *The Public Domain: Its History with Statistics* (New York: Johnson Reprint, 1970), viii.

2. Ibid., viii–ix.

3. The figure was 16 percent for Kansas and 18 percent for Nebraska; see Paul W.

Gates, *Landlords and Tenants on the Prairie Frontier* (Ithaca, N.Y.: Cornell University Press, 1973), 166.

4. United States Census Office, *Statistics of the Population of the United States at the Tenth Census* (June 1, 1880) (Washington, D.C.: Government Printing Office, 1883), xi–xxxiii. For a fuller account of the census see Rudolph Freund, "Turner's Theory of Social Evolution," *Agricultural History* 19 (April 1945): 78–87.

5. A very limited edition was published in San Francisco in 1879. A New York publication followed in January 1880; see Charles A. Barker, *Henry George* (New York: Oxford University Press, 1955): 265–303.

6. George, *Progress and Poverty* (New York: Robert Schalkenbach Foundation, 1960): 389–90.

7. "Bonanza Farms of the West," *Atlantic Monthly* 45 (January 1880): 35–45, 44.

8. An article by Francis A. Walker (superintendent of the Tenth Census, 1880), "The Growth of the United States," *Scribner's Monthly* 24 (October 1882): 920–26, was probably the most important of these efforts. Also influential was Thomas Donaldson's article "The Public Lands of the U.S.," *North American Review* 83 (August 1881): 204–13.

9. See Thomas W. Higginson, "The Great Western March," *Harper's New Monthly Magazine* 69 (June 1884): 118–28; N. C. Frederiksen, "The Development of the West," *Dial* 3 (August 1882), 74–75—a review of Robert P. Porter's *The West from the Census of 1880: A History of the Development from 1800–1880* (Chicago: Rand McNally, 1881); James B. Walker, *Experiences of Pioneer Life in the Early Settlements and Cities of the West* (Chicago: Sumner, 1882), and a review of the book, "The Chronicles of a Western Pioneer," *Dial* 2 (September 1881): 98–100.

10. The book's content was more wide-reaching than the original title suggested. It was subsequently published as *The Land Question: What It Involves and How Alone It Can Be Settled.* Quotations are from the 1898 edition (New York: Doubleday and McLure).

11. Ibid., 73, 74.

12. Donaldson, "The Public Lands of the U.S."

13. *Century Magazine* 25 (December 1882): 599–601.

14. Comments on the 1880 Census results prior to 1882 suggest that the report was not an inaccessible item until that date.

15. *Century Magazine* 25 (December 1882): 599–601.

16. William G. Moody, *Land and Labor in the United States* (New York: Charles Scribner's Sons, 1883), quoted in Jay Martin, *Harvest of Change: American Literature, 1865–1914* (Englewood Cliffs, N.J.: Prentice Hall, 1957), 198. The process that Moody outlined and the reaction to it at the grass-roots level are examined in Michael Cassity's excellent recent study of Sedalia and Pettis County, Missouri, *Defending a Way of Life: An American Community in the Nineteenth Century* (Albany: State University of New York Press, 1989), especially 149–69.

17. Henry George, *Social Problems* (London: Kegan Paul, Trench, 1884), 303, 306–7, 267. Technically, of course, George was wrong on this count. Indeed, more lands would be taken up under the Homestead Act in the first two decades of the twentieth century than in the whole of the nineteenth century; see the statistical appendices in Paul W. Gates, *History of Public Land Law Development* (Washington, D.C.: Government Printing Office, 1968), 799–800. Nevertheless, few could have foreseen in the 1880s that modern-day farming techniques would make this land available to the average homesteader.

18. Donaldson, *The Public Domain*, 530–35.

19. Thomas P. Gill, "Landlordism in America," *North American Review* 142 (January 1886): 53–67.

20. Adam J. Desmond, "America's Land Question," *North American Review* 142 (February 1886): 153–58, 153, 154.

21. Homer E. Socolofsky, *Landlord William Scully* (Lawrence: Regents Press of Kansas, 1970), especially chapter 8, "Scully's Scalpers," 103–19. See also Gates, *Landlords and Tenants*, 284–86, and *History of Public Land Law Development*, 442–43.

22. Edward E. Crapol, *America for Americans: Economic Nationalism and Anglophobia in the Late Nineteenth Century* (Westport, Conn.: Greenwood Press, 1973), 23, 222. By 1900, thirty of the forty-five states had passed statutes that distinguished between foreign and domestic owners.

23. Roy M. Robbins, "The Public Domain in the Era of Exploitation, 1863–1901," *Agricultural History* 13 (April 1939): 99, 106.

24. The complex set of motivations that surrounded the Dawes Act receive excellent discussion in Frederick E. Hoxie's seminal work *A Final Promise: The Campaign to Assimilate the Indians, 1880–1920* (Lincoln: University of Nebraska Press, 1984), especially chapter 1, "The Appeal of Assimilation," 1–39, and chapter 2, "The Campaign Begins," 41–81. See also D. S. Otis, *The Dawes Act and the Allotment of Indian Lands* (Norman: University of Oklahoma Press, 1973).

25. For a quarter century or so after 1889 the Indian Territory would be opened up in fairly small strips; see John W. Morris, Charles R. Goins, and Edwin C. McReynolds, *Historical Atlas of Oklahoma* (Norman: University of Oklahoma Press, 1976), 47–61.

26. See Crapol, *America for Americans*, 112–13, and Gates, *Landlords and Tenants*, 293.

27. John D. Hicks laid great stress on the factor of the closing of the frontier in his pathbreaking work set in the context of the Turner thesis, *The Populist Revolt: A History of the Farmers' Alliance and the People's Party* (Minneapolis: University of Minnesota Press, 1931). Also noteworthy is Solon J. Buck, *The Agrarian Crusade: A Chronicle of the Farmer in Politics* (New Haven, Conn.: Yale University Press, 1920). See Martin Ridge, *Ignatius Donnelly: The Portrait of a Politician* (Chicago: University of Chicago Press, 1962): 324–25; and Norman Pollack, ed., *The Populist Mind* (Indianapolis: Bobbs Merrill, 1967), xxxii, 156–58, 263.

28. John Higham, *Strangers in the Land: Patterns in American Nativism, 1860–1925* (New Brunswick, N.J.: Rutgers University Press, 1955): 35–67.

29. *New York Tribune*, 2 July 1881, 5, quoted in ibid., 38.

30. Donaldson, "The Public Lands of the U.S.," 213.

31. Donaldson, *The Public Domain*, 535–36.

32. George, *Social Problems*, 31, 40.

33. Josiah Strong, *Our Country: Its Possible Future and Its Present Crisis* (New York: Baker and Taylor, 1893): 44–61.

34. Gill, "Landlordism in America," 66. Gill's article expresses concern over abuses of public land policy, over immigration, and over America's nonexpansionism, approaching all three topics from the premise that the frontier was closing.

35. Boyeson, "Dangers of Unrestricted Immigration," *Forum* 3 (July 1887): 532–42, 533, 536.

36. *Congressional Record*, 49th Congress, 1st session, 7831, and 2nd session, 2319–20. See also Higham, *Strangers in the Land*, 41–42.

37. J. Coleman Adams, "Is America Europeanizing?" *Forum* 4 (September 1887), 190–200, 195.

38. William Appleman Williams has pushed this thesis; see especially *The Roots of the Modern American Empire: A Study of the Growth and Shaping of Social Consciousness in a Marketplace Society* (New York: Random House, 1969). But Williams's evidence in this work and others does not lend sufficient support to his elaborate framework.

39. Strong, *Our Country*, 175. John Fiske's influential essay, "Manifest Destiny," *Harpers New Monthly Magazine* 70 (February 1885): 578–90, also stressed the expansionist nature of the Anglo-Saxons.

40. This "National Policy" is given good coverage in Gerald Friesen, *The Canadian Prairies: A History* (Lincoln: University of Nebraska Press, 1984), chapter 8, "Canada's Empire, 1870–1900: The Region and the National Policy," 162–94.

41. Donald F. Warner, *The Idea of Continental Union: Agitation for the Annexation of Canada to the United States, 1849–1893* (Lexington: University of Kentucky Press, 1960); Milton Plesur, *America's Outward Thrust; Approaches to Foreign Affairs, 1865–1890* (De-Kalb: Northern Illinois University Press, 1971), 182–97.

42. Prosper Bender, "The Annexation of Canada," *North American Review* 139 (July 1884): 42–50, 43, 50.

43. The best examples are Alex F. Pririe, "Canadian Prospects and Politics," *North American Review* 142 (January 1886), 36–49; and David A. Poe, "The Position of Canada," *Forum* 3 (July 1887): 441–46.

44. Wiman, "The Greater Half of the Continent," *North American Review* 148 (January 1889): 54–72.

45. Wiman, "What Is the Destiny of Canada?" *North American Review* 148 (June 1889): 665–75; Wiman, "The Capture of Canada," *North American Review* 151 (August 1890): 212–22, 212.

46. Justin S. Morrill, "Is Union with Canada Desirable?" *Forum* 6 (January 1889): 452–64.

47. Remington, "A Few Words from Mr. Remington," *Collier's*, 18 March 1905, quoted in Harold McCracken, *Frederic Remington: Artist of the Old West* (Philadelphia, Penn.: J. B. Lippincott, 1947): 34–35. The *Collier's* piece is discussed in Alex Nemerov, "Frederic Remington: Within and Without the Past," *American Art*, Winter/Spring 1991, 37–59. In 1887, seventy-one of Remington's illustrations appeared in *Outing*. The following year 177 of his pictures were printed in *Harper's Weekly, Outing, Youth's Companion*, and *Century*; see Ben Merchant Vorphal, ed., *My Dear Wister: The Frederic Remington-Owen Wister Letters* (Palo Alto, Calif.: American West, 1972), 22. See also G. Edward White's excellent work, *The Eastern Establishment and the Western Experience: The West of Frederic Remington, Theodore Roosevelt and Owen Wister* (New Haven, Conn.: Yale University Press, 1968), especially 102–21.

48. *Wister's Western Notebook*, 11 July 1885, quoted in Vorphal, *My Dear Wister*, 19.

49. Edgar Wilson Nye quoted in Robert G. Athearn, *The Mythic West in Twentieth-Century America* (Lawrence: University Press of Kansas, 1986), 11–12.

50. Billington, *Land of Savagery, Land of Promise: The European Image of the American Frontier in the Nineteenth Century* (New York: W. W. Norton, 1981), 49; William H. Goetzmann and William N. Goetzmann, *The West of the Imagination* (New York: W. W. Norton, 1986): 292–94.

51. For a fuller account of literary reactions to the closing frontier see Jay Martin, *Harvest of Change: American Literature, 1865–1914* (Englewood Ciffs, N.J.: Prentice Hall, 1967), 116–25; Lucy L. Hazard, *The Frontier in American Literature* (New York: Frederick Ungar, 1967), passim; and Harold P. Simonsen, *The Closed Frontier* (New York: Holt, Rinehart and Winston, 1970), passim. Also fascinating, though unpublished and unavailable, is Warren French's "Death of the Dream," a 114-page seminar paper done under the direction of Walter Prescott Webb at the University of Texas, Austin, c. 1953.

52. Theodore Roosevelt, "Frontier Types," in *The Works of Theodore Roosevelt*, 23 vols. (New York: Charles Scribner's Sons, 1926), vol. 1: *Hunting Trips of a Ranchman, Ranch Life, and the Hunting Trail*, 349.

53. *Century Magazine*, 36 (May–October 1888), 37 (November 1888-April 1889), 38 (May–October 1889). Also interesting in this context are the memoirs of Joseph H. Taylor, who spent more than twenty years hunting and trapping on the Great Plains, *Sketches of Frontier and Indian Life on the Upper Missouri and the Great Plains* (Pottsdown,

Pa.: By the author, 1889). In the book's preface Taylor stated (p. 6) that his intention was "to record . . . some of the passing events in these closing days of frontier and wild Indian life."

54. Achille Loria, *Analisi della proprieta capitalista* (Torino, Italy: Fratelli Bocca, 1889), quoted in Lee Benson, *Turner and Beard: American Historical Writing Reconsidered* (New York: Free Press, 1960), 8.

55. James Bryce, *The American Commonwealth*, 2 vols. (New York: Macmillan, 1908), 2: 311, 850, 851, 857-58.

56. Roosevelt, *Works*, vol. 8: *The Winning of the West, Part I*, xxxiii.

57. *Dial* 10 (August 1889): 71-73.

CHAPTER 3. CRISIS IN THE NINETIES

1. Gilbert C. Fite, *American Farmers: The New Minority* (Bloomington: Indiana University Press, 1981), 9. Although there were some years after 1890 when the value of farm products exceeded that of the nation's industrial production, this tide had turned by 1890.

2. Most notable is an article by the United States Commissioner of Labor, Carroll D. Wright, "How a Census Is Taken," *North American Review* 148 (June 1889): 727-37, which discussed the influence of the 1880 census and the importance of the forthcoming one.

3. *Report on the Population of the United States at the Eleventh Census: 1890, Part I: Progress of the Nation*, (Washington D.C.: Government Printing Office, 1895), xxxiv; this is the most easily accessible source containing the announcement. For an interesting discussion of the 1890 Census and its superintendent, Robert P. Porter, see Gerald D. Nash, "The Census of 1890 and the Closing of the Frontier," *Pacific Northwest Quarterly* 71 (July 1980), 98-100. Nash argues that Porter's assertion that the frontier had closed in 1890 was an "impressionistic" one, rather than a generalization flowing from the close analysis of census data. It ought to be added however, that even if Porter's judgment was impressionistic, he was hardly alone in reaching such a conclusion at the time. Nash provides further biographical information on Porter (a British-born journalist and loyal Republican) in his article, "Where Is the West," *Historian* 49 (November 1986): 1-9, 5-6.

4. U.S. Census Office, 11th Census, 1890, "Distribution of Population According to Density: 1890," *Extra Census Bulletin 2* (April 20, 1891). For a fuller account of the admission of states to the Union see Robert E. Riegel, *America Moves West* (New York: Henry Holt, 1930): 549-51.

5. The mad rush into Oklahoma is recounted in Frederick Merk's *History of the Westward Movement* (New York: Alfred A. Knopf, 1978): 467-69.

6. Francis A. Walker, "The Great Count of 1890," *Forum* 11 (June 1891): 406-18. The psychological effects of the Census Bureau announcement are discussed in Ray Allen Billington, with James Blaine Hedges, *Westward Expansion: A History of the American Frontier* (New York: Macmillan, 1974), 751-53. Lee Benson in "The Historian as Mythmaker: Turner and the Closed Frontier," in David M. Ellis, ed., *The Frontier in American Development* (Ithaca, N.Y.: Cornell University Press, 1969), 3-19, argues that the Census Bulletin did not have any great effect, because it "made no dramatic statement of structural changes in American society" and hardly anyone had heard about it before 1896. Neither of Benson's points holds up very well. The notion of the frontier's unique contribution to American development had been an integral part of the national heritage from the time of independence, and the Census Bureau hardly needed to outline structural changes in American society for readers to ponder the ramifications of the fron-

tier's closing. Furthermore, the census results were given a good deal of coverage in national magazines in the early 1890s. It might also be added that the views Benson put forward in the above essay are, as Billington points out, best negated by reference to Benson's earlier work, "The Historical Background of Turner's Frontier Essay," *Agricultural History* 25 (April 1951): 59-82; see Billington, *The Genesis of the Frontier Thesis: A Study in Historical Creativity* (San Marino, Calif.: Huntington Library, 1971): 75-77.

7. The closed space concept is discussed at length by James C. Malin in his articles, "Mobility and History," *Agricultural History* 27 (April 1944): 65-74, and "The Turner-Mackinder Space Concept of History," in his *Essays on Historiography* (Ann Arbor, Mich.: Edwards Brothers, 1946), 1-44. "The idea of closed-space," Malin says, "is derived from the fact that all unoccupied lands . . . have been appropriated" ("Space and History," 65). The significance of this concept lies in the sense of claustrophobia that an expansive or frontier nation might experience when all its land became occupied.

8. Rodney Welch, "Horace Greeley's Cure for Poverty," *Forum* 8 (January 1890): 586-93, 588.

9. Ibid., 593.

10. Alfred Kazin, *On Native Grounds: An Interpretation of Modern American Prose Literature* (New York: Harcourt Brace Jovanovich, 1970), 18.

11. Charles L. P. Silet, Robert E. Welch, and Richard Bourdeau, eds., *The Critical Reception of Hamlin Garland* (Troy, New York: Whitston, 1985), 98.

12. Garland, *Main-Travelled Roads* (Boston: Arena, 1891); quotations are from the 1899 edition (New York: Harper and Brothers), 195-218, 209, 215.

13. The theme of the closed frontier in Garland's works is discussed in Lucy L. Hazard, *The Frontier in American Literature* (New York: Frederick Ungar, 1967), 261-67; Joseph B. McCullough, *Hamlin Garland* (Boston: Twayne, 1978), 51-62; and Jay Martin, *Harvest of Change: American Literature, 1865-1914* (Englewood Cliffs, N.J.: Prentice Hall, 1967), 126-31. McCullough also illustrates how Garland's adherence to Henry George's "single tax" theory is reflected in his works.

14. Garland, *Jason Edwards, An Average Man* (Boston: Arena, 1892), v.

15. Stark reflections on prairie life also permeated the entirety of Garland's *Prairie Folks; or, Pioneer Life on the Western Prairies* (New York: Garrett Press, 1969), originally published in 1893. See especially the story "Lucretia Burns," 83-117.

16. Walter F. Taylor provides further coverage of this theme in his book *The Economic Novel in America* (Chapel Hill: University of North Carolina Press, 1942), 239-52. Mark Twain's anguished use of the same theme in his novel *A Connecticut Yankee in King Arthur's Court* (New York: Harper and Brothers, 1889), is worth noting. Lee Clark Mitchell describes how Twain had set out to confute sentimental nostalgia by comparing a primitive society with an industrial society to the advantage of the latter, but ended up writing a paean to the pastoral beauty that industrialism had rendered irrecoverable; Mitchell, *Witnesses to a Vanishing America: The Nineteenth Century Response* (Princeton, N.J.: Princeton University Press, 1981), 264.

17. William Dean Howells, "A Traveller from Altruria," in Howells, *The Altrurian Romances* (Bloomington: Indiana University Press, 1968), 7-179, 121.

18. Fuller, *The Cliff-Dwellers* (New York: Harper and Brothers, 1893), quoted in Warner Berthoff, *The Ferment of Realism: American Literature, 1884-1919* (New York: Free Press, 1965), 17.

19. C. Wood Davis, "Why the Farmer Is Not Prosperous," "When the Farmer Will Be Prosperous," "The Exhaustion of the Arable Lands," and "The Probabilities of Agriculture," *Forum* 9 (April, May, June 1890): 231-42, 348-60, 461-74; 10 (November, 1890): 291-305. Davis's articles also appeared in *Country Gentleman*, *Arena*, and in a number of daily newspapers. For a complete listing and a fuller account of the content and impact

of Davis's writings see Lee Benson, "The Historical Background of Turner's Frontier Essay." It is worth pointing out, however, that Benson's emphasis on Davis leads him to postdate the emergence of a significant level of frontier anxiety by a full decade.

20. Davis, "The Exhaustion of the Arable Lands," 474.

21. Erastus Wiman, "The Farmer on Top," *North American Review* 153 (July 1891): 13-22, 14. Wiman's article was reviewed favorably in the *Review of Reviews* 4 (August 1891): 67.

22. Lee Benson points out that farm organizations such as the Southern Alliance were suspicious of these optimistic pronouncements concerning land exhaustion, believing that they had been concocted to placate the farmers and deter them from taking political action ("The Historical Background of Turner's Frontier Essay," 68).

23. Powell, "The Irrigable Lands of the Arid Region," *Century Magazine* 39 (March 1890): 766-76.

24. See Davis, "The Exhaustion of the Arable Lands," 468, and Wiman, "The Farmer on Top," 14-15.

25. James Willis Gleed's "Western Mortgages," *Forum* 9 (March 1890): 93-105, is a particularly interesting example. Benson points to Gleed's probable involvement in the early 1890s, and definite involvement by 1895, with a number of land mortgage companies. Gleed and his brother operated a leading Kansas law firm whose clients included a number of land companies hard hit by the depression. In the light of this evidence, Gleed's reasons for reassuring eastern investors in western mortgages become clear. See Benson, "The Historical Background of Turner's Frontier Essay," 70.

26. See, for example, "The Irrigation of Arid America," *Review of Reviews* 8 (October 1893): 373.

27. Benson, "The Historical Background of Turner's Frontier Essay," 70.

28. The essay appeared in the *AEgis* (a University of Wisconsin student publication), 4 November 1892, 48-52. All quotations are from the reprint in Everett E. Edwards, ed., *The Early Writings of Frederick Jackson Turner* (Freeport, N.Y.: Books for Libraries Press, 1969), 71-83. Herbert Baxter Adams, then secretary of the American Historical Association (AHA), was so impressed with the essay that he invited Turner to deliver a paper at the AHA conference at the Columbian Exposition the following year. It was, as Billington points out, ironic that Adams should give Turner a potential springboard to prominence, as it was the prevalent Teutonic germ theory, which Adams had done so much to popularize, that Turner was reacting against. See Billington, *The Genesis of the Frontier Thesis*, 60-61.

29. Turner, "Problems in American History," 72. It is also worth noting that an earlier essay of Turner's, "American Colonization" (presented to the Madison Literary Club, February 9, 1891), which addressed the factor of the closing of the frontier, was also devoid of any acute concern over that factor. In the essay Turner remarked confidently that "our organism has been completed. We have a national self-consciousness. . . . Will not this organism bud as did the trans-Alleghany organism?" (Frederick Jackson Turner Papers, Henry E. Huntington Library, San Marino, Calif., T.U. file drawer 15 (A), folder: "American Colonization," 1-33, 26. Hereafter, the abbreviation T.U., H.E.H. will be used for material from the Turner Papers.

30. Turner, "The Significance of the Frontier in American History," *The Frontier in American History* (New York: Henry Holt, 1920): 1-38, 1, 38.

31. Ray Allen Billington, "The History of a Theory," in *America's Frontier Heritage* (New York: Holt, Rinehart and Winston, 1966): 1-22; Billington, *The American Frontier Thesis: Attack and Defense* (Washington, D.C.: A.H.A. Pamphlets, 101, 1971); and Billington, ed., *The Frontier Thesis: A Valid Interpretation of American History?* (New York: Holt, Rinehart and Winston, 1966).

32. Turner, "The Significance of the Frontier," 22-23, 15 , 38.

33. James C. Malin discusses the dilemma Turner faced when he suggested that governmental action might offset the loss of the frontier. Turner realized that this suggestion was inconsistent with the premise of his thesis. As Malin puts it, "If man's destiny is determined by one set of environmental circumstances, how can there be an escape from the consequences of a reversal? If government can serve as a substitute [for the loss of the frontier] . . . why could not, or did not, the independent action of the government or of man through other means, suspend the operation of geographical determinism [when the frontier was operative]." Malin, *On the Nature of History: Essays about History and Dissidence* (Ann Arbor, Mich.: Edwards Brothers, 1954), 100. Gene Wise also explores the dilemma Turner faced, describing it as a "paradigm strain." Wise differentiates between the Turner who enthusiastically described the effects of the open frontier and another Turner who could neither face up to the deterministic framework he had imposed nor confidently substitute other factors in place of the frontier (Gene Wise, *American Historical Explanations: A Strategy for Grounded Inquiry* [Minneapolis: University of Minnesota Press, 1973], 179-221). Donald G. Holtgrieve in "Frederick Jackson Turner as a Regionalist," *Professional Geographer* 26 (May 1974): 159-65, downplays Turner's geographic determinism.

34. This point needs to be made because some historians seem to have misinterpreted Turner's work. William Appleman Williams, for example, concludes that Turner clearly implied that American institutions could be "maintained by a foreign policy of expansion" (Williams, "The Frontier Thesis and American Foreign Policy," *Pacific Historical Review* 24 [August 1955]: 379-95, 383). Turner did suggest that Americans would continue to be expansive, but he was not the ardent expansionist that Williams suggested. Chapter five discusses this point further. Turner's thoughts on immigration are discussed further in chapter four.

35. A fuller account of the reactions to the Boone and Crockett Club exhibit can be found in Richard A. Bartlett, *The New Country: A Social History of the American Frontier, 1776-1890* (New York: Oxford University Press, 1974), 444.

36. Billington restages the events in *The Genesis of the Frontier Thesis*, 170-71. He points out that Turner's paper followed five other lengthy addresses that had, in all probability, dulled the audience's concentration considerably by the time Turner took the stage. In all likelihood Turner delivered only a synopsis of his paper that night.

37. The Teutonic germ theory posited that American democratic institutions, along with those of modern Britain and Germany, had first been developed by the Aryo-Teutonic peoples who had occupied Germany's Black Forest in the medieval period. Teutonic germs, then, accounted for American democracy, and not any intrinsically American factors. See Ray Allen Billington's account of the "Teutonic" school of history in *Frederick Jackson Turner: Historian, Scholar, Teacher* (New York: Oxford University Press, 1973), 64-66.

38. *Annual Report of the American Historical Association for 1893* (Washington, D.C.: American Historical Association, 1894), 199-227. The essay first appeared in the *Proceedings of the Forty-First Annual Meeting of the State Historical Society of Wisconsin, 1894* (Madison: State Historical Society of Wisconsin, 1894), 79-112.

39. Elting Morison, ed., *Letters of Theodore Roosevelt*, 8 vols. (Cambridge, Mass.: Harvard University Press, 1951-1954), 1: 363. See also Wilbur Jacobs, *The Historical World of Frederick Jackson Turner* (New Haven, Conn.: Yale University Press, 1968), 4.

40. James A. Skelton, quoted in Reid Badger, *The Great American Fair: The World's Columbian Exposition and American Culture* (Chicago: Nelson Hall, 1979), 100.

41. Theodore Roosevelt, "The Northwest in the Nation" (Biennial Address before the State Historical Society of Wisconsin 24 January 1893), *Proceedings of the Fortieth An-*

nual Meeting of the State Historical Society of Wisconsin, 1893, Theodore Roosevelt Collection, Harvard University Library, Cambridge, Mass., 92-99.

42. Charles H. Pearson, National Life and Character: A Forecast (London: Macmillan and Company, 1913 [1st ed., January 1893]): 1, 16.

43. Richard T. Ely, Outlines of Economics (New York: Hunt and Eaton, 1893): 56-57.

44. Ibid., 57.

45. Ibid., 102. Turner underlined this passage in his personal copy of Ely's book, H.E.H., Rare Books.

46. Ibid., 103.

47. Billington, The Genesis of the Frontier Thesis, 134-42; Lee Benson, "Achille Loria's Influence on American Economic Thought, Including His Contributions to the Frontier Hypothesis," Agricultural History 24 (October 1950): 182-99, reprinted in Turner and Beard: American Historical Writing Reconsidered (New York: Free Press, 1960), 1-40.

48. E. Benjamin Andrews, "Achille Loria's Analisi della proprieta capitalista," Political Science Quarterly 5 (December 1890): 717-19.

49. Ugo Rabbeno, "Loria's Landed System of Social Economy," Political Science Quarterly 8 (June 1892): 258-93.

50. Luna E. Kellie, "Vote for Me," Farmer's Alliance (Lincoln, Nebr., September 6, 1890), quoted in Arthur M. Schlesinger, The Rise of the City, 1878-1898 (New York: Macmillan, 1933), 426.

51. St. Paul Representative, 13 September 1893, quoted in Martin Ridge, Ignatius Donnelly: The Portrait of a Politician (Chicago: University of Chicago Press, 1962), 324-25.

52. St. Paul Representative, 15 November 1893, quoted in Ridge, Ignatius Donnelly, 325. Ridge suggests that Donnelly had probably read news reports of "The Significance of the Frontier in American History" and may even have seen Turner's article, "Problems in American History." Furthermore, Ridge sees similarities of phrasing that he suggests are too striking to be dismissed as coincidence. While all this is possible, it ought to be pointed out that the Chicago address hardly received extensive newspaper coverage, and "Problems in American History" had appeared only in the AEgis—not a major publication by any reckoning. What's more, Donnelly's phrasing is also strikingly similar to Henry George's and Hamlin Garland's, to name but two. As Ridge himself points out, Donnelly recognized, "as did most public men, that the frontier era was drawing to a close" (Ignatius Donnelly, 325).

53. See John W. Morris, Charles R. Goins, and Edwin C. McReynolds, Historical Atlas of Oklahoma (Norman: University of Oklahoma Press, 1976), 47-48.

54. "Opening of the Cherokee Strip," Review of Reviews 8 (October 1893): 372-73, 372.

55. Alice C. Fletcher, "Personal Studies of Indian Life," Century Magazine 45 (January 1894): 441-55, "Personal Studies of Indian Life: Indian Songs," ibid. 47 (January 1894): 421-31; "Personal Studies of Indian Life: Hunting Customs of the Omahas," ibid. 50 (September 1895): 691-702. In the same vein as Fletcher's articles is John Comfort Gilmore's "A Study of Indian Music," ibid. 46 (June 1893): 276-84.

56. Theodore Roosevelt, "In Cowboy Land," Century Magazine 46 (June 1893): 276-84, 276.

57. The end result of this particular collaboration between Remington and Wister was Wister's story, "The Evolution of a Cowpuncher," Harper's Monthly Magazine 91 (September 1895): 602-17; see William H. Goetzmann and William N. Goetzmann's masterly work, The West of the Imagination (New York: W. W. Norton, 1986), 246. Also worthy of mention in the same context is Emerson Hough's book, The Story of the Cowboy (New York: Grosset and Dunlap, 1897). In this work Hough lamented the disappearance of the colorful West of the rough-hewn cowboy—"the men of the wilder and freer

West"—and the rise of the "smart and pretentious . . . [and] less picturesque . . . little city of the new West . . . [with its accompanying] horde of lawyers, doctors, merchants, thieves, and other necessaries" (p. 333).

58. Henry Alden to Owen Wister, 14 July 1893, Owen Wister Papers, Library of Congress; quoted in Richard Etulain, Owen Wister (Boise, Idaho: Boise State College, 1973), 10.

59. Hough, The Story of the Cowboy, 333.

60. During the 1890s dozens of Wister's stories appeared in Harper's and were periodically collected and published in book form: Red Men and White (1895), Lin McLean (1897), and The Jimmyjohn Boss and Other Stories (1900). See Etulain, Owen Wister, 10–11, for a full list. Probably close to 1,000 of Remington's illustrations appeared in those years (see Goetzmann and Goetzmann, The West of the Imagination, 238).

61. Francis Parkman, The Oregon Trail (1892), quoted in Lee Clark Mitchell, Witnesses to a Vanishing America, 42.

62. Richard Harding Davis, The West from a Car Window (New York: Harper and Brothers, 1892), 6.

63. Henry Cabot Lodge and Theodore Roosevelt, Hero Tales from American History (New York: Century, 1905).

CHAPTER 4. INTERNAL SOLUTIONS:
PRESERVING THE FRONTIER

1. Roy M. Robbins discusses the General Revision Act in Our Landed Heritage: The Public Domain (Princeton, N.J.: Princeton University Press, 1942), 296–303. He remarks that in the case of good agricultural lands "the government had . . . locked the barndoor after the horse was stolen" (303). Morton Keller, Affairs of State: Public Life in Nineteenth Century America (Cambridge, Mass.: Harvard University Press, Belknap Press, 1977), 389.

2. Lawrence M. Friedman, A History of American Law (New York: Simon and Schuster, 1973), 366.

3. John Wesley Powell, "The Irrigable Lands of the Arid Region," Century Magazine 39 (March 1890): 766–76. See also E. V. Smalley, "Our Sub-Arid Belt," Forum 21 (June 1896): 483–93. Historian Paul W. Gates's criticism of Powell is worth noting in this context. Gates has pointed to Powell's failure to realize that the large grazing homesteads he proposed for the semiarid West could lead to monopoly. See Gates, A History of Public Law Development (Washington, D.C.: Government Printing Office, 1968): 419–20.

4. Editorial, "The Irrigation of Arid America," Review of Reviews 8 (October 1893): 373.

5. See, for example, Judge J. S. Emery, "Our Arid Lands," Arena 17 (February 1897): 389–98.

6. It is interesting that in the early 1890s, even as conservative a journal as Banker's Magazine featured an article that asked the question, "Have we grown too fast?" H. A. Pierce, "A Review of Finance and Business," Banker's Magazine (February 1894): 563–67, 564.

7. Robbins points out that the Newlands Reclamation Act of 1902 was opposed on the grounds that overproduction of foodstuffs would result if more land were brought into cultivation (Our Landed Heritage, 331).

8. Ibid., 328–30.

9. Emery, "Our Arid Lands," 389–90.

10. *Ellensburg (Washington) Dawn* (18 October 1902), quoted in Robbins, *Our Landed Heritage*, 333.

11. David A. Shannon, *Twentieth Century America: The United States since the 1890s* (Chicago: Rand McNally, 1964), 37.

12. The *Review of Reviews* expressed this sentiment, stressing that the United States could grow as an agricultural nation "only by the intensive cultivation of the soil that we have hitherto been content to occupy extensively" ("The Irrigation of Arid America," *Review of Reviews* 7 [October 1893]: 373).

13. Stewart L. Udall, *The Quiet Crisis* (New York: Holt, Rinehart and Winston, 1963), 54. Udall was John F. Kennedy's secretary of the interior.

14. Russel B. Nye, "The American View of Nature," in *This Almost Chosen People: Essays in the History of American Ideas* (East Lansing: Michigan State University Press, 1966), 256-304. Roderick Nash provides an excellent discussion of the change in American attitudes toward the environment in his essay "The Roots of American Environmentalism," in *Indiana Historical Society Lectures, 1983: Perceptions of the Landscape and Its Preservation* (Indianapolis: Indiana Historical Society, 1984), 29-50. Nash argues that blaming the pioneers for environmental exploitation gains the present generation little, because "what they thought and did was not illogical given the time and place. In the absence of scarcity, there could be no scarcity value." See p. 29.

15. Udall discusses the frenzied raid on resources that lasted for almost a generation after the Civil War in *The Quiet Crisis*, 83-85.

16. Roderick Nash, *Wilderness and the American Mind*, 3rd ed. (New Haven, Conn.: Yale University Press, 1973), 143.

17. The rest of this section deals mainly with the manifestations of this change in attitude toward nature, rather than with the politics of conservation. Those interested in the complicated power struggles between the western states and the federal government and in the struggle between the two wings of the conservation "movement" are referred to Robbin's chapter on the "Rise of Conservation" in *Our Landed Heritage*, 301-24.

18. Friedman, *A History of American Law*, 366.

19. Muir's most noteworthy contributions to *Century Magazine* were: "The Treasures of Yosemite," 40 (August 1890): 483-500; and "A Rival of the Yosemite," 13 (November 1891): 77-97). Notable pieces in the *Atlantic Monthly* included "The American Reservations of the West," 81 (January 1898): 15-28).

20. Muir, "The Wild Parks and Forest Reservations of the West," in our National Parks (Boston: Houghton Mifflin, 1901), 1-36.

21. Jack T. Anderson provides a good discussion of this theme in Turner's writings in his article "Frederick Jackson Turner and Urbanization," *Journal of Popular Culture* 2 (Fall 1968): 292-98.

22. Turner, "The Problem of the West," in *The Frontier in American History* (New York: Henry Holt, 1920), 205-21, 213, 207.

23. Theodore Roosevelt, "The Strenuous Life" (speech before the Hamilton Club, Chicago, 10 April 1899), in Roosevelt, *The Works of Theodore Roosevelt*, 23 vols. (New York: Charles Scribner's Sons, 1926), vol. 13: *American Ideals, The Strenuous Life, Realizable Ideals*, 319-31, 323.

24. Henry George, *Social Problems* (London: Kegan Paul, Trench, 1884), 309-10.

25. Paul K. Conkin, *Tomorrow a New World: The New Deal Community Program* (Ithaca, N.Y.: Cornell University Press, 1959), 14-16, 17.

26. Nye, *This Almost Chosen People*, 286. The first textbooks in the field of nature studies appeared in the 1890s: Wilbur Jackman's *Nature Study for the Common Schools* (New York: Henry Holt, 1891) and Dietrich Lange's *Handbook of Nature Study for Teachers and Pupils in Elementary Schools* (New York: Macmillan, 1898). See Nye, *This Almost*

Chosen People, 291, and Nash, *Wilderness and the American Mind*, 154, for a fuller discussion of the topic.

27. "Parks in and near Large Cities," *Atlantic Monthly* 45 (April 1893): 952–53. Eastern cities such as New York and Boston took the lead in constructing city parks.

28. Eliot, "The Need of Parks," *Souvenir of the Banquet of the Advance Club* (Providence, R.I., 1891), 6: 63, quoted in Nash, *Wilderness and the American Mind*, 155.

29. John Higham, *Strangers in the Land: Patterns of American Nativism, 1860–1925* (New Brunswick, N.J.: Rutgers University Press, 1955), 68–105.

30. Walker's article on "Immigration and Degradation," *Forum* 11 (June 1891): 633–44, clearly indicates the extent of his racism and summarizes his "population theory." A representative sampling of Walker's views on immigration is available in a collection of his writings edited by Davis R. Dewey, *Discussions in Economics and Statistics*, 2 vols. (New York: Augustus M. Kelley, 1971), 2: 429–51.

31. Francis A. Walker, "The Tide of Economic Thought," address given at the Fourth Annual Meeting of the American Economic Association, by the president, Francis A. Walker. Walker used the term "alien breeds" to describe the new immigrants from southern and eastern Europe (*Publications of the American Economic Association* 6 [1891]: 37).

32. See Walker, "Immigration," *Yale Review* 1 (August 1892): 125–45, 125, 126, 129–30.

33. Ibid., 134–35, 139–41, and 144–45.

34. Walker, "Restriction of Immigration," *Atlantic Monthly* 77 (June 1896): 822–29, 826, reprinted in Dewey, ed., *Discussions in Economics and Statistics*, 437–51.

35. Henry Cabot Lodge, "The Restriction of Immigration," *North American Review* 152 (January 1891): 27–36, 31, 32. For more on Shaw's restrictionist views see Lloyd J. Graybar, *Albert Shaw of the Review of Reviews: An Intellectual Biography* (Lexington: University of Kentucky Press, 1974), 86–87, 108–109.

36. Albert Shaw, editorial, *Review of Reviews* 3 (July 1891): 571–72.

37. Turner, "Problems in American History," 82–83. It is worth pointing out, too, that Turner directed a bachelor's thesis on "The Effect of the Settlement of the Public Domain on Immigration." See Lee Benson, "The Historical Background of Turner's Frontier Essay," *Agricultural History* 25 (April 1951): 59–82. For a lengthy and excellent discussion of Turner's views on immigration see Edward N. Saveth, *American Historians and European Immigrants, 1875–1925* (New York: Columbia University Press, 1948), 122–37.

38. As mentioned earlier, "Problems in American History" had only appeared in the University of Wisconsin student publication, *AEgis*, at this early time.

39. See Benson, "The Historical Background of Turner's Frontier Essay," 69. Benson's piece includes an informative discussion of the link between the land exhaustion theme and immigration, but as mentioned earlier, Benson's emphasis on C. Wood Davis as a precursor of Turner leads him to overlook the many expressions of frontier anxiety in the 1880s.

40. Especially noteworthy are the extremely favorable reviews of Walker's 1891 article, "Immigration and Degradation," and his 1896 article, "Restriction of Immigration," which appeared in *Review of Reviews* 4 (August 1891): 174 and 13 (June 1896): 736, respectively. See also Shaw's editorial, "An Opportune Time to Restrict Immigration," *Review of Reviews* 10 (July 1894): 141.

41. Portions of Strong's book, *The New Era or the Coming Kingdom* (New York: Baker and Taylor, 1893), appeared earlier in the *Review of Reviews* (a full listing can be found in the preface of the above edition). Strong's first book, *Our Country: Its Possible Future and Its Present Crisis* (New York: Baker and Taylor, 1885), was published in a revised edition based on the Census of 1890 (Baker and Taylor, 1891). By 1893 the work had sold about

160,000 (see Benson, "The Historical Background of Turner's Frontier Essay," 76). Sales figures for *The New Era* are harder to come by, but it would be safe to assume that the book reached a fairly large audience and had a significant impact on the immigration debate.

42. Josiah Strong, *The New Era*, 80. It is interesting to note that Strong, in a letter to the *Nation* back in 1879, had expressed little concern over the assimilative capacity of the New World, agreeing with an *Encyclopaedia Britannica* article that suggested that the United States would be capable of sustaining a population of nearly 1.2 billion (*Nation*, 18 December 1879, 420).

Concern over the injection of foreign impurities into the national bloodstream was expressed in a number of articles by Sydney G. Fisher, a leading restrictionist. Among the most noteworthy were "Alien Degradation of American Character," *Forum* 14 (January 1893): 608-15, and "Has Immigration Dried Up Our Literature?" *Forum* 16 (December 1893): 560-67, in which he argued that the contamination of the native English stock by foreign blood had led to a deterioration of literary greatness, evidenced in America's failure to produce new literary prophets.

43. Strong, *The New Era*, 79.

44. The intensity of Lodge's racism is apparent in his article "Lynch Law and Unrestricted Immigration," *North American Review* 152 (May 1891): 602-12, in which he condoned the lynching in New Orleans of eleven Italian immigrants who had been tried on a murder charge and acquitted. Lodge's racist views are discussed in John A. Garraty, *Henry Cabot Lodge: A Biography* (New York: Alfred A. Knopf, 1965), 140-45; Karl Schriftgiesser, *The Gentleman from Massachusetts: Henry Cabot Lodge* (Boston: Little, Brown, 1944), 114-17; and William C. Widenor, *Henry Cabot Lodge and the Search for an American Foreign Policy* (Berkeley: University of California Press, 1980), 56-61.

45. William Gibbs McAdoo, "Immigrants and the Tariff," *Forum* 11 (June 1891): 388-405.

46. Edward A. Bradford, "America for Americans," *Harper's New Monthly Magazine* 84 (March 1892): 599-604.

47. John Swinton, *Striking for Life: Labor's Side of the Labor Question* (Philadelphia: American Manufacturing and Publishing, 1894), 39-57, quoted in Higham, *Strangers in the Land*, 71. See also *American Federationist* 1 (1894): 216-17, and 3 (1897): 233-35, also quoted ibid., 71.

48. It is worth mentioning that another aspiring Democrat, Woodrow Wilson, when he became a presidential candidate, had to go to great lengths answering those who raised questions about what he had said in the 1890s regarding the objectionable character of southern and eastern European immigrants; see Saveth, *American Historians and European Immigrants*, 142-43.

49. Edward T. Atkinson, "Incalculable Room for Immigrants," *Forum* 13 (April 1892): 360-70, 361.

50. John B. Weber and Charles Stewart Smith, "Our National Dumping Ground: A Study of Immigration," *North American Review* 154 (April 1892): 424-38.

51. This suggestion, on the part of Weber and Stewart, that the cities were in fact a safety valve for rural discontent, predates by half a century the argument put forward by Fred A. Shannon in his seminal article, "A Post-Mortem on the Labor-Safety-Valve-Theory," *Agricultural History* 19 (January 1945): 31-37.

52. Weber and Smith, "Our National Dumping Ground," 427.

53. Simon Greanleaf Crosswell, "Should Immigration Be Restricted?" *North American Review* 164 (May 1897): 526-36.

54. Higham provides an excellent discussion of this point in *Strangers in the Land*, 104-9.

55. John A. Hawgood, *America's Western Frontiers: The Exploration and Settlement of the Trans-Mississippi West* (New York: Alfred A. Knopf, 1967), 395. See also Benjamin Munn Zeigler, ed., *Immigration: An American Dilemma* (Boston: D. C. Heath, 1966), 17. Zeigler puts the figure at 579,553 for 1892 and records a steady decline in each succeeding year until 1898, when a low for the decade of 229,299 immigrants was reached. Maldwyn A. Jones points out that only about 2 percent of the arrivals were found inadmissible and sent back to Europe; see his *The Limits of Liberty: American History, 1607-1980* (New York: Oxford University Press, 1983), 324.

56. The figure was 448,572 in 1900. Zeigler, *Immigration*, 17.

57. Higham discusses this point in *Strangers in the Land*, 106-11.

CHAPTER 5. EXTERNAL SOLUTIONS:
NEW FRONTIERS

1. These factors are discussed at length in Robert L. Beisner's excellent *From the Old Diplomacy to the New, 1865-1900* (Arlington Heights, Ill.: Harlan Davidson, 1986), 72-95. Beisner's book also includes a useful annotated bibliography.

2. The "markets" thesis is presented by Walter La Feber in *The New Empire: An Interpretation of American Expansion, 1860-1898* (Ithaca, N.Y.: Cornell University Press, 1980); and William Appleman Williams in *The Roots of the Modern American Empire* (New York: Random House, 1969). La Feber argues that the writings of Turner, Strong, Brooks Adams, and Alfred Thayer Mahan, when taken together, amounted to a convincing argument for the expansion of American markets overseas. But La Feber ends up formulating a coherent frontier-based explanation for market expansion that few Americans at the time could possibly have formulated themselves. Williams also constructs a closed-frontier argument for the expansion of American commerce, but presents little hard evidence to support his case. The shortcomings of Williams's analysis are outlined by Lloyd E. Ambrosius in his review of *The Roots of the Modern American Empire*, "Turner's Frontier Thesis and the Modern American Empire," *Civil War History* 17 (December 1971): 332-39.

The general inadequacy of the markets approach is highlighted, in part, in the earlier works of Julius W. Pratt, *Expansionists of 1898; The Acquisition of Hawaii and the Spanish Islands* (Baltimore, Md.: Johns Hopkins University Press, 1936), 22, and "The Large Policy of 1898," *Mississippi Valley Historical Review* 19 (September 1932): 219-42. Pratt showed that businessmen and bankers—whom one would have expected to lend support to American imperialism if its main goal was market expansion—were "generally opposed to expansion, or indifferent to it, until after May 1, 1898." David Healy's *U.S. Expansionism: The Imperialist Urge in the 1890's* (Madison: University of Wisconsin Press, 1970) examines the expedient use of "markets" rhetoric by men whose primary interest was national power. In doing so, he casts doubt on the significance of evidence cited by La Feber, Williams, and others; see Beisner's *From the Old Diplomacy to the New*, 160-61.

3. Raymond Betts discusses the New Imperialism in relation to the closing of the American frontier in his article, "Immense Dimensions: The Impact of the American West on Late Nineteenth-Century European Thought about Expansion," *Western Historical Quarterly* 10 (April 1979): 149-66.

4. Henry Steele Commager discusses the 1890s as a "watershed" in *The American Mind: An Interpretation of American Thought and Character since the 1880's* (New Haven, Conn.: Yale University Press, 1950), 41-54. There is a good deal of credence to this delineation, although shortcomings do arise whenever we "impose divisions upon the contin-

uum of history," as Marcus Cunliffe points out in "American Watersheds," *American Quarterly* 13 (Winter 1961): 480–94.

5. Beisner, *From the Old Diplomacy to the New*, 74.

6. The literature on the safety valve concept is vast. Most of it can be accessed through Vernon E. Mattson and William E. Marion, *Frederick Jackson Turner: A Reference Guide* (Boston: G. K. Hall, 1985). Even as devoted a defender of Turner as Ray Allen Billington admitted that a "direct" safety valve did not operate in nineteenth-century America; see his chapter "Why and How Pioneers Moved Westward," in *America's Frontier Heritage* (New York: Holt, Rinehart and Winston, 1966), 23–46. Notable examples of the literature on the safety valve concept include Carter Goodrich and Sol Davidson, "The Wage-Earner in the Westward Movement" (parts 1 and 2), *Political Science Quarterly* 50 (June 1935): 161–85, and 51 (March 1936): 61–116; Joseph Schafer, "Concerning the Frontier as a Safety Valve," ibid. 52 (September 1937): 407–20; Carter Goodrich and Sol Davidson, "The Frontier as a Safety Valve: A Rejoinder," ibid. 53 (June 1938): 268–71; Fred A. Shannon, "The Homestead Act and Labor Surplus," *American Historical Review* 41 (July 1936): 637–51, and "A Post-Mortem on the Labor-Safety-Valve Theory," *Agricultural History* 19 (January 1945): 31–37; Norman J. Simler, "The Safety-Valve Doctrine Re-Evaluated," *Agricultural History* 32 (October 1958): 250–57; Ellen von Nardroff, "The American Frontier as a Safety Valve: The Life, Death, Reincarnation, and Justification of a Theory," *Agricultural History* 36 (July 1962): 123–42; and most recently, Carlos A. Schwantes, "The Concept of a Wageworkers' Frontier: A Framework for Future Research," *Western Historical Quarterly* 18 (January 1987): 39–55; and William F. Deverell, "To Loosen the Safety Valve: Eastern Workers and Western Lands," *Western Historical Quarterly* 19 (August 1988): 269–85. A thorough review of this literature leads categorically to the conclusion that the notion of the frontier as a direct safety valve (more the brainchild of Turner's disciples than of Turner himself) is unconvincing. Despite the weight of this quantitative evidence, the qualitative evidence suggests that generations of Americans have believed that the frontier did indeed act as a direct safety valve.

7. Richard Hofstadter provided an interesting discussion of this topic in "Manifest Destiny and the Philippines," in Daniel Aaron, ed., *America in Crisis* (New York: Alfred A. Knopf, 1952), 173–200. See also Higham's *Strangers in the Land*, 76.

8. It is interesting that in the debate over extracontinental expansion, frontier-related Malthusian concerns were voiced as often as frontier-related fears of oversurplus. As we saw earlier, this much was also evident in the debate over irrigation.

9. Beisner remarks, perhaps a little too conclusively, that by the late nineties "a speaker was judged remiss if he failed to address the problems of a nation that had lost its frontier safety valve." *From the Old Diplomacy to the New*, 75.

10. See especially Wiman's articles, "Has Not the Time for the Capture of Canada Come?" "Can We Coerce Canada?" and "The Struggle in Canada," *North American Review* 148 (August 1890): 212–22, 152 (January 1891): 91–102, and 152 (March 1891): 339–48, respectively.

11. Wiman, "Has Not the Time for the Capture of Canada Come?" 213, 215.

12. Editorial, *Review of Reviews* 4 (August 1891): 68.

13. Editorial, ibid. (September 1891): 189. In fact, as Donald Warner points out, the dominant trend in the 1880s of migration from the Dominion to the Republic ceased and then reversed itself in the 1890s as U.S. settlers began to take up homestead opportunities on the Canadian prairies (*The Idea of Continental Union: Agitation for the Annexation of Canada to the United States, 1849–1893* [Lexington: University of Kentucky Press, 1960], 241).

14. See especially "Development of the Great Northwest," *Review of Reviews* 8 (October 1893): 373–74; S. A. Thompson, "The Possibilities of the Great Northwest," ibid. 10

(August 1894): 160–64; "The Great Canadian Northwest" (editorial), ibid. 10 (November 1894): 545.

15. Warner, *The Idea of Continental Union*, 226–38.

16. Josiah Strong, *The New Era; or, The Coming Kingdom* (New York: Baker and Taylor, 1893), 78, 79.

17. Ibid., 74, 222.

18. In her article "Josiah Strong and American Nationalism: A Reevaluation," *Journal of American History* 53 (December 1966): 487–503, Dorothea R. Muller argued that historians have overstressed Strong's imperialism and ignored the nature of his religious philosophy. But Muller's evaluation of Strong's major works is at least as selective as that of the historians she admonishes.

19. Some historians have argued that Turner was an avowed expansionist in this period. See, for example, William Appleman Williams's article "The Frontier Thesis and American Foreign Policy," *Pacific Historical Review* 24 (August 1955): 379–95; and Lawrence S. Kaplan's "Frederick Jackson Turner and Imperialism," *Social Science* 27 (January 1952): 12–16. Both of these historians, however, overestimate Turner's own imperialism in their efforts to determine his role in shaping the expansionist temper of the nineties.

20. Frederick Jackson Turner Papers, Huntington Library, file drawer 15 (A), folder: "American Colonization" (paper presented to the Madison Literary Club, 9 February 1891), 32.

21. Turner, "The Significance of the Frontier," in *The Frontier in American History* (New York: Henry Holt, 1920): 1–38, 37.

22. Ibid.

23. Turner applied his environmental determinism on a provincial scale, not a world scale. It was not free land per se that had formed the American character, but the American frontier of free land—"the Great West," "the wilderness," "the American forest," "the stubborn American environment." Turner's frontier was all these things, and always peculiarly American. Turner simply did not feel that new, extracontinental frontiers could offset its loss, even when he radically modified his environmental determinism in his later works.

24. Turner's clippings of the various newspaper reviews of "The Problems of the West" are in T.U., H.E.H., box 54. Among the newspapers that printed reviews were the *Lowell* (Mass.) *Times* (7 September 1896), *Boston Evening Record* (22 August 1896), *Boston Herald* (22 August 1896), and *Chicago Tribune* (30 August 1896).

25. "The Problem of the West," in *The Frontier in American History*, 205–21, 219.

26. Ibid., 221.

27. Wendell H. Stephenson, ed., "The Influence of Woodrow Wilson on Frederick Jackson Turner," *Agricultural History* 19 (October 1945): 249–53.

28. Woodrow Wilson, *Division and Reunion, 1829–1889*, 2d ed. (New York: Longman's, Green, 1929), 4.

29. Ibid., 15.

30. Woodrow Wilson, "Mr. Goldwyn Smith's 'Views' on Our Political History," *Forum* 16 (December 1893): 489–99, 497.

31. Paul C. Nagel, *This Sacred Trust: American Nationality, 1798–1898* (New York: Oxford University Press, 1971), 282. Nagel's examination of Wilson's articles published in the 1890s shows how close he came to advocating further expansion as a logical outgrowth of the frontier process. But Wilson was always more distressed by the loss of the domestic frontier than he was optimistic about the prospects of new compensatory frontiers.

32. Merle E. Curti, *The Growth of American Thought*, 3d ed. (New York: Harper and Row, 1964), 655.

33. See especially General Thomas Jordan, "Why We Need Cuba," *Forum* 11 (June 1891): 559-67; Arthur Curtiss James, "Advantages of Hawaiian Annexation," *North American Review* 165 (December 1897): 758-60; Robert Tudor Hill, "Cuba and Its Value as a Colony," *Forum* 25 (June 1898): 403-15; and a review of Hill's article, "The Wealth of Cuba," *Review of Reviews* 18 (July 1898): 81.

34. Senator Anthony Higgins (Del.), *Congressional Record*, 53d Congress, Senate, 2d Session, March 2, 1895, 3109-10.

35. Senator Orville Platt (Conn.), *Congressional Record*, 53d Congress, Senate, 2d Session, March 2, 1895, 3044-45.

36. Alfred Thayer Mahan, "The Future in Relation to American Naval Power," *Harper's New Monthly Magazine* 91 (October 1895): 767-75; reprinted in Mahan, *The Interest of America in Sea Power: Present and Future* (Boston: Little, Brown, 1903), 137-72, 165, 166.

37. Mahan, *The Interest of America in Sea Power*, 167-68. John William Ward examines this attitude as it was applied to the Indian in the course of America's westward expansion; see his *Andrew Jackson: Symbol for an Age* (New York: Oxford University Press, 1981), 30-45.

38. Mahan, *The Interest of America in Sea Power*, 168.

39. It is interesting to note the utilization of the closed-frontier theme by both Alfred Thayer Mahan and Senators Orville Platt and Anthony Higgins in support of increased naval appropriations.

40. Mahan, "A Twentieth Century Outlook," *Harper's New Monthly Magazine* 95 (September 1897): 521-33; reprinted in *The Interest of America in Sea Power*, 217-68, 220-21.

41. James Bryce, "The Policy of Annexation for America," *Forum* 24 (September 1897): 385-95, 394. Bryce, in *The American Commonwealth*, had foreseen the problems that would arise when America had used up its supply of free land, but his projections for when that day would arise varied widely.

42. "Territorial Expansion" (editorial), *Outlook* 59 (June 1898): 511. Senator Orville Platt asserted that the same population figure of 70 million meant Americans could "no longer shut themselves up within narrow limits" *Congressional Record*, 53d Congress, 2d session, 1894.

43. William D. McCracken, "Our Foreign Policy," *Arena* 44 (July 1893): 145-50, 147, 149.

44. William F. Reddaway, *The Monroe Doctrine*, reprint (New York: G. E. Stechkert, 1924), 141.

45. Edith H. Parker, "William Graham Sumner and the Frontier," *Southwest Review* 41 (Autumn 1956): 357-65. Attempting to establish Sumner as the most important of Turner's precursors, Parker ends up overemphasizing the importance of Sumner's writings on the land-to-man ratio.

46. William Graham Sumner, "Earth Hunger," *Yale Review* 3 (October 1896): 3-32, reprinted in *Earth Hunger and Other Essays* (New Haven, Conn.: Yale University Press, 1913): 31-64; all quotations are from the reprint.

47. The utilization of Darwinian theory to justify expansion is discussed in Richard Hofstadter's *Social Darwinism in American Thought*, 2d ed. (New York: George Braziller, 1969), 170-97. Hofstadter's book also contains an excellent chapter on Sumner, pages 56-78.

48. "Earth Hunger," 31, 44, 45-46.

49. Ibid., 45, 46, 64.

50. Ibid., 63-64.

51. Sumner, "The Conquest of the United States by Spain," *Yale Law Journal* 8 (January 1899): 168-93, reprinted in *War and Other Essays* (New Haven, Conn.: Yale University Press, 1911), 297-334; quotations are from the reprint. See also Sumner's article, "The Fallacy of Territorial Extension," *Forum* 21 (June 1896): 414-19.

52. "The Conquest of the United States by Spain," 324.

53. Ibid., 325-26, 334. Sumner, of course, was not greatly concerned about the probability of the weak getting weaker and the strong getting stronger, but he felt that this should be allowed to happen naturally. In Sumner's mind, inequality was a fact of life, because some people were just more capable than others. At the same time, he felt that conditions of inequality should not be artificially fostered. Thus Sumner was opposed to "political earth hunger" or, more simply, imperialism—just as he was opposed to government intervention on the side of big business—because it created conditions of inequality artificially.

54. Albert J. Beveridge, "The March of the Flag," *Indianapolis Journal*, 17 September 1898, reprinted in Beveridge, *The Meaning of the Times and Other Speeches* (Indianapolis: Bobbs-Merrill, 1908), 47-57; quotations are from the reprint.

55. Beveridge, "The March of the Flag," 47. See, for example, Henry Cabot Lodge, "Our Blundering Foreign Policy," *Forum* 19 (March 1895): 8-17; James C. Fernald, *The Imperial Republic* (New York: Funk and Wagnalls, 1899), especially 37-38; A. Lawrence Lowell, "The Colonial Expansion of the United States," *Atlantic Monthly* 83 (February 1899): 145-54; and W. J. McGee, "National Growth and Character," *National Geographic Magazine* 10 (June 1899): 185-206.

56. Beveridge, "Our Philippine Policy" (speech before the U.S. Senate, January 9, 1900), reprinted in *The Meaning of the Times*, 58-88, 85-86; quotations are from the reprint.

57. Ibid., 64.

58. Beveridge, "The March of the Flag," 52, 57.

59. Turner, "American Colonization," 32.

60. Brooks Adams, *The Law of Civilization and Decay*, reprint (New York: Vintage Books, 1943).

61. Adams, "The Spanish War and the Equilibrium of the World," *Forum* 25 (August 1898): 641-51, 645, 646, 651.

62. Adams, "The New Struggle for Life among Nations," in *America's Economic Supremacy* (New York: Harper and Brothers, 1900, 1947), 84-106, 98-99, 102-3, 106; quotations are from the later edition.

63. David H. Burton makes this point in his essay, "Theodore Roosevelt," in A. E. Campbell, ed., *Expansion and Imperialism* (New York: Harper and Row, 1970), 82-88, 83. Also useful in this context is Burton's article, "The Influence of the American West on the Imperialist Philosophy of Theodore Roosevelt," *Arizona and the West* 14 (January 1962): 5-26. See also Roosevelt's essay, "Expansion and Peace," *Independent*, 21 December 1899, 3401-5; and Lowell, "The Colonial Expansion of the United States."

64. Roosevelt, *The Wilderness Hunter* (New York: G. P. Putnam and Sons, 1893), reprinted in *The Works of Theodore Roosevelt*, 23 vols. (New York: Charles Scribner's Sons, 1926), 2: xvi, xxi, xxix; quotations are from the reprint.

65. David Healy provides a useful examination of Roosevelt's concern over the deterioration of the American character in his *U.S. Expansionism: The Imperialist Urge in the 1890's* (Madison: University of Wisconsin Press, 1970): 115-20.

66. Elting E. Morison, ed., *The Letters of Theodore Roosevelt*, 8 vols. (Cambridge, Mass.: Harvard University Press, 1951-1954), Roosevelt to Granville Stanley Hall, 29 November 1899, 2: 1100.

67. Roosevelt to Francis V. Greene, 23 September 1897, quoted in Howard K. Beale,

Theodore Roosevelt and the Rise of America to World Power (Baltimore, Md.: Johns Hopkins University Press, 1956), 37.

68. James to the editor, *Springfield Republican*, 4 June 1900, quoted in Beale, *Roosevelt and the Rise of America to World Power*, 37.

69. Theodore Roosevelt, *The Rough Riders* (New York: Charles Scribner's Sons, 1899), reprinted in *Works* 9: 15-16; quotations are from the reprint. Actually many of the Rough Riders were northeastern college students and graduates who had never been in the West.

70. Roosevelt, *Works* 5: "The Strenuous Life" (speech before the Hamilton Club, Chicago, 10 April 1899), 319-31, 323, 331.

CHAPTER 6. THE FADING FRONTIER

1. Woodrow Wilson, "Democracy and Efficiency," *Atlantic Monthly* 87 (March 1901): 289-99, reprinted in Woodrow Wilson, *College and State*, R. S. Baker and W. E. Dodd, eds. (New York: Harper and Brothers, 1925), 398-415.

2. Woodrow Wilson, "The Ideals of America" (address delivered on the 125th anniversary of the Battle of Trenton, 26 December 1901), reprinted in *Atlantic Monthly* 90 (December 1902): 721-34, 726. The general notion that extracontinental expansion had followed naturally and inevitably the completion of the nation's internal expansion was outlined by the historian Edwin Erle Spark in *The Expansion of the American People: Social and Territorial* (Chicago: Scott Foresman, 1900).

3. Portions of Roosevelt's speech appeared in *Nation*, 7 May 1903), 366-67.

4. Ibid., 367.

5. J. M. Scanland, "Expansion: Past and Prospective," *Arena* 23 (April 1900): 337-52.

6. Benjamin O. Flower, "An Army of Wealth Creators Versus an Army of Destruction," *Arena* 25 (May 1901): 521-26. Those interested in William E. Smythe's writings are referred to his influential book *The Conquest of Arid America* (Seattle: University of Washington Press, 1969, first published in 1899, revised 2d edition, 1905) and two of his articles: "The Irrigation Idea and Its Coming Congress," *Review of Reviews* 8 (October 1893): 394-406 (the first account of irrigation published in the national periodical press); and "The Struggle for Water in the West," *Atlantic Monthly* 86 (November 1900): 646-54. Another frontier-related, antiexpansionist argument, by former Secretary of State (1895-1897) Richard Olney, appeared in the *Atlantic Monthly* in the early months of the century. Olney argued that the nation's landed resources were sufficient to meet the needs of its growing population long into the future, and furthermore, that the Philippines' tropical climate would prove wholly inhospitable to the white race. Olney, "Growth of Our Foreign Policy," *Atlantic Monthly* 85 (March 1900): 289-301.

7. There was of course one remaining continental frontier, Alaska, which at the turn of the century had a population of only 5,000.

8. Theodore Roosevelt, *The Strenuous Life*, 2d ed. (New York: Century, 1901), 44. Roosevelt elaborated at length on this theme in a speech he gave in Colorado in early August (included in *The Strenuous Life*).

9. "March of Events," *World's Work* 1 (November 1900): 3-4.

10. Editorial, *The Independent* 54 (May 1902): 1201-2, quoted in Warren French, "Death of the Dream" (unpublished doctoral seminar paper for Walter Prescott Webb, University of Texas, Austin, c. 1953), 41.

11. Frank Norris, "The Frontier Gone at Last," *World's Work* 3 (February 1902): 1728-31. The essay is reprinted in Frank Norris's *The Responsibilities of a Novelist* (Garden City, N.Y.: Doubleday Doran, 1928), 53-61—a work that contains other essays by

Norris on the closing of the frontier. The piece is also included in Roderick Nash, ed., *The Call of the Wild: 1900-1916* (New York: George Braziller, 1970), 69-75. Nash's collection also contains George S. Evans's essay "The Wilderness" (quoted on the first page of Part Three of this book), 75-78. Evans's piece first appeared in the *Overland Monthly* 18 (January 1904): 31-33. All quotations from Norris's essay are taken from *World's Work*.

12. Norris, "The Frontier Gone at Last," 1728-29.

13. Ibid., 1729-30.

14. Ibid., 1731.

15. Charles Grant Miller, "The Trust Question: Its Development in America," *Arena* 23 (January 1900): 40-50, 40-41.

16. Richard T. Ely, *Studies in the Evolution of Industrial Society* (New York: Macmillan, 1903), 59. Quotations are taken from Frederick Jackson Turner's copy of the book (H.E.H. Special Collections), in which Turner underlined Ely's statements on population density in the United States.

17. William E. Smythe, *Constructive Democracy: The Economics of a Square Deal* (New York: Macmillan, 1905), 335. For further information on Smythe, see Patricia Nelson Limerick's cynical assessment of his irrigation schemes and his boundless optimism in her *Desert Passages: Encounters with the American Deserts* (Albuquerque: University of New Mexico Press, 1985), 77-90. For a more favorable evaluation of Smythe's efforts see Martin E. Carlson, "William E. Smythe: Irrigation Crusader," *Journal of the West* 7 (January 1968): 41-47.

18. Ibid., 357, 385. See also E. E. Miller, "The American Farmer as a Co-operator," *Forum* 52 (October 1914): 595-622. Miller commented that the American farmer's individualism was often given as the reason for the failure of cooperative efforts, which had been more successful in European countries, but he concluded that cooperative agricultural efforts could work in the United States.

19. The quotation is from Frederick Jackson Turner's personal copy of the book by Algie M. Simons, *The American Farmer* (Chicago: Charles H. Kerr, 1902): 178; H.E.H., acc. no. 126733. Turner underlined the quoted material.

20. Smythe, *Constructive Democracy*, 345.

21. Ibid., 348.

22. See, for example, J. M. Scanland, "Will the Chinese Migrate?" *Arena* 24 (July 1900): 21-30; John Chetwood, "The Problems of Immigration: The Argument for Suspension," ibid. 27 (March 1902): 254-60; Truxton Beale, "Why the Chinese Should Be Excluded," *Forum* 33 (March 1902): 53-58; and Charles Denby, "Chinese Exclusion," *Forum* 34 (July 1902): 131-37.

23. For a thorough discussion of this topic, including the reaction of the American Chinese population to the exclusion acts, see Ronald Takaki's excellent *Strangers from a Different Shore: A History of Asian Americans* (New York: Penguin Books, 1990), 79-131.

24. Kate Holladay Claghorn, "Our Immigrants and Ourselves," *Atlantic Monthly* 86 (October 1900): 535-48, 545.

25. Edward Alsworth Ross, *Social Control: A Survey of the Foundations of Order* (New York: Johnson Reprint, 1970), 17, 42, 83-84, 86-87, quoted in R. Jackson Wilson, *In Quest of Community: Social Philosophy in the United States, 1860-1920* (New York: John Wiley and Sons, 1968), 109.

26. Wilson, *In Quest of Community*, 109.

27. Frederick Jackson Turner, "The Stream of Immigration into the United States," *Chicago Herald Tribune*, 25 September 1901.

28. Turner, "Jewish Immigration," *Chicago Herald Tribune*, 16 October 1901. Turner's contributions were part of a series of articles on the topic of immigration that ran in the *Herald Tribune* in the summer and fall of 1901. All of these articles were clipped and col-

lected by Turner; see H.E.H., T.U. file drawer 15C, folder: "General Views of Immigration." Turner's writings in the Herald Tribune are also discussed in Edward N. Saveth's American Historians and European Immigrants, 1875–1925 (New York: Columbia University Press, 1948), 127–35.

29. Walter Weyl, "New Americans," Harper's Magazine 129 (September 1914): 615–23.

30. See, for example, W. Jett Lauck's articles, "The Vanishing American Wage-Earner," Atlantic Monthly 110 (November 1912): 691–96, "A Real Myth," ibid. (September 1912): 389–93 and "The Real Significance of Recent Immigration," North American Review 195 (February 1912): 201–11; and Prescott F. Hall, "The Future of American Ideals," North American Review 195 (January 1912): 94–102.

31. Henry Pratt Fairchild, "Some Immigration Differences," Yale Review (old series) 19 (May 1910): 79–97. See also Fairchild's collection of essays on the topic, Immigration, A New World Movement and Its American Significance (New York: Macmillan, 1913).

32. Edward Alsworth Ross, "Racial Consequences of Immigration," Century 87 (February 1914): 615–22, 621, 620.

33. See, for example, A. Piatt Andrew, "The Crux of the Immigration Question," North American Review 99 (June 1914): 866–78.

34. Ray Allen Billington, "Frederick Jackson Turner and the Closing of the Frontier," in Roger Daniels, ed., Essays in Western History in Honor of Professor T. A. Larson (Laramie: University of Wyoming Publications, October 1971), 37: 45–56, 46.

35. Frederick Jackson Turner, "The Middle West," International Monthly (December 1901); the essay is included in The Frontier in American History (New York: Henry Holt, 1920), 126–156, 155; the quotation is from the reprint.

36. Turner, "Contributions of the West to American Democracy," Atlantic Monthly (January 1903), reprinted in The Frontier in American History, 243–68, 244, 258, and 261; quotations are from the reprint.

37. Turner, "Pioneer Ideals and the State University," in The Frontier in American History, 269–89.

38. Turner, "Social Forces in American History" (presidential address before the American Historical Association, Indianapolis, 28 December 1910), American Historical Review 16 (January 1911): 217–33, reprinted in The Frontier in American History, 311–34, 319; the quotation is from the reprint.

39. Turner's mention in this period of the possibilities offered by Alaska is worthy of note; see "The West and American Ideals," Washington Historical Quarterly 5 (October 1914): 243–57; reprinted in The Frontier in American History, 290–310, 296. Turner's numerous clippings of articles on Alaska and the Canadian West from the period 1911–1913 are interesting, too, and suggest that Turner gave serious consideration to this region as a new frontier that might offset some of the "post-frontier" problems the nation was experiencing.

40. H.E.H., T.U. file drawer L (2), folder: "Sequence to End of Frontier." The newspaper clippings contained in this file (the latest dated February 1909) give us a clue to the rough date of these notes. The folder title, "Sequence to End of Frontier," bears a close resemblance to the line "sequence to the extinction of the frontier" contained in Turner's 1910 American Historical Association address, "Social Forces in American History." It seems likely that these notes were made in early preparation for the speech.

41. Herbert D. Croly, The Promise of American Life, reprint (Cambridge, Mass.: Harvard University Press, Belknap Press, 1965), 7, 13. Large sections of Croly's book treat the theme of the closing of the frontier. Of particular note are pages 1–26 and 100–117. Gerald Nash also discusses Croly's utilization of the closed-frontier theme; see his Creat-

ing the West: Historical Interpretations, 1890–1990 (Albuquerque: University of New Mexico Press, 1991), 11–12.

42. Croly, *The Promise of American Life*, 17–18, 22–23.

43. Theodore Roosevelt, "The Pioneer Spirit and American Problems," *Outlook* 96 (September 1910): 56–60, reprinted in *The Works of Theodore Roosevelt*, 23 vols. (New York: Charles Scribner's Sons, 1926), 16: American Problems, 21–25, 21–22. Quotations are from the reprint.

44. Robert Tudor Hill, *The Public Domain and Democracy: A Study of Social, Economic and Political Problems in the United States in Relation to Western Development* (New York: Columbia University Press, 1910), 217, 219.

45. Walter F. Weyl, *The New Democracy: An Essay on Certain Political and Economic Tendencies in the United States* (New York: Harper and Row, 1964), 22, 36. Gerald Nash also provides discussion of the closed-frontier theme in Weyl's book; see his *Creating the West*, 12–13.

46. Weyl, *The New Democracy*, 24–25, 32.

47. The various phases of London's career and their relation to the theme of the closing of the frontier are outlined in William Judson Bogard's "The West as a Cultural Image at the End of the Nineteenth Century" (Ph.D dissertation, Tulane University, 1971), 176–77. Bogard's dissertation also contains useful discussion of Theodore Roosevelt's and Owen Wister's reactions to the closing of the frontier. Also worth mentioning in this context is Clell Peterson's "Jack London and the American Frontier" (M.A. thesis, University of Minnesota, 1951).

48. Jack London, "The Class Struggle," *Independent*, 5 November 1903, 2603–10. The essay was reprinted in the major work of London's socialist phase, *The War of the Classes* (London: W. M. Heinemann, 1905), 3–49, 7–9. The book was first published in New York, in April 1905, by the Macmillan Company. All quotations are from the 1905 London edition. The essay is also included and discussed in Philip S. Foner, ed., *Jack London: American Rebel: A Collection of His Social Writings Together with an Extensive Study of the Man and His Times* (New York: Citadel Books, 1947). Foner also provides some useful commentary on London's thinking about the frontier. The reader is also directed to Earle Labor's excellent "Jack London" and to the bibliography of books by and about London in Thomas J. Lyon et al., eds., *A Literary History of the American West* (Fort Worth: Texas Christian University Press, 1987), 381–97.

49. Jack London, *The People of the Abyss* (New York: Macmillan, 1903). The closed frontier theme in the book is discussed in Bogard, "The West as a Cultural Image at the End of the Nineteenth Century," 182–83, and in Foner, *Jack London: American Rebel*, 49.

50. Jack London, "How I Became a Socialist," in *The War of the Classes*, 267–78, 267, 269, 271. Another interesting commentary in this period on the claustrophobic effects of the closed frontier on the laboring classes is Frederic C. Howe's "The Lure of the Land," *Scribner's Magazine* 46 (October 1909): 431–36.

51. London, "How I Became a Socialist," 273, 274, 278.

52. London, "The Class Struggle," 9–10.

53. Ibid., 49.

54. Algie M. Simons, *Social Forces in American History* (New York: Macmillan, 1911), chapter 12, "The Westward March of a People," 134–42, 134, 140, 318. Gerald Nash provides further discussion of Simons in *Creating the West*, 15. Nash points out that Simons, in a personal letter to Turner, noted how influential the frontier thesis had been in molding his own thinking. Nash also notes the interesting duplication of Simons's forthcoming book title by Turner in his presidential address to the American Historical Association in December 1910.

55. William J. Trimble, "The Influence of the Passing of the Public Lands," *Atlantic Monthly* 113 (June 1914): 755–57, 759, and 763.

CHAPTER 7. BACK TO UNTAMED NATURE

1. Gilbert C. Fite, *American Farmers: The New Minority* (Bloomington: Indiana University Press, 1981), 9.

2. United States Bureau of the Census, *Historical Statistics of the United States: Colonial Times to 1970* (Washington, D.C.: Government Printing Office, 1975), chapter K, 457.

3. Charles Moreau Harger, "The Passing of the Promised Land," *Atlantic Monthly* 104 (October 1909): 461–66, 466.

4. Agnes C. Laut, "The Last Trek to the Last Frontier: The American Settler in the Canadian Northwest," *Century Magazine* 78 (May 1909): 99–111, 99, 102. See also L. A. Chase, "The Last American Frontier," *History Teacher's Magazine* 6 (February 1915): 37–40; Lawrence J. Burpee, "The Lure of the Land West," *Dial* 54 (April 1913): 343–45; and Philip R. Kellar, "The American Farm Landlord-Tenant Problem," *Forum* 52 (July 1914): 81–88.

5. Paul F. Sharp, "When Our West Moved North," *American Historical Review* 55 (October 1949): 286–300, 289. "The Last Best West" was the title of the Canadian Department of the Interior's most effective promotional pamphlet. For more on this topic see Harold Martin Trooper, *Only Farmers Need Apply: Official Canadian Government Encouragement of Immigration from the United States, 1896–1911* (Toronto: Griffin House, 1972); and Marcus L. Hansen, *The Mingling of the Canadian and American Peoples* (New Haven, Conn.: Yale University Press, 1940).

6. C. C. Georgeson, "The Possibilities of Alaska," *National Geographic Magazine* 13 (March 1902): 81–85, 84, 85. See also C. C. Georgeson, "Agricultural Capacity of Alaska: What Population Can the Territory Support?" ibid. 20 (July 1909): 676–79.

7. The *Dial* is a particularly good source for reviews of frontier histories in this period. See volumes 28–43 (1900–1907).

8. Reviews of books on birds, flowers, gardening, and related "nature topics" in the *Dial* in the early years of the twentieth century are too numerous to list. The reader is referred to particularly representative items in volumes 39 (September 1900): 120–22; 31 (July 1901): 14–17, and (September 1901): 185–87; 32 (June 1902): 281–84, 33 (October 1902): 236–37; 34 (February 1903): 82–83, and (June 1903): 362–64. Some particularly interesting examples of this theme in *Harper's Magazine* are: Julius Norregard, "The Joys of Gardens," 104 (March 1902): 606–11; Edward S. Martin, "The Country," ibid. (April 1902): 825–32, and "Wister in the Country," ibid. 107 (November 1903): 845–52. Also well worth noting in this context is the slick publication *Country Life*, begun in 1900. *Collier's Magazine* was another repository for the writings of nature enthusiasts, especially after 1910. The nature enthusiast Bolton Hall sought to educate the public in the practice of gardening in his works *Three Acres and Liberty* (New York: Grosset and Dunlap, 1907), and *The Garden Yard: A Handbook of Intensive Farming* (Philadelphia: David McKay, 1909).

9. This theme is stressed in William L. Bowers's useful study *The Country Life Movement in America, 1900–1920* (Port Washington, N.Y.: Kennikat Press, 1974). Another useful overview of the movement is provided in Stanford J. Layton's *To No Privileged Class: The Rationalization of Homesteading and Rural Life in the Early Twentieth Century American West* (Salt Lake City: Brigham Young University, Charles Redd Center for Western Studies, 1988), 5–20. Barbara Allen's *Homesteading the High Desert* (Salt Lake City: University

of Utah Press, 1987) also includes useful discussion of the "back-to-nature" strain in American thought, linking it to the theme of the closing of the frontier, 114-26.

10. For a brief and excellent discussion of Stratton-Porter's popularity in this period see Roderick Nash, *The Nervous Generation: American Thought, 1917-1930* (Chicago: Ivan R. Dee, 1990), 137-39. Also on this theme of "tamed nature," see Peter J. Schmitt, *Back to Nature: The Arcadian Myth in Urban America* (New York: Oxford University Press, 1969).

11. George S. Evans, "The Wilderness," *Overland Monthly* 43 (January 1904): 31-33, reprinted in Roderick Nash, ed., *The Call of the Wild, 1900-1916* (New York: George Braziller, 1973): 75-78. Quotations are from the reprint, 75, 75, 77, and 78.

12. Roderick Nash, *Wilderness and the American Mind*, 3d. ed. (New Haven, Conn.: Yale University Press, 1982), 143.

13. Ernest Thompson Seton is quoted in Nash, *Wilderness and the American Mind*, 147-48.

14. The quotation is from London's autobiographical story, "At the Rainbow's End," which is included in his *The God of His Fathers* (New York: McClure Phillips, 1901). It is cited in William Judson Bogard, "The West as a Cultural Image of the End of the Nineteenth Century" (Ph.D. dissertation, Tulane University, 1971), 163.

15. Peter Schmitt, "Wilderness Novels in the Progressive Era," *Journal of Popular Culture* 3 (Summer 1960): 72-90, 74. Schmitt's article provides an excellent treatment of the theme of wilderness as an antidote to the ills of civilization. London's wilderness tales also appeared in the *Atlantic Monthly*; especially noteworthy is "An Odyssey of the North," 85 (January 1900): 85-100.

16. Jack London, "In a Far Country," *Overland Monthly* (June 1899): 47-63; reprinted in Dale L. Walker, ed., *In a Far Country: Jack London's Tales of the West* (Ottawa, Ill.: Jameson Books, 1987). The quotation is from the reprint, 49.

17. See Nash, *Wilderness and the American Mind*, 156.

18. Jack London, "Economics of the Klondike," *Review of Reviews* 21 (January 1900): 70-74, 74; cited in Bogard, "The West as a Cultural Image," 178.

19. Bogard, "The West as a Cultural Image," 177. The reader is also directed to Earle Labor's excellent essay, "Jack London," in Thomas J. Lyon et al., eds., *A Literary History of the American West* (Fort Worth: Texas Christian University Press, 1987): 381-97.

20. Nash recounts Knowles's adventure in his excellent chapter on "The Wilderness Cult," in *Wilderness and the American Mind*, 141-60.

21. Walter Prichard Eaton, "The Park of the Many Glaciers," *Harper's Magazine* 135 (June 1917): 1-12, 8, 6.

22. Cyrus C. Adams, "Unexplored Regions of the Earth," *Harper's Magazine* 114 (January 1907): 305-11, 310.

23. Vilhjalmur Stefansson, "Wintering among the Eskimos," *Harper's Magazine* 117 (June 1908): 38-48.

24. H. W. Newman, "Through the African Wilderness," *Harper's Magazine* 113 (June 1908): 28-36; Roy C. Andrews, "The Wilderness of North Korea," ibid. 117 (May 1913): 828-39; Charles Wellington Furlong, "Through the Heart of the Suriname Jungle," ibid. 128 (February 1914): 327-39; Hiram Bingham, "Along the Unchartered Pampaconas," ibid. 129 (August 1914): 452-63; A. Hyatt Verrill, "My Boat Trip Through the Guiana Wilderness," ibid. 134 (January 1917): 242-53; Roy Chapman Andrews, "The Frontier of the Forbidden Land," ibid. 136 (May 1918): 894-905; Vilhjalmur Stefansson, "Solving the Problems of the Arctic," ibid. 139 (June 1919): 36-47; Burt McConnell, "Over the Ice with Stefansson," ibid. 130 (April 1915): 672-85. See also Frank E. Schoonovar, "The Edge of the Wilderness," *Scribner's* 37 (April 1905): 441-53; Theodore Roosevelt, "A Colorado Bear Hunt," ibid. 38 (October 1905): 387-408, and "A Wolf Hunt in Okla-

homa," ibid. (November 1905): 513-32; Andrew J. Stone, "Hunting the Great Alaskan Bear," ibid. 41 (February 1907): 205-9.

25. Theodore Roosevelt's wilderness adventures in Africa and then Brazil were recounted in *Scribner's* 46-48 (July 1909–September 1910) and 56 (July–December 1914), respectively.

26. Theodore Roosevelt, "Is Polar Exploration Worth While?" *Outlook*, 1 March 1913, 485-86; reprinted in Roosevelt's *Literary Essays* (New York: Charles Scribner's Sons, 1923), 440-44, 441; the quotation is from the reprint..

27. Theodore Roosevelt, "The World Movement" (address delivered at the University of Berlin, 12 May 1910, in *Literary Essays*, 368-76.

28. Reverend Ethlebert Talbot, "In Western Camps," *Harper's Magazine* 112 (December 1905): 506-12.

29. Richard Etulain, *Owen Wister* (Boise, Idaho: Boise State College, 1973), 11.

30. Owen Wister, *The Virginian: A Horseman of the Plains* (New York: Grosset and Dunlap, 1929), x. This publication includes the original preface dated 31 March 1902.

31. The quotation is from Mathew Johnson Herron, "The Passing of the Cowman," *Overland Monthly* 55 (February 1910): 195-99, 193.

32. Roderick Nash, *The Nervous Generation*, 140-41.

33. See William H. Hutchinson's discussion of this genre in his essay "The Cowboy in Short Fiction," in Thomas J. Lyon et al., eds., *A Literary History of the American West* (Fort Worth: Texas Christian University Press, 1987): 515-21.

34. See, for example: Mathew Johnson Herron, "The Passing of the Cowman"; George A. Lipp, "Passing of the Old Cattle Ranges," *Overland Monthly* 58 (February 1914): 131-38; Max McD, "The Passing of the Buffalo," ibid. 65 (May 1915): 437-41, and "The Passing of the Cowboy," ibid. 66 (July 1915): 53-56.

35. See, for example: George Bird Grinnell, "Portraits of Indian Types," *Scribner's* 36 (March 1905): 258-73; Edward S. Curtis, "Vanishing Indian Tribes: The Tribes of the Southwest," ibid. 39 (May 1906): 514-29, "Vanishing Indian Tribes: Tribes of the Northwest Plains," ibid. (June 1906): 657-71, and "Indians of the Stone Houses," ibid. 45 (February 1909): 161-75; G. W. Miles, "My Experience with Geronimo's Indians in Arizona in the Summer of 1885," *Overland Monthly* 66 (July 1915): 44-52; and Howard C. Kegley, "Ulte Fiesta in Garden of the Gods," ibid., 57-59.

36. Charles Moreau Harger, "The Next Commonwealth: Oklahoma," *Outlook* 67 (February 1901): 273-81, 273.

37. Charles Moreau Harger, "The New Westerner," *North American Review* 185 (August 1907): 748-58, 757, 758.

38. Robert G. Athearn makes this point in *The Mythic West in Twentieth-Century America* (Lawrence: University Press of Kansas, 1986), 45.

39. Ray Stannard Baker, "The Great Southwest, Part II: The Desert," *Century Magazine* 64 (June 1902): 213-25, 225.

40. Ray Stannard Baker, "The Western Spirit of Restlessness," *Century Magazine* 76 (July 1908): 467-69.

41. Ray Stannard Baker, "The New Pioneering and Its Heroes," *American Monthly Magazine* 77 (April 1914): 61-62. An excellent discussion of Baker's argument can be found in Warren French, "Death of the Dream" (unpublished seminar paper for Walter Prescott Webb, University of Texas, Austin, c. 1953), 38-41.

42. Ray Stannard Baker, "The New Pioneering and Its Heroes," 62.

43. Charles Moreau Harger, "The West's New Vision," *Atlantic Monthly* 120 (July 1917): 121-28.

44. Charles Wellington Furlong, "The Epic Drama of the West," *Harper's Magazine* 133 (August 1916): 368-77. For another interesting example of the unwillingness to ac-

cept that the frontier had closed and the Old West had passed, see Charles M. Harvey, "Epic of the West's Expansion," *North American Review* 285 (July 1907): 518–29.

45. Waldo R. Smith, "Is the Old West Passing?" *Overland Monthly* 67 (March 1916): 243–52.

46. Henry Seidel Canby, "Back to Nature," *Yale Review* (New Series) 6 (July 1917): 755–67, 755, 757.

47. Emerson Hough, *The Passing of the Frontier: A Chronicle of the Old West* (New Haven, Conn.: Yale University Press, 1918), 172. Gerald Nash provides further discussion of the closed frontier theme; see *Creating the West: Historical Interpretations, 1890–1990* (Albuquerque: University of New Mexico Press, 1991), 15–16. Nash also discusses Hamlin Garland's article, "The Passing of the Frontier" *Dial*, 4 October 1919, which commented upon Hough's book and similarly lamented the loss of the frontier, but, like Hough, remained confident concerning the preservation of pioneer traits in the future.

48. Hamlin Garland, "The Passing of the Frontier," *Dial* 6 (October 1919): 285–86. Nash provides further discussion of the Garland piece in *Creating the West*, 16.

49. This point is made by Athearn in *The Mythic West*, 57–58.

50. Willa Cather, *One of Ours* (New York: Alfred A. Knopf, 1922), 118. Cather's treatment of the theme of the closed frontier in the novel is discussed in John J. Murphy, "Willa Cather," in Fred Erisman and Richard W. Etulain, eds., *Fifty Western Writers: A Bio-Bibliographical Sourcebook* (Westport, Conn.: Greenwood Press, 1982), 51–62.

51. Barbara Allen provides an excellent discussion of the changes in farming techniques in this period in relation to the theme of the closing of the frontier in *Homesteading the High Desert*, 115–41.

52. Theodore Roosevelt, "Opening Address by the President," in Newton C. Blanchard, ed., *Proceedings of a Conference of Governors in the White House* (Washington, D.C.: Government Printing Office, 1909): 3–12; reprinted in Roderick F. Nash, ed., *American Environmentalism: Readings in Conservation History*, 3rd ed. (New York: McGraw Hill, 1990), 84–90; the quotation is from Nash, 88. Nash discusses the impact that the realization of the closing of the frontier had on the conservation movement in *American Environmentalism*, 69–71. The most thorough account of the conservationist impulse in the Progressive era is Samuel P. Hays, *Conservation and the Gospel of Efficiency: The Progressive Conservation Movement, 1890–1920* (Cambridge, Mass.: Harvard University Press, 1959).

53. Theodore Roosevelt, "Opening Address by the President," 89.

54. William J. Trimble, "Influence of the Passing of the Public Lands," *Atlantic Monthly* 113 (June 1914): 755–67, 758.

55. Robert Tudor Hill, *The Public Domain and Democracy: A Study of Economic and Political Problems in the United States in Relation to Western Development* (New York: Columbia University Press, 1910): 235–36. See also Witt Bowden, "The New Source of Economic Opportunity," *Forum* 53 (February 1915): 202–12.

CHAPTER 8. RUGGED INDIVIDUALISM REVISITED

1. The response to Turner's collection is discussed in Ray Allen Billington, *Frederick Jackson Turner: Historian, Scholar, Teacher* (New York: Oxford University Press, 1973), 360–62, and in Gerald D. Nash's chapter on "The West as Frontier, 1890–1945," in *Creating the West: Historical Interpretations, 1890–1990* (Albuquerque: University of New Mexico Press, 1991), 3–48, especially 21–25.

2. See Roderick Nash, *The Nervous Generation: American Thought, 1917–1930* (Chicago: Ivan R. Dee, 1990).

3. Percy H. Boynton, *The Rediscovery of the Frontier* (New York: Greenwood Press, 1969), 53.

4. Nash's chapter on "Henry Ford: Symbol of an Age," in *The Nervous Generation*, 153–63, provides an excellent account of this apprehensiveness about modernization and technological progress. Another useful commentary on this theme is John W. Ward, "The Meaning of Lindbergh's Flight," *American Quarterly* 10 (Spring 1958): 3–16.

5. That is the premise of Boynton's *The Rediscovery of the Frontier*.

6. Frederick Jackson Turner Papers, Henry E. Huntington Library, San Marino, Calif. (hereafter referred to as T.U., H.E.H.), file drawer 15D, folder 22: *"Frontier in American History,* 'Reviews.' " It is worth pointing out that Emerson's book, like Turner's, was the subject of some remarkably positive reviews. One particularly laudatory review of the book, by Lincoln MacVeagh, was clipped by Turner and is included in folder 22 (above).

7. Guy Emerson, *The New Frontier: A Study of the American Liberal Spirit, Its Frontier Origin, and Its Application to Modern Problems* (New York: Henry Holt, 1920); Emerson to Turner (6 December 1919), T.U. box 29 (1).

8. Emerson, *The New Frontier*, 33–34. The press release was saved by Turner; see T.U., H.E.H., file drawer 15D, folder 22: *"Frontier in American History,* 'Reviews.' "

9. Emerson, *The New Frontier*, 12, 61.

10. Ibid., 31, 282.

11. The Turner-Emerson correspondence spanned almost a decade, from early 1919 through late 1927; see T.U., H.E.H., boxes 29 to 37.

12. Emerson to Turner (2 January 1919), and Emerson to Turner (7 October 1919), T.U., H.E.H., box 29 (1); Emerson to Turner (18 October 1920), T.U. box 30 (64). Ray Allen Billington provides some discussion of the Turner-Emerson correspondence in *"Dear Lady": The Letters of Frederick Jackson Turner and Alice Forbes Perkins Hooper, 1910–1932* (San Marino, Calif.: The Huntington Library, 1970), 267.

13. See folders: "Children of the Pioneers" and "Revised Children of the Pioneers," T.U., H.E.H., file drawer C. The essay was read before the Madison Literary Club in November 1925, published in the *Yale Review* 15 (July 1926): 645–70, and is reprinted in Turner's *The Significance of Sections in American History* (New York: Henry Holt, 1932), 256–86; quotations are from the reprint, 283, 286. The essay is discussed in Billington, *Frederick Jackson Turner: Historian, Scholar, Teacher*, 399–400.

14. Herbert Hoover, "American Individualism," *World's Work* 43 (April 1922): 584–88; Hoover, *American Individualism* (Garden City, N.Y.: Doubleday, Page, 1922); reprinted in a double edition, Hoover, *American Individualism/The Challenge to Liberty* (West Branch, Iowa: Herbert Hoover Presidential Library Association, 1989), 19–62; quotations are from the reprint.

15. See George H. Nash's introduction to *American Individualism/The Challenge to Liberty*, 1–18, 9–10. Hoover's essay is also discussed in Nash, *The Nervous Generation*, 132–33.

16. Nash, introduction to *American Individualism/The Challenge to Liberty*, 10; Turner to Herbert Hoover (January 1923), T.U., H.E.H., box 32 (3). The correspondence is also discussed in Billington, *Frederick Jackson Turner: Historian, Scholar, Teacher*, 441–42.

17. See Billington, *Frederick Jackson Turner: Historian, Scholar, Teacher*, 442.

18. Hoover, *American Individualism/The Challenge to Liberty*, 58–59.

19. Ibid., 59–60, 61.

20. Robert D. Dripps, *New Pioneers for New Frontiers* was published as an eight-page pamphlet (New York: Buffalo Bill American Association, 1924), 1–5. Turner's copy of the publication is in the Henry E. Huntington Library, Rare Books Collection, accession number 126620.

21. Ibid., 5–8.

22. Duncan Aikman, ed., *The Taming of the Frontier*, reprint (Freeport, N.Y.: Books for Libraries Press, 1967), xv, xi.

23. Owen P. White, "El Paso," in ibid., 3-23, 3.

24. Bernard De Voto, "Ogden: The Underwriters of Salvation," in ibid., 27-60, 30.

25. Willa Cather, *A Lost Lady* (New York: Alfred A. Knopf, 1923), 55, quoted in Warren French, "Death of the Dream" (unpublished seminar paper, University of Texas, Austin, c. 1953), 62. French's treatment of Cather's novel (60-67) is excellent. For those interested in literary reactions to the closing of the frontier, French's paper also contains a lengthy treatment of the theme in Sinclair Lewis's writings (67-81).

26. Cather, *A Lost Lady*, 106, quoted in French, "Death of the Dream," 64.

27. Philip Ashton Rollins, *The Cowboy; His Characteristics, His Equipment, and His Part in the Development of the West* (New York: Charles Scribner's Sons, 1922), 347.

28. Ibid., 347, 351, and 353.

29. See, for example, James Stevens, "The Uplift of the Frontier," *American Mercury* 1 (April 1924): 413-18; Harvey Fergusson, "Billy the Kid," ibid. 5 (June 1925): 224-31; Bernard De Voto, "Utah," ibid. 7 (March 1926): 317-23, and "The Mountain Men," ibid. 9 (December 1926): 472-79; Stanley Vestal, "Ballads of the Old West," ibid. 7 (April 1926): 402-3; George Sterling, "The Pathfinders," ibid. 8 (June 1926): 144-47; H. L. Davis, "Back to the Land: Oregon, 1907," ibid. 16 (March 1929): 314-23; Harrison Rhodes, "Is There a West?" *Harper's Magazine* 141 (June 1920): 70-81; Arthur Ruhl, "What Happens to Pioneers," ibid. 145 (July 1922): 137-47, "Fast and Loose with the Homesteaders," ibid. (August 1922): 378-90, and ". . .And Points West," ibid. (October 1922): 561-72; Katherine Fullerton Gerould, "Our Northwestern States," ibid. 150 (March 1925), 412-28; Bernard De Voto, "Footnote on the West," ibid. 155 (November 1927): 713-22; Will James, "Bucking Horses and Bucking-Horse Riders," *Scribner's Magazine* 73 (March 1923): 297-305, "A Cowpuncher Speaks," ibid. (April 1923): 417-26, "Cattle Rustlers," ibid. 74 (August 1923): 181-89, "Cowboys, North and South," ibid. (December 1923): 707-16, "Winter Months in a Cow Camp," ibid. 75 (February 1924): 153-62, "The Makings of a Cow-Horse," ibid. (April 1924): 381-90, and "The Longhorns," ibid. (June 1924): 625-35; Richard Nygren, "Dead Man's Hand," ibid. 74 (October 1923), 487-96; Frank A. Waugh, "Frontiering," *Survey* 52 (June 1924): 290-92; John Gould Fletcher, "The Passing of the West," *New Republic*, 23 June 1920, 124-26.

30. See Roderick Nash, *The Nervous Generation*, 77-90, especially 81. The wilderness theme in the 1920s is given only a cursory treatment here because the ground has been so well covered by Nash and others, including Peter J. Schmitt in his *Back to Nature: The Arcadian Myth in Urban America* (New York: Oxford University Press, 1969), especially 146-89.

31. Calvin Coolidge's shortcomings as a conservationist are outlined by Roderick F. Nash in his edited volume, *American Environmentalism: Readings in Conservation History* (New York: McGraw Hill, 1990), 118. Herbert Hoover's generally overlooked role in the conservation movement is the topic of a highly informative article by Carl E. Krog, "Organizing the Production of Leisure: Herbert Hoover and the Conservation Movement in the 1920s," *Wisconsin Magazine of History* 67 (Spring 1984): 199-218. The contributions of Hough and Leopold to the wilderness preservation movement are discussed in Nash, *The Nervous Generation*, 84-86. Leopold's contributions receive further treatment in Roderick Nash's chapter, "Aldo Leopold: Prophet," in his *Wilderness and the American Mind* (New Haven, Conn.: Yale University Press, 1982), 182-99.

32. Aldo Leopold, "Wilderness as a Form of Land Use," *Journal of Land and Public Utility Economics* 1 (1925): 401; quoted in Nash, *Wilderness and the American Mind*, 188.

33. Henry Steele Commager provided an interesting examination of the frontier

theme in American literature in his essay, "The Literature of the Pioneer West," *Minnesota History* 8 (December 1927): 319–28.

34. John D. Hicks, "The People's Party in Minnesota," *Minnesota History* 5 (November 1924): 531–60. This theme was fleshed out in Hicks's classic work *The Populist Revolt: A History of the Farmer's Alliance and the People's Party* (Minneapolis: University of Minnesota Press, 1931).

35. Frederic Logan Paxson, *When the West Is Gone: The Colver Lectures in Brown University, 1929* (New York: Henry Holt, 1930). For more on Paxson see Richard W. Etulain's excellent essay, "After Turner: The Western Historiography of Frederic Logan Paxson," in Etulain, ed., *Writing Western History: Essays on Major Western Historians* (Albuquerque: University of New Mexico Press, 1991), 137–65.

36. Arthur M. Schlesinger, "Geographic Factors in American History," in *New Viewpoints in American History* (New York: Macmillan, 1922), 23–46.

37. Archer Butler Hulbert, *Frontiers: The Genius of American Nationality* (Boston: Little, Brown, 1929): 246–47.

38. On the popularization of the frontier thesis, see, for example, Mark Sullivan's popular six-volume work, *Our Times: The United States, 1920–1925* (New York: Charles Scribner's Sons, 1926–1935), vol. 1: *The Turn of the Century* (1926), especially 136–50. Other important treatments of the theme in the period are John Carl Parish, "The Persistence of the Westward Movement," *Yale Review* 15 (April 1926): 461–77; and C. W. Wright, "The Significance of the Disappearance of Free Land in Our Economic Development," *American Economic Review* 16 (March 1926): 265–71. The early attacks on the frontier thesis receive such excellent treatment in Nash's *Creating the West*, 20–29, that treating them here would prove unproductive and overly derivative. Of these attacks, particularly worthy of note, though, is John C. Almack's "The Shibboleth of the Frontier," *Historical Outlook* 16 (May 1925): 197–202. Almack's essay was so harsh in tone that it prompted Arthur Schlesinger, Sr., to write reassuringly to Turner that no one would take the piece seriously (Schlesinger to Turner [2 May 1925] T.U., H.E.H., box 34). Also on the topic of Almack's essay see Turner to Schlesinger (5 May 1925), Turner to Frederick Merk (6 May 1925), and Merk to Turner (18 May 1925), all in T.U., H.E.H., box 34 (49).

39. Alfred Booth Kuttner, "A Study of American Intolerance, Part One: The Unacknowledged Historical Background," *Dial*, 14 March 1918, 223–25, 223, 225; the second part of Kuttner's study appeared in ibid., 28 March 1918, 282–85. Kuttner reiterated his theme in an essay entitled "Nerves," in Harold E. Stearns's important collection, *Civilization in the United States: An Inquiry by Thirty Americans* (New York: Harcourt, Brace, 1922), 427–42.

40. John Dewey, "The American Intellectual Frontier," *New Republic*, 10 May 1922, 303–5. Nash also provides discussion of Dewey's essay in *Creating the West*, 22.

41. Waldo Frank, "The Land of the Pioneer," in *Our America* (New York: Boni and Liverwright, 1919), 13–58, 20, 21, 23, 30.

42. Waldo Frank, *The Re-discovery of America: An Introduction to a Philosophy of American Life* (New York: Charles Scribner's Sons, 1929). A fine analysis of the book is provided in Paul J. Carter, *Waldo Frank* (New York: Twayne, 1967), 84–92. Also worth mentioning in this context is a work by another author, Paul A. Carter. His *Revolt against Destiny: An Intellectual History of the United States* (New York: Columbia University Press, 1989), does not deal with Waldo Frank, but does focus on the wider theme of America's failure, in part because of its adherence to the agrarian myth, to come to terms with its decidedly unagrarian destiny.

43. This point is cogently made in Charles C. Alexander, *Here the Country Lies: Nationalism and the Arts in Twentieth Century America* (Bloomington: Indiana University

Press, 1980), 90–92. Alexander analyzes Harold Stearns's edited collection of essays, *Civilization in the United States*, a book that has been regarded as "the classic expression of disillusionment and alienation of the twenties," and demonstrates that the outlook of many of the contributors to the volume was far more positive than has been assumed. Alexander also provides some discussion of Frank's *Our America* in *Here the Country Lies*, 86–87.

44. Brooks's book is placed into a wider context in Richard Hofstadter's *Anti-Intellectualism in American Life* (New York: Vintage Books, 1963), 410–11; the quotation is from ibid., 411.

45. Van Wyck Brooks, "The Literary Life," in Stearns, ed., *Civilization in the United States*, 180–97. See also Alexander, *Here the Country Lies*, 91. Brooks provides a fascinating account of Stearns's volume, playing up the "lost generation" stereotypes, in a chapter of reminiscences about the decade, "Thirty against America," in his book *Days of the Phoenix: The Nineteen-Twenties I Remember* (New York: E. P. Dutton, 1957), 159–69.

46. Harold E. Stearns, "The Intellectual Life," in Stearns, ed., *Civilization in the United States*, 135–50, 136, 150,

47. Deems Taylor, "Music," in Stearns, ed., *Civilization in the United States*, 199–214, 203.

48. Paul Rosenfeld, *An Hour with American Music* (Philadelphia: J. B. Lippincott, 1929), 26–32, 60, quoted in Alexander, *Here the Country Lies*, 132.

49. Henry L. Mencken, "The Husbandman," in *Selected Prejudices* (New York: Alfred A. Knopf, 1927), 59–77, and "The Anglo-Saxon," *Baltimore Evening Sun*, July 1923, reprinted in Alistair Cooke, ed., *The Vintage Mencken* (New York: Vintage Books, 1955), 127–37.

50. Donald L. Miller, *Lewis Mumford: A Life* (New York: Weidenfeld and Nicolson, 1989), 245. Those interested in Mumford's cultural criticism are directed to an excellent new collection of essays edited by Thomas P. Hughes and Agatha C. Hughes, *Lewis Mumford: Public Intellectual* (New York: Oxford University Press, 1990); see also Van Wyck Brooks, "Lewis Mumford: American Prophet," *Harper's Magazine* 205 (June 1952): 46–53.

51. Lewis Mumford, *Sticks and Stones: A Study of American Architecture and Civilization* (New York: W. W. Norton, 1924), 81–82, 84.

52. Lewis Mumford, *The Golden Day: A Study in American Experience and Culture* (New York: Boni and Liverwright, 1926), 73, 74, 80–81.

53. Lewis Mumford, "Life by Rule of Thumb," *Freeman*, 12 April 1922, 102–3, quoted in Miller, *Lewis Mumford*, 246.

54. Charles P. Howland, "America's Coming of Age," *Survey*, 1 August 1927, 437–40, 440. Howland's article provides an interesting parallel to Frank Norris's much earlier essay, "The Frontier Gone at Last," *World's Work* 3 (February 1902): 1728–31.

CHAPTER 9. MALTHUS REVISITED

1. Frederick Jackson Turner, "Sections and Nation," *Yale Review* 12 (October 1922): 1–21; reprinted in *The Significance of Sections in American History* (New York: Henry Holt, 1932), 315–39. Michael C. Steiner draws much-needed attention to Turner's sectional thesis in his essay, "Frederick Jackson Turner and Western Regionalism," in Richard W. Etulain, ed., *Writing Western History: Essays on Major Western Historians* (Albuquerque: University of New Mexico Press, 1991), 103–35; see also Steiner's earlier article, "The Significance of Turner's Sectional Thesis," *Western Historical Quarterly* 10 (October 1979): 437–66.

2. Frederick Jackson Turner, "The Children of the Pioneers," *Yale Review* 15 (July 1926): 645–70; reprinted in *The Significance of Sections in American History*, 256–86. The quotation is from the reprint, 286.

3. Frederick Jackson Turner, "Since the Foundation of Clark University," *Publications of the Clark University Library* 7 (February 1924): 9–29; reprinted in *The Significance of Sections in American History*, 207–34, 212, 221. Quotations are from the reprint.

4. Ibid., 232.

5. The acuteness of Turner's concern over the closing of the frontier in the 1920s is clearly evident in his unpublished writings of the period. See Frederick Jackson Turner Papers, Henry E. Huntington Library, San Marino, Calif., especially: box 56 (21), "Outline and Notes for a Lecture on the History of the West" (1924); file drawer 10B (5), folder: "Liberty and the New Nationalism, 1876–1917," (1922); file drawer 10B (7), folder: "History of Liberty Lectures" (1919–1922); these lectures are discussed in Ray Allen Billington, *Frederick Jackson Turner: Historian, Scholar, Teacher* (New York: Oxford University Press, 1973): 350–52. Also critical to an understanding of Turner's concerns are: file drawer 15B (35), folder: "The New Era of Gold and Prosperity, and Social and Political Change, 1896–1907" (c. early to mid 1920s); file drawer 15C (2), folder: "Notes for Shop Club Lecture" (1923); file drawer 20C (28), folder: "Skyscrapers" (c. early 1920s). Turner's massive collection of Malthusian Alarmist writings and his extensive notes on the topic are contained in file drawer 10A (1), folder: "Alarmist Arguments" (c. early to mid 1920s); and 10A (2), folder: "Strategies for a Saturated Earth" (c. early to mid 1920s); file drawer 22B (notes for Harvard course on the West, 1924), folders 1 and 15; file drawer 22C (lecture notes on presidents), folders 10 and 11; black box No. 10 (Malthusian clippings). See also Turner's personal library in the Rare Books Collection, H.E.H. Steiner pays some attention to these Malthusian concerns in "Frederick Jackson Turner and Western Regionalism," 119.

6. See Ray Allen Billington, "Frederick Jackson Turner and the Closing of the Frontier," in Roger Daniels, ed., *Essays in Western History in Honor of Professor T. A. Larson* (Laramie: University of Wyoming Publications, 1971), 37: 45–56.

7. Turner himself noted that the war was a catalyst to the Malthusian thinking of the period in "Since the Foundation of Clark University," 232. Also noteworthy is an eight-part series entitled "War and Peace," which appeared in *Forum* between July 1925 and June 1926 (vols. 74 and 75). It discussed Malthusian issues in relation to war.

8. Ray Allen Billington's excellent but obscure essay, "Frederick Jackson Turner and the Closing of the Frontier," is the only source I have found that discusses the "Malthusian Alarmism" of the post–World War I years. Considering the sheer bulk of Malthusian literature in the period, it is surprising that historians have paid so little attention to the topic.

9. Frederick Jackson Turner, "Social Forces in American History," *American Historical Review* 16 (January 1911): 217–33; reprinted in *The Frontier in American History*, 311–34.

10. Walter Weyl, "An Experiment in Population," *Atlantic Monthly* 103 (February 1909): 261–67; and "Depopulation in France," *North American Review* 195 (March 1912): 343–55. Charles Forcey provides some discussion of Weyl's Malthusian predilections in *The New Democracy* in *The Crossroads of Liberalism: Croly, Weyl, Lippman and the Progressive Era, 1900–1925* (New York: Oxford University Press, 1967), 64, 80, 85, as well as the closed frontier theme in the writings of Herbert Croly, 26, 76, 142–44. It is worth noting, as Forcey does, that Weyl's Malthusian thinking in *The New Democracy* ran counter to the teachings of Simon Nelson Patten, his mentor, who held that greater wealth would come from the increase in population.

11. Roy Hinman Holmes, "The Passing of the Farmer," *Atlantic Monthly* 110 (October 1912): 517-23, 517.

12. Robert W. Bruere, "The Rural Reformation," *Harper's Monthly Magazine* 129 (November 1914): 941-47, and "The Control of Soil Fertility," ibid. (April 1915): 696-704; William J. Trimble, "The Influence of the Passing of the Public Lands," *Atlantic Monthly* 113 (June 1914): 755-67; Warren S. Thompson, *Population: A Study in Malthusianism* (New York: Columbia University, 1915), 115, 164.

13. Marcel Aurousseau, "The Distribution of Population: A Constructive Problem," *Geographical Review* 11 (October 1921): 563-93, 563, 586.

14. See T.U., H.E.H., file drawer 10A (1), folder: "Alarmist Arguments." Aurousseau's ideas on the theme of urban to rural migration were fleshed out more fully in his article "Geographical Study of Population," *Geographical Review* 13 (September 1923): 266-82.

15. Oliver E. Baker, "The Increasing Importance of the Physical Conditions in Determining the Utilization of Land for Agricultural and Forest Production in the United States," *Annals of the Association of American Geographers* 11 (1921): 17-46, 45, 46.

16. Baker, "Land Utilization in the United States. Geographical Aspects of the Problem," *Geographical Review* 13 (January 1923): 1-26.

17. Raymond Pearl, "World Overcrowding: Saturation Point for Earth's Population Soon Will Be in Sight," *New York Times*, 8 October 1922, 3. See also Pearl's article, "The Population Problem," *Geographical Review* 12 (October 1922): 634-45.

18. John Maynard Keynes, introduction to Harold Wright, *Population* (New York: Harcourt, Brace, 1923), vii. Harold Wright, a Fellow of King's College, Cambridge, was not an alarmist. His study was one of the more level-headed treatments of the population question in the period. On the topic of the centrality of the population problem, see Raymond Pearl, "The Population Problem"; Pearl asserted that the problem was "perhaps the most significant facing mankind today" (645).

19. Griffith Taylor, "The Distribution of Future White Settlement," *Geographical Review* 12 (July 1922): 387-402, 387.

20. Halford J. Mackinder, *Democratic Ideals and Reality: A Study in the Politics of Reconstruction* (New York: Henry Holt, 1919). Mackinder's analysis was enthusiastically summarized by Frederick J. Teggart in his article, "Geography as an Aid to Statecraft: An Appreciation of Mackinder's *Democratic Ideals and Reality*," *Geographical Review* 8 (October-November 1919): 227-42. Also worthy of mention is Charles Redway Dryer's highly critical review of the book, "Mackinder's 'World Island' and Its American Satellite," *Geographical Review* 9 (March 1920): 205-7.

21. All of these questions were addressed in *Forum's* eight-part "War or Peace" series, which included Henry Pratt Fairchild, "The Land Hunger Urge to War," 74 (September 1925): 413-20; Frederick Adams Woods, "The Biology of War," ibid. (October 1925): 533-42; Edward M. East, "The Fool Value of Food," ibid. (November 1925): 668-78; Havelock Ellis, "Life Versus Life," ibid. (December 1925): 815-24; Vilhjalmur Stefansson, "Polar Pastures," 75 (January 1926): 9-20; Herbert Joseph Spinden, "Also the Friendly Tropics," ibid. (February 1926): 204-11; John Treadwell Nicholls, "Farming the Ocean," ibid. (April 1926): 560-67; and Ellsworth Huntington, "Where Can Man Best Live?" ibid. (May 1926): 708-17.

22. Raymond Pearl, *The Biology of Population Growth* (New York: Alfred A. Knopf, 1925). See also Pearl's synopsis of his findings, "The Biology of Population Growth," *American Mercury* 3 (November 1924): 293-305. Pearl's work is treated more extensively in Billington's "Frederick Jackson Turner and the Closing of the Frontier," 48-49. Pearl's analysis of the population problem was considerably less alarmist in 1925 than it had been a few years earlier (see "The Population Problem" above).

23. Don D. Lescohier, "Population and Agriculture," in Louis I. Dublin, ed., *Population Problems in the United States and Canada* (Boston: Houghton Mifflin, 1926), 77–93. Dublin's nineteen-essay volume is indicative of the centrality of this topic during the 1920s.

24. Don D. Lescohier, "Will the American Standard of Living Limit Population Growth?" *American Review* 3 (December 1925): 690–98, 698.

25. Among the more optimistic assessments of the problem was Edward S. Martin, "The Population Problem," *Harper's Monthly Magazine* 149 (November 1924): 802–5.

26. T.U., H.E.H., file drawer 15C, folder: "Notes for Shop Club Lecture, 1923."

27. Ibid., and file drawer 10A, folder: "Alarmist Arguments."

28. Ibid., file drawer 10A (2), folder: "Strategy for a Saturated Earth." It seems quite likely, considering Turner's extensive notes on this theme and his mass of references to the current literature on the topic, that he was planning to write a scholarly paper on it. Turner's notes for the lecture on "The Outcome of the Western Movement" are in ibid., file drawer 15C, folder: "Notes For Shop Club Lecture, 1923."

29. T.U., H.E.H., file drawer 22B, folders 1 and 15 (both untitled); file drawer 22C, folders 10: "Agriculture," 11: (untitled), and 16: "Immigration."

30. See T.U., H.E.H., file drawer 15C, folder: "Notes for Shop Club Lecture, 1923." Turner's primary concern in his files on the population problem is with the situation of the United States. Even when he mentions the "internationalization of resources," his accompanying question is "How would [the] U.S. fare?" The meeting of the World Agriculture Society in April 1924 is discussed in the *New York Times*, 27 April 1924, 18.

31. Edward M. East, *Mankind at the Crossroads* (New York: Charles Scribner's Sons, 1923), 152, 303–4.

32. Ibid., 304, 311–13. See also East's "Overseas Politics and the Food Supply," *Scribner's Magazine* 75 (January 1924): 109–15, and "Our Changing Agriculture," ibid. (March 1924): 297–304.

33. Roderick Nash provides excellent coverage of Grant and the eugenicist position in *The Nervous Generation*, 68–72. See also Charles C. Alexander, "Prophet of American Racism: Madison Grant and the Nordic Myth," *Phylon* 23 (Spring 1962): 73–90.

34. Raymond Pearl, "World Overcrowding," 3.

35. Vernon Kellogg, "Race and Americanization," *Yale Review* (New Series) 10 (July 1921): 729–40.

36. Isaiah Bowman, *Supplement to the New World: Problems in Political Geography* (Yonkers-on-Hudson: World Book, 1923), 1–15. See also *The New World: Problems in Political Geography* (Yonkers-on-Hudson: World Book, 1921).

37. Editorial, "Do We Want Coolie Labor," *Saturday Evening Post*, 24 February 1923, 24 quoted in *Congressional Record—House* 64 (3 March 1923): 5436.

38. Earl C. Michener, *Congressional Record—House* 65 (5 April 1924): 5908, 5909.

39. Louis I. Dublin, "The Statistician and the Population Problem," in Dublin, ed., *Population Problems in the United States and Canada*, 3–18. A good example of Dublin's proposed detachment and sophistication is A. B. Wolfe's essay in the volume, "The Optimum Size of Population," 63–76; see also Louis I. Dublin, "The Fallacious Propaganda for Birth Control," *Atlantic Monthly* 137 (February 1926): 186–94.

40. Selections from East's lecture are reprinted in the *New York Times*, 3 August 1925, 8. Further selections are reprinted ibid., 12 August 1923, 1. East's argument was commented on in a number of editorials and letters in the same newspaper, including; "Garfield Rebukes East on Italians" (August 6, 1925, 7); "Italy's Overpopulation" (August 6, 1925, 7); "Overpopulation" (August 23, 1925, 3); and "The Problem of Population" (August 27, 1925, 27). Future Secretary of Agriculture Henry A. Wallace also spoke at the round table on agriculture and population and predicted that the world would face a

food shortage within five or ten years. Wallace's speech is summarized in the *New York Times*, 7 August 1925, 2. The *New York Times* featured dozens of articles, letters, and editorials on the Malthusian debate in the mid-1920s. Especially noteworthy are: Carroll Binder, "Future Has Big Food Problems" 1 February 1925, 1; "Malthus Cross-Examined" (5 April 1925), 4; Edward M. East, "Population: New York's Growing Problem" (16 August 1925, 1); T. R. Ybabra, "Great Food Lack Threatens World" (10 August 1926, 1); "Shortage in Food Called Unlikely" (11 August 1926, 2); and "Methusela and Malthusianism" (11 August 1926, 4).

41. Edward Alsworth Ross, *Standing Room Only* (New York: Arno Press, 1977): 345–46, 339.

42. See, for example, Bernard Ostrolente, "The Surplus Farmer," *Atlantic Monthly* 143 (April 1929): 539–45.

CHAPTER 10. THE NEW DEAL FRONTIER

1. Charles Morrow Wilson, "The Surviving American Frontier," *Current History* 34 (May 1931): 189–92, 189; see also Wilson's "Land for the Taking," *American Magazine* 113 (March 1932): 54–56, 102. For more on Appalachia and how it has been perceived, see Henry D. Shapiro, *Appalachia on Our Mind: The Southern Mountains and Mountaineers in the American Consciousness, 1870–1920* (Chapel Hill: University of North Carolina Press, 1978).

2. John A. Piquet, "Our Unconquered Frontier," *Scribner's Magazine* 96 (December 1934): 354–58, 354–55. Piquet's essay is a fascinating precursor to Frank J. Popper's more recent essay, "The Strange Case of the Contemporary American Frontier," *Yale Review* 76 (December 1986): 101–21; see also Frank J. Popper and Deborah E. Popper, "The Reinvention of the American Frontier," *Amicus Journal* 13 (Summer 1991): 4–7.

3. Isaiah Bowman, *The Pioneer Fringe* (New York: American Geographical Society, 1931), 1–2; Bowman, "The Jordan Country," *American Geographical Review* 21 (January 1931): 25–55; Turner to Bowman (24 December 1931), Bowman to Turner (5 January 1932), Turner to Bowman (12 January 1932), in the Frederick Jackson Turner Papers, Henry E. Huntington Library, box 46 (94) and box 47 (6), respectively. The correspondence is reprinted and discussed in Wilbur Jacobs, *The Historical World of Frederick Jackson Turner* (New Haven, Conn.: Yale University Press, 1968), 168–72; further commentary is provided in Gerald D. Nash, *Creating the West: Historical Interpretations, 1890–1990* (Albuquerque: University of New Mexico Press, 1991), 31–32. Also interesting in the context of Bowman's wide-ranging analysis are W. L. G. Joerg, ed., *Pioneer Settlement: Cooperative Studies by Twenty-Six Authors* (New York: American Geographical Society, 1932); G. L. Wood, "Pioneer Settlement," *The Economic Record* 9 (June 1933): 49–57; and Bowman, ed., *Limits of Land Settlement: A Report on Present-Day Possibilities* (New York: Council on Foreign Relations, 1937).

4. See, for example: Bradford K. Daniels, "My Last Frontier," *Atlantic Monthly* 148 (December 1931): 710–18; Charles Adams Jones, "On the Last Frontier," ibid. 153 (June 1934): 681–89; and Bernard De Voto, "Jonathon Dyer, Frontiersman: A Paragraph in the History of the West," *Harper's Magazine* 167 (September 1933): 491–501. Such confident treatises on surviving physical frontiers and reminiscences about the vigor of life on last frontiers were less evident in the 1930s than in earlier decades. Charles R. Hearn provides some coverage of this interesting undercurrent in *The American Dream in the Great Depression* (Westport, Conn.: Greenwood Press, 1977): 63–64.

5. This point is also made in Charles C. Alexander, *Nationalism in American Thought, 1930–1945* (Chicago: Rand McNally, 1971), 3–4. See also: Theodore Rosenof, *Dogma,*

Depression, and the New Deal: The Debate of Political Leaders over Recovery (Port Washington, N.Y.: Kennikat Press, 1975), especially 20–33 and 113–32, and "Young Bob La Follette on American Capitalism," *Wisconsin Magazine of History* 55 (Winter 1971–1972): 130–39; Curtis Nettels, "Frederick Jackson Turner and the New Deal," *Wisconsin Magazine of History* 17 (March 1934): 257–65, reprinted in Lawrence Burnette, Jr., ed., *Wisconsin Witness to Frederick Jackson Turner* (Madison: The State Historical Society of Wisconsin, 1961), 45–53 (quotations from original); Steven Kesselman, "The Frontier Thesis and the Great Depression," *Journal of the History of Ideas* 29 (April 1968): 253–68 (this and Rosenof's works [above] are the only really substantive studies of the closed-frontier theme in the depression years); Orlando W. Miller, *The Frontier in Alaska and the Matanuska Colony* (New Haven, Conn.: Yale University Press, 1975), 1–13; Donald K. Pickens, "Westward Expansion and the End of American Exceptionalism: Sumner, Turner, and Webb," *Western Historical Quarterly* 14 (October 1981): 409–18; Paul A. Carter, *Revolt against Destiny: An Intellectual History of the United States* (New York: Columbia University Press, 1989), 17–18; Arthur A. Ekirch, Jr., *Ideologies and Utopias: The Impact of the New Deal on American Thought* (Chicago: Quadrangle Books, 1969); Gerald Nash, *Creating the West*, 28–44; Ray Allen Billington, *Frederick Jackson Turner: Historian, Scholar, Teacher* (New York: Oxford University Press, 1973), 446–47; and J. R. Pole, *The Pursuit of Equality in American History* (Berkeley: University of California Press, 1978), 255. Historians have paid more attention to the closed-frontier theme in the New Deal years than to the Malthusian Alarmism of the preceding decade, yet the extent of that coverage—a handful of articles and a number of passing mentions—is still rather meager for a theme that is so central to the sociopolitical thought of the era.

6. A. L. Burt, "Our Dynamic Society," *Minnesota History* 13 (March 1932): 3–23, 13.

7. John Steinbeck, "The Leader of the People," first published in *The Long Valley* (New York: Viking Press, 1938), 283–303. The story later appeared as a chapter in Steinbeck's *The Red Pony* (New York: Viking Press, 1945), 107–131. Warren French provides a more extensive analysis of the closed-frontier theme in "The Leader of the People" in his "Death of the Dream" (unpublished Ph.D. seminar paper, University of Texas, Austin, for Walter Prescott Webb, c. 1953): 88–91.

8. *To a God Unknown* was written before *The Pastures of Heaven*, though it was published after that work.

9. John Steinbeck, *The Grapes of Wrath* (New York: Penguin Books, 1986), 107.

10. Warren French provides a useful treatment of the closed-frontier theme in *The Grapes of Wrath* in "Death of the Dream," 91–97. Another interesting treatment of the theme is Walter Rundell, Jr., "Steinbeck's Image of the West," *American West* 1 (Spring 1964): 4–17, 79.

11. See Archibald MacLeish, "Corporate Entity," in *Poems: 1924–1933* (Boston: Houghton Mifflin, 1933), 182.

12. Archibald MacLeish, *Land of the Free* (New York: Harcourt, Brace, 1938), 18, 21, 29, 32, 52–53, 84, 87–88.

13. Dorothea Lange and Paul Schuster Taylor, *An American Exodus: A Record of Human Erosion in the 1930's* (New York: Reynal and Hitchcock, 1939), 107. The story of the environmental disaster that precipitated the mass exodus that Lange and Taylor, MacLeish, and Steinbeck examined is recounted in Donald Worster's *Dust Bowl: The Southern Plains in the 1930s* (New York: Oxford University Press, 1979).

14. Carey McWilliams, "Myths of the West," *North American Review* 232 (November 1931): 424–32.

15. Carey McWilliams, *Factories in the Field: The Story of Migratory Farm Labor in California* (Boston: Little, Brown, 1939), 22. McWilliams elaborated on this theme in *Ill Fares*

the Land: Migrants and Migratory Labor in the United States (Boston: Little, Brown, 1942), 188–89, 282, 332.

16. Among the most important of these attacks on the frontier theory were: Carter Goodrich and Sol Davidson, "The Wage-Earner in the Westward Movement," parts 1 and 2, *Political Science Quarterly* 50 (June 1935): 161–85, and 51 (March 1936): 61–116; and "The Frontier as a Safety Valve: A Rejoinder," ibid. 53 (June 1938): 268–71; Fred A. Shannon, "The Homestead Act and the Labor Surplus," *American Historical Review* 41 (July 1936): 637–51; Paul Wallace Gates, "The Homestead Law in an Incongruous Land System," *American Historical Review* 41 (July 1936): 652–81. Less well known but also interesting is Benjamin F. Wright, Jr., "American Democracy and the Frontier," *Yale Review* 20 (September 1930): 349–65. Gerald D. Nash provides insightful coverage of these writings in his *Creating the West*, 28–44.

17. Steven Kesselman provides some interesting discussion of the "present-mindedness" of historical writing in the 1930s in "The Frontier and the Great Depression."

18. Fascinating in this regard is the correspondence between Turner and Beard in the 1920s that was sparked by Beard's critical review of *The Frontier in American History* in the *New Republic*, 16 February 1921, 349–50; see Wilbur Jacobs, ed., *Frederick Jackson Turner's Legacy: Unpublished Writings in American History* (San Marino, Calif.: Huntington Library, 1965), 36–38; and Billington, *Frederick Jackson Turner: Historian, Scholar, Teacher*, 361–62.

19. Henry Steele Commager, "Farewell to Laissez-Faire," *Current History* 38 (August 1933): 513–20. Also interesting in this context is William Trufant Foster, "Economic Consequences of the New Deal," *Atlantic Monthly* 152 (December 1933): 748–55. One cannot help seeing a resemblance between such critiques of the settlement of the continent in the 1930s and those of the New Western Historians today.

20. Ibid., 518.

21. James Truslow Adams, "Rugged Individualism Analyzed," *New York Times Sunday Magazine*, 18 March 1934, 1–2, 11.

22. Ibid., 11. Also of interest in this context is Ernest Boyd, "Drugged Individualism," *American Mercury* 33 (November 1934): 308–14.

23. Nettels, "Frederick Jackson Turner and the New Deal," 257–65. See also Dwight W. Michener, "Economic Repercussions from the Passing of the Frontier," *Analist*, 21 December 1934, 853–54.

24. The fascinating story of the publication crisis that surrounded the book is told by Walter Rundell, Jr., "Walter Prescott Webb's *Divided We Stand*: A Publishing Crisis," *Western Historical Quarterly* 13 (October 1982): 391–407. Rundell outlines the impact of the book in more detail in his posthumously published article, "A Historian's Impact on Federal Policy: W. P. Webb as a Case Study," *Prologue* 15 (Winter 1983) 215–28. *Divided We Stand* is also discussed in Elliott West's excellent recent essay, "Walter Prescott Webb and the Search for the West," in Richard W. Etulain, ed., *Writing Western History: Essays on Major Western Historians* (Albuquerque: University of New Mexico Press, 1991): 167–91, 179–80; West's essay also includes a useful bibliography of writings on Webb.

25. Walter Prescott Webb, *Divided We Stand: The Crisis of a Frontierless Democracy* (New York: Farrar and Rinehart, 1937), 157.

26. Elliott West provides illuminating discussion of this point in "Walter Prescott Webb and the Search for the West," 170–79.

27. Webb, *Divided We Stand*, 158–59.

28. Ibid., 163–64.

29. Ibid., 169, 170–72.

30. Rundell, "W. P. Webb's *Divided We Stand*," 391.

31. Alexander, *Nationalism in American Thought*, 1. See, for example, Charles Angoff,

"The End of an Epoch," *American Mercury* 32 (August 1934): 458–59; and Howard F. Barker, "The World Faces Eastward," *American Mercury* 30 (October 1933): 129–37.

32. James Truslow Adams, Henry Seidel Canby, Stuart Chase, and Howard Mumford Jones, "Dark Days Ahead: A Dialogue on the Bankruptcy of Business Leadership," *Forum* 84 (October 1930): 200–207.

33. *Capital Times* (Madison, Wisc.), 15 January 1931, quoted in Ray Allen Billington, ed., *"Dear Lady": The Letters of Frederick Jackson Turner and Alice Forbes Perkins Hooper, 1910–1932* (San Marino, Calif.: Huntington Library, 1970), 445–46, and in *Frederick Jackson Turner: Historian, Scholar, Teacher*, 446. See also Nettels, "Frederick Jackson Turner and the New Deal," 262.

34. Daniel R. Fusfeld, *The Economic Thought of Franklin D. Roosevelt and the Origins of the New Deal* (New York: Columbia University Press, 1956), 24–25. Billington discusses the course in *Frederick Jackson Turner: Historian, Scholar, Teacher*, 238. Rexford G. Tugwell points out in *The Democratic Roosevelt: A Biography of Franklin D. Roosevelt* (Garden City, N.Y.: Doubleday, 1957), 56, that Turner was away in the Caribbean for much of Turner's course. Tugwell does add that FDR was "familiar with the range of history Turner taught" from reading "Uncle Ted's books."

35. Franklin D. Roosevelt, "Commonwealth Club Address" (23 September 1932), in *The Public Addresses of Franklin D. Roosevelt* (New York: Random House, 1938): 742–56, 747–48. Useful commentary on the speech is provided in Arthur Schlesinger, Jr., *The Crisis of the Old Order, 1919–1933* (Boston: Houghton Mifflin, 1957): 425–26; Carter, *Revolt against Destiny*, 17–18; Alexander, *Nationalism in American Thought*, 3–4; Nash, *Creating the West*, 41–42; and Ekirch, *Ideologies and Utopias*, 83–84.

36. Roosevelt, "Commonwealth Club Address," 750–51, 754.

37. Stuart Chase, *A New Deal* (New York: Macmillan, 1933). The book first appeared in August, the month before the Commonwealth Club speech and a month after Roosevelt had used the phrase "New Deal" in his acceptance speech in Chicago.

38. Chase, *A New Deal*, 66–67.

39. See, for example, George Soule, *A Planned Society* (New York: Macmillan, 1932), and *The Coming American Revolution* (New York: Macmillan, 1934); Charles A. Beard, "A 'Five Year Plan' for America," *Forum* 86 (July 1931): 1–11; Beard, "The World As I Want It," ibid. 91 (June 1934): 332–34; and Beard, ed., *America Faces the Future* (Boston: Houghton Mifflin, 1932), especially "The Rationality of a Planned Economy," 400–410; and Howard Scott, "Technology Smashes the Price System," *Harper's* 166 (January 1933): 129–142. Thorstein Veblen's critique of the wastefulness of capitalism is given excellent coverage in Vernon Mattson and Rick Tilman, "Thorstein Veblen, Frederick Jackson Turner, and the America Experience," *Journal of Economic Issues* 20 (December 1986): 219–35.

40. Excellent coverage of the "social planners" is provided in Richard H. Pells, *Radical Visions and American Dreams: Culture and Social Thought in the Depression Years* (Middletown, Conn.: Wesleyan University Press, 1973): 69–76; Alexander, *Nationalism in American Thought*, 6–11; Otis L. Graham, Jr., *Toward a Planned Society: From Roosevelt to Nixon* (New York: Oxford University Press, 1977), 13–15; and Kesselman, "The Frontier Thesis and the Great Depression," passim.

41. Franklin Delano Roosevelt, *Looking Forward* (New York: John Day, 1933), 21, 25.

42. See Nettels, "Frederick Jackson Turner and the New Deal," 264.

43. Rexford G. Tugwell, "The Ideas behind the New Deal," *New York Times Sunday Magazine*, 16 July 1933, 1. See also Tugwell, "No More Frontiers," *Today*, 22 June 1935, 3–4, 21; and Rexford G. Tugwell and Howard C. Hill, "Laissez-Faire Versus Social Control," in *Our Economic Society and Its Problems: A Study of American Levels of Living and How to Improve Them* (New York: Harcourt Brace, 1934), 497–505.

44. Harold Ickes, "The National Domain and the New Deal," *Saturday Evening Post*, 23 December 1933, 10; quoted in Richard Lowitt, *The New Deal and the West* (Bloomington: Indiana University Press, 1984), 115.

45. "10,000 Hear Mayor Protest C.W.A. Cuts," *New York Times*, 22 January 1934, 1, 3.

46. Henry A. Wallace, *New Frontiers* (New York: Reynal and Hitchcock, 1934), 5, 11. See also Wallace, *America Must Choose: The Advantages and Disadvantages of World Trade and of a Planned Middle Course* (New York and Boston: Foreign Policy Foundation and World Peace Foundation, 1934); "America Must Choose," *New York Times*, 25 February 1934, 1, 6; and *The General Welfare* (Chapel Hill: University of North Carolina Press, 1937). Theodore Rosenof provides an excellent overview of Wallace's views on the closing of the frontier in "The Economic Ideas of Henry A. Wallace, 1933-1948," *Agricultural History* 41 (April 1967): 143-54.

47. Henry A. Wallace, *New Frontiers*, 287, 280.

48. Harold Ickes, *The New Democracy* (New York: W. W. Norton, 1934), 11; also quoted in Kesselman, "The Frontier Thesis and the Great Depression," 263-64.

49. Rexford G. Tugwell, *The Battle for Democracy* (New York: Columbia University Press, 1935): 5-6, 7, 54-55.

50. Herbert Hoover (October 31, 1932), in Aaron Singer, ed., *Campaign Speeches of American Presidential Candidates, 1928-1972* (New York: Frederick Ungar, 1976), 103-21, 116. Ekirch, also quotes this passage in *Ideologies and Utopias*, 84; and Rosenof discusses this speech in *Dogma, Depression, and the New Deal*, 27-28. A similar point to Hoover's was made by Henry Pratt Fairchild, "The Great Economic Paradox," *Harper's Magazine* 164 (May 1932): 641-52.

51. See George H. Nash's introduction to Herbert Hoover, *American Individualism/The Challenge to Liberty* (West Branch, Iowa: Herbert Hoover Presidential Library Association, 1989), 17.

52. Herbert Hoover, *The Challenge to Liberty* (New York: Charles Scribner's Sons, 1934): 147-48; this passage is also quoted in Kesselman, "The Frontier Thesis and the Great Depression," 262.

53. Hoover, *The Challenge to Liberty*, 149. Fascinating in this context is Peter Van Dresser, "The Conquest of Outer Space: An Approach to Astronautics," *Harper's Magazine* 171 (September 1935): 442-49. Dresser argued that with the landed frontier settled and the oceans explored, it was inevitable that "eternal adventurers" would "sooner or later blaze a new trail through or beyond the skies" to new frontiers in space. See also Van Dresser, "New Tools for Democracy," *Harper's Magazine* 178 (March 1939): 397-403.

54. Hoover, *Addresses upon the American Road 1933-38* (New York, Charles Scribner's Sons, 1938) 59-60; quoted in Ralph Henry Gabriel, *The Course of American Democratic Thought*, 3d ed. (New York: Greenwood Press, 1986), 430. See also Hoover, "The Crisis and the Political Parties," *Atlantic Monthly* 160 (September 1937): 257-68.

55. Alfred M. Landon, *America at the Crossroads* (Port Washington, N.Y.: Kennikat Press, 1971): 14-15.

56. See, for example, Ralph E. Flanders, *Platform for America* (New York: McGraw-Hill, 1936); Ogden L. Mills, *Liberalism Fights On* (New York: Macmillan, 1936); and Newton D. Baker, "The Decay of Self-Reliance," *Atlantic Monthly* 154 (December 1934): 726-33. Theodore Rosenof provides extensive coverage of the conservative response to the closed-frontier argument in *Dogma, Depression, and the New Deal*, 25-29.

57. *Congressional Record* (hereafter C.R.), House, 74th Congress, 2d session, 80 (January 22, 1936), 832.

58. C.R., Senate, 75th Congress, 1st session, 81 (28 July 1937), 7745.

59. C.R., House, 75th Congress, 2d session, 82 (14 December 1937), Appendix, 455-

56; *C.R.*, House, 75th Congress, 3d session, 83 (9 April 1938), Appendix, 1429–34; *C.R.*, House, 75th Congress, 3rd Session, 83 (16 June 1938), Appendix, 2855–58.

60. Portions of La Follette's speech were printed in the *New York Times*, 5 June 1938, 41, and 28 April 1938, 1, 4. See also Philip La Follette, "The Party of Our Time," *Vital Speeches of the Day*, 15 May 1938; and *The Progressive*, 9 January 1937, 5–6; ibid., 22 May 1937, 7; ibid., 7 July 1937, 1–2.

61. For a fuller treatment of Corey see Pells, *Radical Visions and American Dreams*, 91–95. Quotations are from Lewis Corey, *The Decline of American Capitalism* (New York: Covici Friede, 1934), 31, 75, 515. See also Corey, *The Crisis of the Middle Class* (New York: Covici Friede, 1935).

62. Anna Rochester, *Rulers of America: A Study of Finance Capital* (New York: International Publishers, 1936): 16–18.

63. See, for example, Norman Thomas, *Human Exploitation in the United States* (New York: Frederick A. Stokes, 1934), 260; George S. Counts, *Dare the School Build a New Social Order?* (New York: John Day, 1932): 32–34; Samuel Everett, *Democracy Faces the Future* (New York: Columbia University Press, 1935), passim.

64. Ronald Radosh, "America's Dissident Fascist: Lawrence Dennis," in *Prophets on the Right: Profiles of Conservative Critics of American Globalism* (New York: Simon and Schuster, 1975), 275–95.

65. Lawrence Dennis, *Is Capitalism Doomed?* (New York: Harper and Brothers, 1932), 9–10. See also Dennis, "The Class War Comes to America," *American Mercury* 45 (December 1938): 385–93; and *The Dynamics of War and Revolution* (New York: Weekly Foreign Letter, 1940), especially, 67–70. See also J. B. Mathews and R. E. Shallcross, "Must America Go Fascist?" *Harper's Magazine* 169 (June 1934): 1–15.

66. Alexander, *Nationalism in American Thought*, 18–19. See also Paul K. Conkin's excellent book, *The Southern Agrarians* (Knoxville: University of Tennessee Press, 1988). Also useful are Edward S. Shapiro's articles, "American Conservative Intellectuals, the 1930's, and the Crisis of Ideology," *Modern Age* 23 (Fall 1979): 370–80, and "Decentralist Intellectuals and the New Deal," *Journal of American History* 58 (March 1972): 938–57. One of the most interesting (in the present context) of the many works produced in the decade by the various Southern Agrarians is Herman Clarence Nixon, *Forty Acres and Steel Mules* (Chapel Hill: University of North Carolina Press, 1938). Nixon differed from many of his fellow Agrarians in that he praised the TVA and the various other government resettlement schemes.

67. Franklin D. Roosevelt, "Back to the Land," *Review of Reviews* 84 (October 1931): 63–64.

68. Donald Holley, *Uncle Sam's Farmers: The New Deal Communities in the Lower Mississippi Valley* (Urbana: University of Illinois Press, 1975), 20.

69. "Return of Jobless from City to Farm Is Roosevelt's Aim," *New York Times*, 17 January 1933, 1, 5.

70. Roosevelt Urges Forestry on Boys," *New York Times*, 13 June 1933.

71. The Subsistence Homestead Program has been too well covered by Paul K. Conkin in *Tomorrow a New World: The New Deal Community Program* (Ithaca, N.Y.: Cornell University Press, 1959) to warrant extensive coverage here.

72. See Orlando W. Miller's fine study, *The Frontier in Alaska and the Matanuska Colony* (New Haven, Conn.: Yale University Press, 1975). Miller treats the media's coverage of the colony in his chapters, "The Press, a Hero of Self-Help, and Some Rebels," 145–60, and "Promoting the Last Frontier: The Closed Safety Valve," 161–79.

73. M. L. Wilson, "The Subsistence Homesteads Program," *Proceedings of the Institute of Public Affairs, 1934* 8 (1934): 171–72; quoted in Conkin, *Tomorrow a New World*, 102–3; Conkin provides extensive coverage of Wilson, 93–130. See also Wilson's articles,

"The Place of Subsistence Homesteads in Our National Economy," *Journal of Farm Economics* 16 (1934): 73-87, and "A New Land-Use Program: The Place of Subsistence Homesteads," *Journal of Land and Public Utility Economics* 10 (February 1934): 1-12.

74. See William E. Leverette, Jr., and David Shi, "Agrarianism for Commuters," *South Atlantic Quarterly* 79 (Spring 1980): 204-18, and Paul K. Conkin, *Tomorrow a New World* 107-8. Good firsthand introductions to Borsodi's thinking are *This Ugly Civilization* (New York: Simon and Schuster, 1929); and O. E. Baker, Ralph Borsodi, and M. L. Wilson, *Agriculture in Modern Life* (New York: Harper and Brothers, 1939); see also his articles "Subsistence Homesteads: President Roosevelt's New Deal Land and Population Policy," *Survey Graphic* 23 (January 1934): 11-14, and "Land Tenure," *American Magazine* 7 (October 1936): 556-63. For more on Borsodi see William H. Issel, "Ralph Borsodi and the Agrarian Response to Industrial America," *Agricultural History* 41 (April 1967): 155-66. David E. Shi provides ample coverage of Borsodi and other decentralist agrarian thinkers in a chapter on "Prosperity, Depression, and Simplicity" in his book *The Simple Life: Plain Living and High Thinking in American Culture* (New York: Oxford University Press, 1985), 215-47. Other useful commentaries on decentralist agrarian thought in the period include William E. Leverette, Jr., and David E. Shi, "Herbert Agar and *Free America*: A Jeffersonian Alternative to the New Deal," *Journal of American Studies* 16 (1982): 189-206; Edward S. Shapiro, "Catholic Agrarian Thought and the New Deal," *Catholic Historical Review* 65 (October 1969): 583-99, "American Conservative Intellectuals, the 1930's, and the Crisis of Ideology," and "Decentralist Intellectuals and the New Deal."

75. See, for example, Maurice G. Kains, *Five Acres and Independence: A Handbook for Small Farm Management* (New York: Dover, 1973 [first published 1935]); Charles Allen Smart, "Landscape with Farmers," *Harper's* 176 (December 1937): 79-88; and "Invitation to the Country: Notes from an Ohio Farm," ibid. (January 1938): 158-67; Anna Steese Richardson, "The Call of the Old Home Town," *Forum* 91 (March 1934): 173-77; and Arthur Pond, "Land Ho!" *Atlantic Monthly* 151 (June 1933): 714-21. An interesting attack on the notion of subsistence farming as an alternative to urban unemployment is Russell Lord, "Back to the Farm?" *Forum* 39 (February 1933): 97-103. Lord argued that in the closed-frontier age the country needed fewer and better farmers, not more untrained ones.

EPILOGUE

1. Jack Kerouac, *On the Road* (New York: Signet Books, 1972), 66.

2. "A Brush with the Old West," Los Angeles Times, (4 June 1990), E1, E8.

3. FDR to Vannevar Bush, 17 November 1944, reprinted in Vannevar Bush, *Science: The Endless Frontier* (Washington, D.C.: Office of Scientific Research and Development, 1945). Also interesting in this regard is Gerard K. O'Neil, *The High Frontier: Human Colonies in Space* (Garden City, N.Y.: Anchor Press, 1982). O'Neil states that "the exponential growth of population, on what has become not only a finite but now a strictly limited planet, is almost certain to make the decades ahead on Earth very difficult, and perhaps catastrophic. In the United States, even cushioned as it is by previous wealth, we are feeling the pinch of unemployment, rapid inflation, and conflict between industrial efficiency and environmental protection" (29).

4. Paul A. Carter discusses the very different uses of the frontier theme by these two men in *Revolt against Destiny: An Intellectual History of the United States* (New York: Columbia University Press, 1989), 18.

SELECTED BIBLIOGRAPHY

PRIMARY SOURCES

Periodicals

Agricultural History
American Historical Review
American Mercury
Arena
Arizona and the West
Atlantic Monthly
Century Magazine
Congressional Record
Dial
Forum
Geographic Review
Harper's Magazine
Huntington Library Quarterly
Journal of American History
Journal of Popular Culture
Journal of the West
McClure's
Mississippi Valley Historical Review
New York Times
Nation
New Mexico Historical Review
New Republic
North American Review
Outlook
Overland Monthly
Pacific Historical Review
Review of Reviews
Scribner's Monthly
Utah State Historical Quarterly

Works cited are not necessarily first editions.

Western Historical Quarterly
Wisconsin Magazine of History
World's Work
Yale Review

Archives

The Frederick Jackson Turner Papers, Henry E. Huntington Library, San Marino, California.

Books and Articles

Adams, Andy. *Log of a Cowboy* (Boston: Houghton Mifflin, 1903).
Adams, Brooks. *America's Economic Supremacy* (New York: Harper and Brothers, 1947).
————. *The Law of Civilization and Decay* (New York: Vintage Books, 1943).
————. *The New Empire* (New York: Macmillan, 1902).
————. "The Spanish War and the Equilibrium of the World," *Forum* 25 (August 1898): 641–651.
Adams, Cyrus C. "Unexplored Regions of the Earth," *Harper's Magazine* 114 (January 1907): 305–11.
Adams, J. Coleman. "Is America Europeanizing?" *Forum* 4 (September 1887): 190–200.
Adams, James Truslow. *The Epic of America* (Boston: Little, Brown, 1931).
Adams, James Truslow, Henry Seidel Canby, Stuart Chase, and Howard Mumford Jones. "Dark Days Ahead: A Dialogue on the Bankruptcy of Business Leadership," *Forum* 84 (October 1930): 200–207.
Aikman, Duncan, ed. *The Taming of the Frontier* (Freeport, N.Y.: Books for Libraries Press, 1967).
Alexander, Franz. *Our Age of Unreason: A Study of the Irrational Forces in Social Life* (Philadelphia: J. B. Lippincott, 1942).
Almack, John C. "The Shibboleth of the Frontier," *Historical Outlook* 16 (May 1925): 197–202.
Atkinson, Edward T. "Incalculable Room for Immigrants," *Forum* 13 (April 1892): 360–70.
Aurousseau, Marcel. "The Distribution of Population: A Constructive Problem," *Geographical Review* 11 (October 1921): 563–93.
————. "Geographical Study of Population," *Geographical Review* 13 (September 1923): 266–82.
Baker, Newton D. "The Decay of Self-Reliance," *Atlantic Monthly* 154 (December 1934): 726–33.
Baker, Oliver E. "The Increasing Importance of the Physical Conditions in Determining the Utilization of Land for Agricultural and Forest Production in the United States," *Annals of the Association of American Geographers* 11 (1921): 17–46.
————. "Land Utilization in the United States: Geographical Aspects of the Problem," *Geographical Review* 13 (January 1923): 1–26.
Baker, O. E., Ralph Borsodi, and M. L. Wilson. *Agriculture in Modern Life* (New York: Harper and Brothers, 1939).
Baker, Ray Stannard. "The Great Southwest, Part II: The Desert," *Century Magazine* 64 (June 1902): 213–25.
————. "The New Pioneering and Its Heroes," *American Monthly Magazine* 77 (April 1914): 61–62.
————. "The Western Spirit of Restlessness," *Century Magazine* 76 (July 1908): 467–69.

Beard, Charles A. *The Idea of National Interest* (New York: Macmillan, 1934).
_____. "The Myth of the Rugged American Individual," *Harper's Magazine* 164 (December 1931): 13–22.
_____. ed. *America Faces the Future* (Boston: Houghton Mifflin, 1932).
Bender, Prosper. "The Annexation of Canada," *North American Review* 139 (July 1884): 42–50.
Bentley, Arthur F. *The Condition of the Western Farmer* (Baltimore, Md.: Johns Hopkins University Press, 1893).
Beveridge, Albert J. *The Meaning of the Times and Other Speeches* (Indianapolis: Bobbs-Merrill, 1908).
Borsodi, Ralph. *This Ugly Civilization* (New York: Simon and Schuster, 1929).
Bowman, Isaiah, ed. *Limits of Land Settlement: A Report on Present-Day Possibilities* (New York: Council on Foreign Relations, 1937).
_____. *The New World: Problems in Political Geography* (Yonkers-on-Hudson, N.Y.: World Book, 1921).
_____. *The Pioneer Fringe* (New York: American Geographical Society, 1931).
_____. *Supplement to New World: Problems in Political Geography* (Yonkers-on-Hudson, N.Y.: World Book, 1923).
Boyesen, H. H. "Dangers of Unrestricted Immigration," *Forum* 3 (July 1887): 532–42.
_____. *Immigration* (New York: Evangelical Alliance for the United States, 1888).
Boynton, Percy H. *The Rediscovery of the Frontier* (Chicago: University of Chicago Press, 1931).
Bradford, E. A. "America for Americans," *Harper's New Monthly Magazine* 84 (March 1892): 599–604.
Brigham, Albert Perry. *Geographical Influences in American History* (Boston: Ginn, 1903).
Brockett, Linus. *Our Western Empire; or, The New West Beyond the Mississippi* (Philadelphia: Bradley Garretson, 1881).
Bruce, H. A. *Daniel Boone and the Wilderness Road* (New York: Macmillan, 1921).
Bryce, James. *The American Commonwealth*, 2 vols. (New York: Macmillan, 1893–1895), vol. 2.
_____. "The Policy of Annexation for America," *Forum* 24 (September 1897): 385–95.
Buck, Solon J. *The Agrarian Crusade: A Chronicle of the Farmer in Politics* (New Haven, Conn.: Yale University Press, 1920).
Buckman, George R. "Ranches and Rancheros of the Far West," *Lippincott's Magazine* 29 (May 1882): 425–35.
Burt, A. L. "Our Dynamic Society," *Minnesota History* 13 (March 1932): 3–23.
Bush, Vannevar. *Science: The Endless Frontier* (Washington, D.C.: Office of Research and Development, 1945).
Butler, J. A. "Some Western Resorts," *Harper's Magazine* 65 (August 1882): 325–41.
Canby, Henry Seidel. "Back to Nature," *Yale Review* 6 (July 1917): 755–67.
Cather, Willa. *A Lost Lady* (New York: Alfred A. Knopf, 1923).
_____. *My Antonia* (Boston: Houghton Mifflin, 1918).
_____. *O Pioneers!* (Boston: Houghton Mifflin, 1913).
_____. *One of Ours* (New York: Alfred A. Knopf, 1922).
Chase, L. A. "The Last American Frontier," *History Teacher's Magazine* 6 (February 1915): 37–40.
Chase, Stuart. "Disaster Rides the Plains," *American Magazine* 124 (September 1937): 46–47, 66–70.
_____. *Government in Business* (New York: Macmillan, 1935).
_____. *A New Deal* (New York: Macmillan, 1933).

Clough, Wilson O. "The American Frontier as a Metaphor," *Rendezvous* 4 (January 1969): 1–13.

Commager, Henry Steele. "Farewell to Laissez-Faire," *Current History* 38 (August 1933): 513–20.

————. "The Literature of the Pioneer West," *Minnesota History* 8 (December 1927): 319–28.

————. *The Search for a Usable Past* (New York: Alfred A. Knopf, 1967).

Cook, James H. *Fifty Years on the Old Frontier* (New Haven, Conn.: Yale University Press, 1923).

Corey, Lewis. *The Crisis of the Middle Class* (New York: Covici Friede, 1935).

————. *The Decline of American Capitalism* (New York: H. Wolff, 1934).

Cox, Harold. *The Problem of Population* (New York: G. P. Putnam's Sons, 1923).

Crèvecoeur, Hector St. John de. *Letters from an American Farmer* (New York: Fox, Duffield, 1904).

————. *Sketches of 18th Century America: More Letters from an American Farmer* (New Haven, Conn.: Yale University Press, 1925).

Croly, Herbert. *The Promise of American Life* (Cambridge, Mass.: Harvard University Press, Belknap Press, 1965).

Davis, C. Wood. "The Exhaustion of the Arable Lands," *Forum* 9 (June 1890): 461–74.

————. "The Probabilities of Agriculture," *Forum* 10 (November 1890): 291–305.

————. "When the Farmer Will Be Prosperous," *Forum* 9 (May 1890): 348–60.

————. "Why the Farmer Is Not Prosperous," *Forum* 9 (April 1890): 231–42.

Davis, Richard Harding. *The West from a Car Window* (New York: Harper and Brothers, 1892).

Dennis, Lawrence. "The Class War Comes to America," *American Mercury* 45 (December 1938): 385–93.

————. *The Dynamics of War and Revolution* (New York: Weekly Foreign Letter, 1940).

————. *Is Capitalism Doomed?* (New York: Harper and Brothers, 1932).

Desmond, Adam J. "America's Land Question," *North American Review* 142 (February 1886): 153–58.

De Voto, Bernard. "The West: A Plundered Province," *Harper's* 169 (August 1934): 355–64.

Dewey, John. "The American Intellectual Frontier," *New Republic*, 10 May 1922, 303–5.

Dixon, William Hepworth. *White Conquest*, 2 vols. (London: Chatto and Windus, 1876), 2: 363–65.

Donaldson, Thomas. "The Public Domain," *House Miscellaneous Document 45, Part IV*, 47th Congress, 2d session, 1884.

————. *The Public Domain: Its History with Statistics*, 1884 edition (New York: Johnson Reprint, 1970).

————. *The Public Domain: Its History with Statistics* (Washington, D.C.: Government Printing Office, 1881).

————. "The Public Lands of the U.S.," *North American Review* 83 (August 1881): 204–13.

Douglas, Lewis W. *The Liberal Tradition: A Free People and a Free Economy* (New York: D. Van Nostrand, 1935).

Dripps, Robert D. *New Pioneers for New Frontiers* (New York: Buffalo Bill American Association, 1924).

Dryer, Charles Redway. "Mackinder's 'World Island' and Its American 'Satellite,'" *Geographical Review* 9 (March 1920): 205–7.

Dublin, Louis I. "The Fallacious Propaganda for Birth Control," *Atlantic Monthly* 137 (February 1926): 186–94.

————. *The New World: Problems in Political Geography* (Yonkers-on-Hudson, N.Y.: World Book, 1921).

————, ed. *Population Problems in the United States and Canada* (Boston: Houghton Mifflin, 1926).

East, Edward M. "The Agricultural Limits of Our Population," *Scientific Monthly* 12 (June 1921): 551–57.

————. *Mankind at the Crossroads* (New York: Charles Scribner's Sons, 1923).

————. "Our Changing Agriculture," *Scribner's Magazine* 75 (March 1924): 297–304.

————. "Overseas Politics and the Food Supply," *Scribner's Magazine* 75 (January 1924): 109–15.

————. "Population," *Scientific Monthly* 10 (June 1920): 603–24.

Eaton, Walter Prichard, "The Park of the Many Glaciers," *Harper's Magazine* 135 (June 1917): 1–12.

Eliot, William. *Charles Eliot: Landscape Architect* (Boston: Houghton Mifflin, 1902).

Ely, Richard T. *Outlines of Economics* (New York: Hunt and Eaton, 1893).

————. *Studies in the Evolution of Industrial Society* (New York: Macmillan, 1903).

Emerson, Guy. *The New Frontier: A Study of the American Liberal Spirit, Its Frontier Origin, and Its Application to Modern Problems* (New York: Henry Holt, 1920).

Everett, Samuel. *Democracy Faces the Future* (New York: Columbia University Press, 1935).

Fairchild, Henry Pratt. *Immigration, A New World Movement and Its American Significance* (New York: Macmillan, 1913).

————. "Some Immigration Differences," *Yale Review* (May 1910): 79–97.

Faris, John T. *On the Trail of the Pioneers: Romance, Tragedy and Triumph of the Path of Empire* (New York: George H. Doran, 1920).

Fernald, James C. *The Imperial Republic* (New York: Funk and Wagnalls, 1899).

Fish, Carl Russel. "The Frontier: A World Problem," *Wisconsin Magazine of History* 1 (December 1917): 121–41.

Fiske, John. "Manifest Destiny," *Harper's New Monthly Magazine* 70 (February 1885): 578–90.

Fitzhugh, George. *Cannibals All? (Or Slaves without Masters)* (Cambridge, Mass.: Harvard University Press, 1960).

Flanders, Ralph E. *Platform for America* (New York: McGraw Hill, 1936).

Fletcher, John Gould. "The Passing of the West," *New Republic* 23 June 1920, 124–26.

Ford, Worthington C. "Public Lands of the United States." In John J. Lalor, ed., *Cyclopaedia of Political Science, Political Economy, and of the Political History of the United States* (Chicago: M. B. Cary, 1884), 2: 460–79.

Foster, William Trufant. "Economic Consequences of the New Deal," *Atlantic Monthly* 152 (December 1933): 748–55.

Frank, Waldo. *Our America* (New York: Boni and Liverwright, 1919).

————. *The Re-discovery of America: An Introduction to a Philosophy of American Life* (New York: Charles Scribner's Sons, 1929).

Fuller, Henry Blake. *The Cliff Dwellers* (New York: Harper and Brothers, 1893).

Furlong, Charles Wellington. "The Epic Drama of the West," *Harper's Magazine* 133 (August 1916): 368–77.

Garland, Hamlin. *Jason Edwards, An Average Man* (Boston: Arena Publishing, 1892).

————. "The Land Question: Relations to Art and Literature," *Arena* 9 (January 1894): 165–75.

————. *Main Travelled Roads* (New York: Harper and Brothers, 1899).

————. *Other Main Travelled Roads* (New York: Harper and Brothers, 1892).

————. "The Passing of the Frontier," *Dial* 67 (October 1919): 285–86.

_____. *Prairie Folks: or, Pioneer Life on the Western Prairies* (New York: Garrett Press, 1969).
_____. *A Son of the Middle Border* (New York: Macmillan, 1920).
_____. *Under the Wheel* (Boston: Barta Press, 1880).
_____. *The Westward March of American Settlement* (Chicago: American Library Association, 1927).
Garnsey, Morris. *America's New Frontier: The Mountain West* (New York: Alfred A. Knopf, 1950).
Gates, Paul Wallace. "The Homestead Law in an Incongruous Land System," *American Historical Review* 41 (July 1936): 652–81.
George, Henry. *The Land Question: What It Involves and How Alone It Can Be Settled* (New York: Doubleday and McClure, 1898).
_____. *Our Land and Land Policy, National and State* (New York: Doubleday Page, 1904).
_____. *Progress and Poverty* (New York: Robert Schalkenbach Foundation, 1960).
_____. *Social Problems* (London: Kegan Paul, Trench, 1884).
Gill, Thomas P. "Landlordism in America," *North American Review* 42 (January 1886): 52–67.
Godkin, Edwin L. *Problems in Modern Democracy* (Cambridge, Mass.: Harvard University Press, Belknap Press, 1966).
_____. *Reflections and Comments, 1865–1895* (New York: Charles Scribner's Sons, 1895).
_____. *Unforeseen Tendencies of Democracy* (Boston: Houghton Mifflin, 1898).
Goodrich, Carter, and Sol Davidson. "The Frontier as a Safety Valve: A Rejoinder," *Political Science Quarterly* 53 (June 1938): 268–71.
_____. "The Wage-Earner in the Westward Movement," parts 1 and 2, *Political Science Quarterly* 50 (June 1935): 161–85, and 51 (March 1936): 61–116.
Goodwin, Cardinal. *The Trans-Mississippi West 1803–53: A History of Its Settlement and Acquisition* (New York: D. Appleton, 1922).
Greeley, Horace. *Glances at Europe* (New York: Denitt and Davenport, 1851).
Guthrie, A. B. *The Big Sky* (New York: W. Sloane, 1947).
_____. *The Way West* (New York: W. Sloane, 1949).
Hacker, Louis M. "Sections—or Classes?" *Nation,* 26 July 1933, 108–110.
Hall, Bolton. *Three Acres and Liberty* (New York: Grosset and Dunlap, 1907).
Hamilton, William Thomas. *My Sixty Years on the Plains: Trapping, Trading, and Indian Fighting* (Norman: University of Oklahoma Press, 1960).
Harger, Charles Moreau. "Brighter Skies Out West," *American Monthly Review of Reviews* 70 (October 1924): 420–23.
_____. "The New Westerner," *North American Review* 185 (August 1907): 748–58.
_____. "The Next Commonwealth: Oklahoma," *Outlook* 67 (February 1901): 273–81.
_____. "The Passing of the Promised Land," *Atlantic Monthly* 114 (October 1909): 461–66.
_____. "The Revival in Western Land Values," *American Monthly Review of Reviews* 35 (January 1907): 63–65.
_____. "To-day's Chance for the Western Settler," *Outlook* 78 (December 1904): 980–82.
_____. "The West's New Vision," *Atlantic Monthly* 120 (July 1917): 121–28.
Hart, A. B. "Disposition of Our Public Lands," *Quarterly Journal of Economics* 1 (October 1880): 169–83.
Harvey, William H. *Coin's Financial School* (Chicago: Coin's Publishing School, 1894).

Hayden, Ferdinand Vandeever. *The Great West: Its Attractions and Resources* (Philadelphia: Franklin Publishing, 1880).

Hazard, Lucy L. *The Frontier in American Literature* (New York: Frederick Ungar, 1967).

Hazen, General William Babcock. "The Great Middle Region of the United States, and Its Limited Space of Arable Land," *North American Review* 120 (January 1875): 1–36.

_____. *Our Barren Lands: The Interior of the United States West of the One-Hundredth Meridian and East of the Sierra Nevadas* (Cincinnati, Ohio: Clarke, 1875).

Heaton, Herbert. "Migration and Cheap Land: The End of Two Chapters," *Sociological Review* 26 (July 1934): 231–48.

_____. "Other Wests Than Ours," *Journal of Economic History*, 6 (1946): 50–62.

Hegel, G. W. F. *Lectures on the Philosophy of History*, translated by J. Sibree (New York: Colonial Press, 1900).

Hibbard, Benjamin H. "Tenancy in the North Central States," *Quarterly Journal of Economics* 25 (August 1911): 710–29.

Hicks, John D. "The People's Party in Minnesota," *Minnesota History* 5 (November 1924): 531–60.

_____. *The Populist Revolt: A History of the Farmer's Alliance and the People's Party* (Minneapolis: University of Minnesota Press, 1931).

Higginson, Thomas W. "The Great Western March," *Harper's New Monthly Magazine* 69 (June 1884): 118–28.

Hill, Robert Tudor. "Cuba and Its Value as a Colony," *Forum* 25 (June 1898): 403–15.

_____. *The Public Domain and Democracy: A Study of Social, Economic, and Political Problems of the United States in Relation to Western Development* (New York: Columbia University Press, 1910).

Hinsdale, Burke A. *The Old Northwest* (New York: Silver, Burdett, 1899).

Hollon, W. Eugene. *The Great American Desert: Then and Now* (New York: Oxford University Press, 1966).

Holmes, Roy Hinman. "The Passing of the Farmer," *Atlantic Monthly* 110 (October 1912): 517–23.

Hoover, Herbert. *Addresses upon the American Road: 1933–38* (New York, Charles Scribner's Sons, 1938).

_____. *American Individualism* (Garden City, N.Y.: Doubleday Page, 1922).

_____. *American Individualism/The Challenge to Liberty* (West Branch, Iowa: Herbert Hoover Presidential Library Association, 1989).

_____. *The Challenge to Liberty* (New York: Charles Scribner's Sons, 1934).

_____. "The Crisis and the Political Parties," *Atlantic Monthly* 160 (September 1937): 257–68.

Hough, Emerson. *Covered Wagon* (New York: D. Appleton, 1922).

_____. *The Girl at the Halfway House* (New York: D. Appleton, 1900).

_____. *The Passing of the Frontier* (New Haven, Conn.: Yale University Press, 1918).

_____. "The Settlement of the West: A Study in Transportation," *Century Illustrated Monthly Magazine* 63 (November 1901): 91–107.

_____. *Story of the Cowboy* (New York: D. Appleton, 1897).

Howard, Randall R. "The Passing of the Cattle King," *Outlook* 96 (May 1911): 146–204.

Howe, Frederic C. "The Lure of the Land," *Scribner's Magazine* 46 (October 1909): 431–36.

Howells, William Dean. *The Altrurian Romances* (Bloomington: Indiana University Press, 1968).

Howland, Charles P. "America's Coming of Age," *Survey*, 1 August 1927, 437–40.

Hulbert, Archer Butler. *Frontiers: The Genius of American Nationality* (Boston: Little, Brown, 1929).

Ickes, H. L. *The New Democracy* (New York: W. W. Norton, 1934).

Ingersoll, Ernest. *The Crest of the Continent: A Summer's Ramble in the Rocky Mountains and Beyond* (Chicago: R. R. Donnelley and Sons, 1885).

Irving, Washington. *Astoria; or, Enterprise beyond the Rockies* (Boston: Twayne Publishers, 1976).

Jackson, Helen Hunt. *A Century of Dishonor* (New York: Harper and Brothers, 1881).

———. *Ramona* (Boston: Little, Brown, 1913).

Joerg, W. L. G., ed. *Pioneer Settlement: Cooperative Studies by Twenty-Six Authors* (New York: American Geographical Society, 1932).

Jordan, General Thomas. "Why We Need Cuba," *Forum* 11 (June 1891): 559–67.

Josephson, Mathew. "The Frontier and Literature," *New Republic*, 2 September 1931, 77–78.

Kains, Maurice G. *Five Acres and Independence: A Handbook for Small Farm Management* (New York: Dover, 1973).

Keller, B. C. *Where to Go to Become Rich* (Chicago: Belford, Clarke, 1880).

Kellogg, Vernon. "Race and Americanization," *Yale Review* 10 (July 1921): 729–40.

Kerouac, Jack. *On the Road* (New York: Signet Books, 1972).

Kuttner, Alfred Booth. "A Study of American Intolerance, Part One: The Unacknowledged Historical Background," *Dial*, 14 March 1918, 223–25.

Landon, Alfred M. *America at the Crossroads* (Port Washington, N.Y.: Kennikat Press, 1936).

Lange, Dorothea, and Paul Schuster Taylor. *An American Exodus: A Record of Human Erosion in the 1930's* (New York: Reynal and Hitchcock, 1939).

Laut, Agnes C. "The Last Trek to the Last Frontier: The American Settler in the Canadian Northwest," *Century Magazine* 78 (May 1909): 99–111.

Lescohier, Don D. "Will the American Standard of Living Limit Population Growth?" *American Review* 3 (December 1925): 690–98.

Lighton, William R. "Where Is the West?" *Outlook* 18 (July 1903): 703–4.

Lodge, Henry Cabot. "The Distribution of Ability in the United States," *Century Magazine* 42 (September 1891): 687–94.

———. "Our Blundering Foreign Policy," *Forum* 19 (March 1895): 8–17.

———. "The Restriction of Immigration," *North American Review* 152 (January 1891): 27–36.

———. *The War with Spain* (New York: Harper and Brothers, 1899).

———. ed. *Selections from the Correspondence of Theodore Roosevelt and Henry Cabot Lodge, 1884–1918* (New York: Charles Scribner's Sons, 1925).

Lodge, Henry Cabot, and Theodore Roosevelt. *Hero Tales from American History* (New York: Century, 1905).

London, Jack. *The Call of the Wild* (New York: Macmillan, 1903).

———. "Economics of the Klondike," *Review of Reviews* 21 (January 1900): 70–74.

———. *The People of the Abyss* (New York: Macmillan, 1903).

———. *The Son of the Wolf: Tales of the Far North* (Boston: Houghton Mifflin, 1900).

———. *The War of the Classes* (London: W. M. Heinemann, 1905).

———. *White Fang* (New York: Macmillan, 1906).

Lord, Russell. "Back to the Farm?" *Forum* 39 (February 1933): 97–103.

Lowell, A. Lawrence. "The Colonial Expansion of the United States," *Atlantic Monthly* 83 (February 1899): 145–54.

McAdoo, William Gibbs. "Immigrants and the Tariff," *Forum* 11 (June 1891): 388–405.

McCabe, James D. *History of the Grange Movement* (Philadelphia: National Publishing, 1873).

McCoy, Donald R. *Landon of Kansas* (Lincoln: University of Nebraska Press, 1966).

McCracken, William D. "Our Foreign Policy," *Arena* 44 (July 1893): 145–50.

McElrath, Francis. *The Rustler, a Tale of Love and War in Wyoming* (New York: Funk and Wagnalls, 1902).

Mackinder, Halford J. *Democratic Ideals and Reality: A Study in the Politics of Reconstruction* (New York: Henry Holt, 1919).

MacLeish, Archibald. *Land of the Free* (New York: Harcourt Brace, 1938).

————. *Poems: 1924–1933* (Boston: Houghton Mifflin, 1933).

McMurtry, Larry. *Buffalo Girls* (New York: Simon and Schuster, 1990).

————. *The Last Picture Show* (New York: Dial Press, 1966).

————. *Lonesome Dove* (New York: Simon and Schuster, 1985).

McWilliams, Carey. *Factories in the Fields: The Story of Migratory Farm Labor in California* (Boston: Little, Brown, 1939).

————. *Ill Fares the Land: Migrants and Migratory Labor in the United States* (Boston: Little, Brown, 1942).

————. "The Myths of the West," *North American Review* 222 (November 1931): 426–28.

Mahan, Alfred Thayer. *The Influence of Sea Power upon History* (Boston: Little, Brown, 1917).

————. *The Interest of America in Sea Power, Present and Future* (Boston: Little, Brown, 1898).

————. *Lessons of the War with Spain and Other Articles* (Boston: Little, Brown, 1899).

March, Alden. *A New History of the Spanish-American War Including the Past, Present and Future Destiny of Our New Possessions* (Philadelphia: American Book and Bible House, 1899).

Martin, Edward S. "The Population Problem," *Harper's Monthly Magazine* 149 (November 1924): 802–5.

Mencken, Henry L. *Selected Prejudices* (New York: Alfred A. Knopf, 1927).

Michener, Dwight W. "Economic Repercussions from the Passing of the Frontier," *Analist*, 21 December 1934, 853–54.

Miller, Charles Grant, "The Trust Question: Its Development in America," *Arena* 23 (January 1900): 40–50.

Mills, Ogden L. *Liberalism Fights On* (New York: Macmillan, 1936).

Moody, William G. *Land and Labor in the United States* (New York: Charles Scribner's Sons, 1883).

Muir, John. "The American Forests," *Century Magazine* 80 (August 1897): 147–57.

————. *Our National Parks* (Boston: Houghton Mifflin, 1901).

Mumford, Lewis. *The Golden Day: A Study in American Experience and Culture* (New York: Boni and Liverwright, 1926).

————. *Sticks and Stones: A Study of American Architecture and Civilization* (New York: W. W. Norton, 1924).

Murphy, Frank. *Selected Addresses of Frank Murphy Governor of Michigan January 1, 1937 to September 30, 1938* (East Lansing: Michigan State University Press, 1938).

Nettels, Curtis. "Frederick Jackson Turner and the New Deal," *Wisconsin Magazine of History* 17 (March 1934): 257–65.

Nixon, Herman Clarence. *Forty Acres and Steel Mules* (Chapel Hill: University of North Carolina Press, 1938).

Nordhoff, Charles. *The Communist Societies of the United States: From Personal Visit and Observation* (New York: Hilary House, 1961).

Norris, Frank. "The Frontier Gone at Last," *World's Work* 3 (February 1902): 1728–31.

————. *The Octopus* (New York: Doubleday Page, 1901).

————. *The Responsibilities of a Novelist* (Garden City, N.Y.: Doubleday Doran, 1928).

Noyes, Reinold C. "The Weather Chart of Population," *Yale Review* 12 (July 1923): 813–25.

Oberholtzer, Ellis P. *A History of the United States since the Civil War* (New York: Macmillan, 1922).

Ogg, Frederick A. *The Old Northwest* (New Haven, Conn.: Yale University Press, 1919).

———. *The Reign of Andrew Jackson: A Chronicle of the Frontier in Politics* (New Haven, Conn.: Yale University Press, 1919).

O' Henry. *The Heart of the West* (Garden City, N.Y.: Doubleday Doran, 1919).

O'Neill, Gerard K. *The High Frontier: Human Colonies in Space* (Garden City, N.Y.: Anchor Press, 1982).

Oswald, Felix L. "The Preservation of Forests," *North American Review* 128 (January 1879): 35–46.

Page, Walter Hines. "The War with Spain and After," *Atlantic Monthly* 81 (June 1898): 721–27.

Parish, John Carl. "The Persistence of the Westward Movement," *Yale Review* 15 (April 1926): 461–77.

Parkman, Francis. *The Oregon Trail* (Boston: Little, Brown, 1892).

Parton, James. *Life of Horace Greeley* (Boston: Fields, Osgood, 1869).

Paxson, Frederic L. "A Generation of the Frontier Hypothesis, 1893–1932," *Pacific Historical Review* 11 (March 1933): 34–51.

———. *History of the American Frontier—1763–1893* (Boston: Houghton Mifflin, 1924).

———. *The Last American Frontier* (New York: Macmillan, 1918).

———. "The New Frontier and the Old American Habit," *Pacific Historical Review* 4 (December 1935): 308–27.

———. "The Pacific Railroads and the Disappearance of the Frontier in America," *American Historical Review, Annual Report for 1907* (1907): 105–22.

———. "The West and the Growth of the National Ideal," *Transactions of the Illinois State Historical Society* 15 (1910): 24–33.

———. *When the West Is Gone: The Colver Lectures in Brown University, 1929* (New York: Henry Holt, 1931).

Pearl, Raymond. *The Biology of Population Growth* (New York: Alfred A. Knopf, 1925).

———. "The Biology of Population Growth," *American Mercury* 3 (November 1924): 293–305.

———. "The Population Problem," *Geographical Review* 12 (October 1922): 634–45.

Pearson, Charles H. "The Land Question in the United States," *Contemporary Review* 9 (November 1868): 347–56.

———. *National Life and Character: A Forecast* (London: Macmillan and Company, 1893).

Pell, Charles Edward. *The Law of Births and Deaths* (London: T. Fishor Unwin, 1922).

Perry, Bliss. *The American Mind* (Boston: Houghton Mifflin, 1912).

———. *The American Spirit in Literature* (New Haven, Conn.: Yale University Press, 1918).

Peters, Edward T. "Evils of Our Public Land Policy," *Century Magazine* 25 (February 1883): 599–601.

Pinchot, Gifford. *Breaking New Ground* (New York: Harcourt Brace, 1947).

———. *The Fight for Conservation* (Seattle: University of Washington Press, 1967).

Piquet, John A. "Our Unconquered Frontier," *Scribner's Magazine* 96 (December 1934): 354–58.

Pitkin, W. B. *Must We Fight Japan?* (New York: Century, 1921).

Porter, Robert P. *The West from the Census of 1880: A History of the Industrial, Commercial,*

Social, and Political Development of States and Territories of the West from 1800 to 1880 (Chicago: Rand McNally, 1882).

Powell, G. W. "American Forests," *Harper's New Monthly Magazine* 59 (August 1879): 371–74.

Powell, John Wesley. "The Irrigable Lands of the Arid Region," *Century Magazine* 39 (March 1890): 766–76.

———. *Report of Explorations in 1873 of the Colorado River of the West and Its Tributaries, under the Direction of the Smithsonian Institution* (Washington, D.C.: Government Printing Office, 1874).

Pusey, W. A. *The Wilderness Road to Kentucky; Its Location and Features* (New York: Charles H. Doran, 1921).

Reddaway, W. F. *The Monroe Doctrine* (New York: G. E. Stechkert, 1924).

Remington, Frederic. *Crooked Trails* (New York: Bonanza Books, 1974).

———. "A Few Words from Mr. Remington," *Colliers*, 18 March 1905.

———. *John Ermine of the Yellowstone* (Ridgewood, N.J.: Gregg Press, 1968).

———. *Men with the Bark On* (New York: Harper and Brothers, 1900).

———. "On the Indian Reservations," *Century Magazine* 38 (July 1889): 394–405.

———. *Pony Tracks* (Columbus, Ohio: Longs College Book Company, 1951).

Reuter, E. B. *Population Problems*, (Philadelphia, Penn.: J. B. Lippincott, 1923).

Riegel, R. E. *America Moves West*, (New York: Henry Holt, 1930).

Rochester, Anna. *Rulers of America: A Study of Finance Capital* (New York: International Publishers, 1936).

Rollins, Philip Ashton. *The Cowboy: His Characteristics, His Equipment, and His Part in the Development of the West* (New York: Charles Scribner's Sons, 1922).

Roosevelt, Franklin D. "Back to the Land," *Review of Reviews* 84 (October 1931): 63–64.

———. *Commonwealth Campaign Speech* (San Francisco: Democratic Campaign Club Committee, 1932).

———. *Looking Forward* (New York: John Day, 1933).

———. *The Public Addresses of Franklin D. Roosevelt* (New York: Random House, 1938).

———. "Text of Governor Roosevelt's Speech at Commonwealth Club, San Francisco," *New York Times*, 24 September 1932.

Roosevelt, Theodore. *Autobiography* (New York: Charles Scribner's Sons, 1913).

———. "Big Game Disappearing in the West," *Forum* 15 (August 1893): 767–74.

———. "Frontier Types," *Century Magazine* 36 (October 1888): 832–43.

———. *Hunting Trips of a Ranchman* (New York: G. P. Putnam's Sons, 1904).

———. *Hunting Trips on the Prairie and in the Mountains* (New York: G. P. Putnam's Sons, 1900).

———. *Life and Times of Thomas Hart Benton* (New York: Houghton Mifflin, 1887).

———. *Literary Essays* (New York: Charles Scribner's Sons, 1923).

———. *The New Nationalism* (Englewood Cliffs, N.J.: Prentice Hall, 1961).

———. "The Northwest in the Nation," *Proceedings of the Fourth Annual Meeting of the Wisconsin State Historical Society, 1893*, Theodore Roosevelt Collection, Harvard University Library, Cambridge, Mass.

———. "Ranch Life in the Far West," *Century Magazine* 13 (February 1888): 495–510.

———. *The Rough Riders* (New York: Charles Scribner's Sons, 1899).

———. *Through the Brazilian Wilderness* (New York: Charles Scribner's Sons, 1914).

———. "What Americanism Means," *Forum* 13 (April 1894): 196–206.

———. *The Wilderness Hunter* (New York: G. P. Putnam's Sons, 1893).

———. "The Wilderness Hunter," *Atlantic Monthly* 75 (June 1895): 826–30.

———. *The Winning of the West*, 4 vols. (New York: G. P. Putnam's Sons, 1889–1896).

_____. *The Works of Theodore Roosevelt*, 23 vols. (New York: Charles Scribner's Sons, 1926).

Roosevelt, Theodore, and George Bird Grinnell. *American Big-Game Hunting, the Book of the Boone and Crockett Club* (New York: Forest and Stream Publishing, 1893).

Roosevelt, Theodore, and Henry Cabot Lodge. *Hero Tales from American History* (New York: Century, 1905).

Ross, Edward Alsworth. *The Old World in the New: The Significance of Past and Present Immigration to the American People* (New York: Century, 1914).

_____. "Racial Consequences of Immigration," *Century* 87 (February 1914): 615–22.

_____. *Social Control: A Survey of the Foundations of Order* (New York: Johnson Reprint, 1970).

_____. *Standing Room Only* (New York: Arno Press, 1977).

Sanger, Margaret. *The Pivot of Civilization* (New York: Brentanos Publishers, 1922).

Sanders, A. M. Carr. *The Population Problem: A Study in Human Evolution* (New York: Oxford University Press, 1922).

Schafer, Joseph. "Concerning the Frontier as a Safety Valve," *Political Science Quarterly* 52 (September 1937): 407–20.

_____. "Was the West a Safety-Valve for Labor?" *Mississippi Valley Historical Society* 24 (December 1937): 299–314.

Schlesinger, Arthur M. *New Viewpoints in American History* (New York: Macmillan, 1926).

_____. *The Rise of the City, 1878–1898* (New York: Macmillan, 1933).

Semple, Ellen Churchill. *American History and Its Geographic Conditions* (Boston: Houghton Mifflin, 1903).

Shaler, Nathaniel Southgate. *Nature and Man in America* (New York: Charles Scribner's Sons, 1891).

Shannon, Fred A. "The Homestead Act and the Labor Surplus," *American Historical Review* 41 (July 1936): 637–51.

Simons, Algie M. *The American Farmer* (Chicago: Charles H. Kerr, 1902).

_____. *Social Forces in American History* (New York: Macmillan, 1913).

Skinner, C. L. *Pioneers of the Old Southwest: A Chronicle of the Dark and Bloody Ground* (New Haven, Conn.: Yale University Press, 1921).

Smith, Russel J. *The World's Food Resources* (New York: Henry Holt, 1919).

Smith, Waldo R. "Is the Old West Passing?" *Overland Monthly* 67 (March 1916): 243–52.

Smythe, William E. *The Conquest of Arid America* (Seattle: University of Washington Press, 1969).

_____. *Constructive Democracy: The Economics of a Square Deal* (New York: Macmillan, 1905).

_____. "The Irrigation Idea and Its Coming Congress," *Review of Reviews* 8 (October 1893): 394–406.

_____. "Real Utopias in the Arid West," *Atlantic Monthly* 79 (May 1897): 599–609.

_____. "The Struggle for Water in the West," *Atlantic Monthly* 86 (November 1900): 646–54.

Soule, George. *The Coming American Revolution* (New York: Macmillan, 1934).

_____. *A Planned Society* (New York: Macmillan, 1932).

Spalding, John. "Is Our Social Life Threatened?" *Forum* 5 (March 1888): 16–26.

Spark, Edwin Erle. *The Expansion of the American People: Social and Territorial* (Chicago: Scott Foresman, 1900).

Spofford, A. F. "Homestead and Exemption Laws," in John J. Lalor, ed., *Encyclopaedia of Political Science, Political Economy and the Political History of the United States*, 3 vols. (New York: Charles E. Merrill, 1888–1890), 2: 462–464.

Stearns, Harold E. *Civilization in the United States: An Inquiry by Thirty Americans* (New York: Harcourt, Brace, 1922).

————. ed. *America Now: An Inquiry into Civilization in the United States* (New York: Charles Scribner's Sons, 1938).

Stefansson, Vilhjalmur. *Hunters of the Great North* (New York: Harcourt, Brace, 1922).

————. *The Northward Course of Empire* (New York: Macmillan, 1924).

Steinbeck, John. *In Dubious Battle.* (New York: Covici-Friede, 1936).

————. *To a God Unknown* (New York: Ballou, 1933).

————. *The Grapes of Wrath* (New York: Penguin Books, 1986).

————. *Of Mice and Men: A Play in Three Acts* (New York: Covici-Friede, 1937).

————. *The Pastures of Heaven* (New York: Brewer, Warren and Putnam, 1932).

————. *The Red Pony* (New York: Viking Press, 1945).

Stoddard, Theodore Lothrop. *The Rising Tide of Color* (New York: Charles Scribner's Sons, 1920).

Strong, Josiah. *Expansion under New World Conditions* (New York: Garland Publishing, 1971).

————. *The New Era; or, The Coming Kingdom* (New York: Baker and Taylor, 1893).

————. *Our Country: Its Possible Future and Its Present Crisis* (New York: Baker and Taylor, 1885).

Sullivan, Mark. *Our Times: The United States, 1920–1925,* 6 vols. (New York: Charles Scribner's Sons, 1926–1935).

Sumner, William Graham. *Earth Hunger and Other Essays* (New Haven, Conn.: Yale University Press, 1913).

————. *War and Other Essays* (New Haven, Conn.: Yale University Press, 1913).

————. *What Social Classes Owe to Each Other* (New York: Harper and Brothers, 1911).

Swinburne, J. *Population and the Social Problem* (New York: Macmillan, 1924).

Talbot, Reverend Ethlebert. "In Western Camps," *Harper's Magazine* 112 (December 1905): 506–12.

Taylor, Griffith. "The Distribution of Future White Settlement," *Geographical Review* 12 (July 1922): 375–402.

Taylor, Joseph Henry. *Sketches of Frontier and Indian Life* (Pottstown, Pa.: n.p., 1889).

Teggart, Frederick J. "Geography as an Aid to Statecraft: An Appreciation of Mackinder's *Democratic Ideal and Reality,*" *Geographical Review* 8 (October–November 1919): 227–42.

Thomas, Jean. *Blue Ridge Country* (New York: Duell, Sloan and Pearce, 1942).

Thomas, Norman. *The Choice before Us* (New York: Macmillan, 1934).

————. *Human Exploitation in the United States* (New York: Frederick A. Stokes, 1934).

Thompson, Warren S. *Population: A Study in Malthusianism* (New York: Columbia University, 1915).

Tocqueville, Alexis de. *Democracy in America* (Henry Reeve Text as revised by Francis Bowen), ed. Phillips Bradley, 2 vols. (New York: Macmillan, 1945).

Trimble, William J. "The Influence of the Passing of the Public Lands," *Atlantic Monthly* 113 (June 1914): 755–67.

Tugwell, Rexford G. *The Battle for Democracy* (New York: Columbia University Press, 1935).

————. "No More Frontier," *Today,* 22 June 1936, 3–4, 21.

Tugwell, Rexford G. and Howard C. Hill. *Our Economic Society and Its Problems: A Study of American Levels of Living and How to Improve Them* (New York: Harcourt, Brace, 1934).

Turner, Frederick Jackson. *The Early Writings of Frederick Jackson Turner,* compiled by Everett E. Edwards (New York: Books for Libraries Press, 1975).

_____. *The Frontier in American History* (New York: Henry Holt, 1920).

_____. *The Significance of Sections in American History* (New York: Henry Holt, 1932).

Turner, Frederick Jackson, and Frederick Merck. *List of References on the History of the West* (Cambridge, Mass.: Harvard University Press, 1922).

Twain, Mark. *Adventures of Huckleberry Finn* (Berkeley and Los Angeles: University of California Press, 1985).

_____. *A Connecticut Yankee in King Arthur's Court* (New York: Harper and Brothers, 1889).

Veblen, Thorstein. *The Engineers and the Price System* (New York: B. W. Huebsch, 1921).

Viele, General Egbert L. "The Frontiers of the United States," *Journal of the American Geographical Society of New York* 14 (1882): 166–204.

Villard, Oswald G. "The West: Tamed and Combed," *The Nation* (10 December 1924): 617–18.

Walker, Francis A. *Discussions in Economics and Statistics*, edited by Davis R. Dewey, 2 vols. (New York: Augustus M. Kelley, 1971), vol. 2: *Statistics, National Growth, Social and Economic*.

_____. "The Great Count of 1890," *Forum* 11 (June 1891): 406–18.

_____. "The Growth of the United States," *Scribner's Monthly* 24 (October 1882): 920–26.

_____. "Immigration, " *Yale Review* 1 (August 1892): 129–38.

_____. "Immigration and Degradation," *Forum* 11 (June 1891): 633–44.

_____. "Restriction of Immigration," *Atlantic Monthly* 77 (June 1896): 822–29.

_____. "The Tide of Economic Thought," address at the Fourth Annual Meeting of the American Economic Association, *Publications of the American Economic Association* 6 (1891): 37.

Walker, James B. *Experiences of Pioneer Life in Early Settlements and Cities of the West* (Chicago: Sumner, 1881).

Wallace, Henry A. *America Must Choose: The Advantages and Disadvantages of World Trade, and of a Planned Middle Course* (New York and Boston: Foreign Policy Association and the World Peace Foundation, 1934).

_____. *New Frontiers* (New York: Reynal and Hitchcock, 1934).

Waugh, Frank. "Frontiering," *Survey* 52 (June 1924): 290–92.

Webb, Melody. *The Last Frontier* (Albuquerque: University of New Mexico Press, 1985).

Webb, Walter Prescott. "The American West: Perpetual Mirage," *Harper's Magazine* 214 (May 1957): 25–31.

_____. *Divided We Stand: The Crisis of a Frontierless Democracy* (New York: Ginn, 1944).

_____. "Ended: Four Hundred Year Boom: Reflections on the Age of the Frontier," *Harper's Magazine* 23 (October 1951): 25–33.

_____. *The Great Frontier* (Boston: Houghton Mifflin, 1952).

_____. *The Great Plains* (New York: Ginn, 1931).

_____. "The West and the Desert," *Montana: Magazine of Western History* 8 (January 1958): 2–12.

Weber, John B., and Charles Stewart Smith. "Our National Dumping Ground: A Study of Immigration," *North American Review* 154 (April 1892): 424–38.

Weinberg, Albert K. *Manifest Destiny* (Baltimore: Johns Hopkins University Press, 1935).

Welch, Rodney. "Horace Greeley's Cure for Poverty," *Forum* 8 (January 1890): 586–93.

Weyl, Walter. "Depopulation in France," *North American Review* 195 (March 1912): 343–55.

_____. "An Experiment in Population," *Atlantic Monthly* 103 (February 1909): 261–67.

_____. "New Americans," *Harper's Magazine* 129 (September 1914): 615–23.

_____. *The New Democracy: An Essay on Certain Political and Economic Tendencies in the United States* (New York: Harper and Row, 1964).
Whelpton, Pascal K. "The Extent, Character, and Future of the New Landward Movement," *Journal of Farm Economics*, 15 January 1933, 57–72.
White, Horace. "The Question of the Birth Rate," *Nation*, 11 June 1903, 468–69.
Wilcox, Walter F. "On the Future Distribution of White Settlement," *Geographical Review* 12 (October 1922): 646–47.
Wilson, Charles Morrow. *Backwoods America* (Chapel Hill: University of North Carolina Press, 1934).
_____. "Land for the Taking," *American Magazine* 113 (March 1932): 54–56.
_____. "The Surviving American Frontier," *Current History* 34 (May 1931): 189–92.
Wilson, Woodrow. *College and State* (New York: Harper and Brothers, 1925).
_____. *Division and Reunion, 1829–1889* (New York: Longman's, Green, 1893).
_____. "The Ideals of America," *Atlantic Monthly* 90 (December 1902): 721–34.
_____. "The Making of a Nation," *Atlantic Monthly* 80 (July 1897): 1–14.
_____. "Mr. Goldwin Smith's Views on Our Political History," *Forum* 16 (December 1893): 489–99.
_____. *The New Democracy* (New York: Harper and Brothers, 1926).
_____. "The Proper Perspective of American History," *Forum* 19 (July 1895): 544–59.
Wiman, Erastus. "Can We Coerce Canada?" *North American Review* 152 (January 1891): 91–102.
_____. "The Capture of Canada," *North American Review* 151 (August 1890): 212–22.
_____. "The Farmer on Top," *North American Review* 153 (July 1891): 13–22.
_____. "The Greater Half of the Continent," *North American Review* 148 (January 1889): 54–72.
_____. "Has Not the Time for the Capture of Canada Come?" *North American Review* 148 (August 1890): 212–22.
_____. "The Struggle in Canada," *North American Review* 152 (March 1891): 339–48.
_____. "What Is the Destiny of Canada?" *North American Review* 148 (June 1889): 665–75.
Winsor, Justin. *The Westward Movement* (New York: Houghton Mifflin, 1897).
Wister, Owen. "The Evolution of a Cowpuncher," *Harper's Monthly Magazine* 91 (September 1895): 602–17.
_____. "How Lin McLean Went East," *Harper's New Monthly Magazine* 86 (December 1892): 135–46.
_____. *Roosevelt: The Story of a Friendship* (New York: Macmillan, 1930).
_____. *The Virginian: A Horseman of the Plains* (New York: Grosset and Dunlap, 1929).
Wood, Robert E. "The Gulf Coast, Our New Frontier," *Reader's Digest* 53 (September 1948): 17–20.
Wright, Benjamin F., Jr. "American Democracy and the Frontier," *Yale Review* 20 (September 1930): 349–65.
Wright, C. W. "The Significance of the Disappearance of Free Land in Our Economic Development," *American Economic Review* 16 (March 1926): 265–71.
Wright, Harold. *Population* (New York: Harcourt, Brace, 1923).

SECONDARY SOURCES

Aaron, Daniel. *Men of Good Hope. A Story of American Progressives* (New York: Oxford University Press, 1967).

Alexander, Charles C. *Here the Country Lies: Nationalism and the Arts in Twentieth Century America* (Bloomington: Indiana University Press, 1980).

————. *Nationalism in American Thought, 1930–1945* (Chicago: Rand McNally, 1971).

————. "Prophet of American Racism: Madison Grant and the Nordic Myth," *Phylon* 23 (Spring 1962): 73–90.

Allen, Barbara. *Homesteading the High Desert* (Salt Lake City: University of Utah Press, 1987).

Allen, Gay Wilson. "The Influence of Space on the American Imagination," in Clarence Ghodes, ed., *Essays on American Literature in Honor of Jay B. Hubbell* (Durham, N.C.: Duke University Press, 1967): 329–42.

Allen, Walter. *The Urgent West: The American Dream and Modern Man* (New York: E. P. Dutton, 1969).

Ambrosius, Lloyd E. "Turner's Frontier Thesis and the Modern American Empire," *Civil War History* 17 (December 1971): 332–39.

Anderson, Clifford B. "The Metamorphosis of American Agrarian Idealism in the 1920's and 1930's," *Agricultural History* 35 (October 1961): 182–88.

Anderson, David. *Ignatius Donnelly* (Boston: Twayne Publishers, 1980).

Anderson, George. "The Administration of Federal Land Laws in Western Kansas, 1880–1890: A Factor in Adjustment to a New Environment," *Kansas Historical Quarterly* 20 (November 1952): 233–51.

Anderson, Jack T. "Frederick Jackson Turner and Urbanization," *Journal of Popular Culture* 2 (Fall 1968): 292–98.

Anderson, Per Sveaas. *Westward Is the Course of Empire: A Study in the Shaping of an American Idea: Frederick Jackson Turner's Frontier* (Oslo, Norway: Oslo University Press, 1956).

Anderson, Thornton. *Brooks Adams, Constructive Conservative* (Ithaca, N.Y.: Cornell University Press, 1951).

Armstrong, William M. *E. L. Godkin and American Foreign Policy, 1865–1900* (New York: Bookman Associates, 1957).

Athearn, Robert G. "The American West: An Enduring Mirage?" *Colorado Quarterly* 26 (Autumn 1977): 3–16.

————. "The Ephemeral West," *Colorado Quarterly* 28 (Autumn 1979): 5–14.

————. *The Mythic West in Twentieth-Century America* (Lawrence: University Press of Kansas, 1986).

————. *Westward the Briton* (Lincoln: University of Nebraska Press, 1953).

Badger, Reid R. *The Great American Fair: The World's Columbian Exposition and American Culture* (Chicago: Nelson Hall, 1979).

Baldwin, Donald N. "Wilderness: Concept and Challenge" *Colorado Magazine* 44 (Summer 1967) 224–40.

Baritz, Lon. "The Idea of the West," *American Historical Review* 66 (April 1961): 618–39.

Barker, Charles A. *Henry George* (New York: Oxford University Press, 1955).

Bartlett, Richard A. "Freedom and the Frontier: A Pertinent Re-Examination," *Mid-America* 40 (July 1958): 131–38.

————. *The New Country: A Social History of the American Frontier, 1776–1890* (New York: Oxford University Press, 1974).

Beale, Howard K. *Theodore Roosevelt and the Rise of America to World Power* (Baltimore: Johns Hopkins University Press, 1956).

Beisner, Robert L. *From the Old Diplomacy to the New, 1865–1900* (Arlington Heights, Ill.: Harlan Davidson, 1986).

Bennett, James D. *Frederick Jackson Turner* (Boston: Twayne, 1975).

Benson, Lee. "The Historical Background of Turner's Frontier Essay," *Agricultural History* 25 (April 1951): 59–82.

———. *Turner and Beard; American Historical Writing Reconsidered* (New York: Free Press, 1960).

Beringause, Arthur. *Brooks Adams: A Biography* (New York: Alfred A. Knopf, 1955).

Bernstein, Richard. "Ideas and Trends: Among Historians the Frontier Is Turning Nastier with Each Revision," *New York Times*, 17 December 1989, E, 4–6.

Betts, Raymond F. "Immense Dimensions: The Impact of the American West on Late Nineteenth-Century European Thought about Expansion," *Western Historical Quarterly* 10 (April 1979): 149–66.

Billington, Ray A. *The American Frontier Thesis: Attack and Defense* (Washington, D.C.: American Historical Association Pamphlets, 1971).

———. *America's Frontier Heritage* (New York: Holt, Rinehart and Winston, 1966).

———. "Cowboys, Indians, and the Land of Promise: The World Image of the American Frontier," in Waldo W. Braden, ed., *Representative American Speeches, 1975–1976.* (New York: H. W. Wilson, 1976): 79–99.

———. *"Dear Lady": The Letters of Frederick Jackson Turner and Alice Forbes Perkins Hooper, 1910–1932* (San Marino, Calif.: Huntington Library, 1970).

———. *The Far Western Frontier* (New York: Harper and Row, 1956).

———. *Frederick Jackson Turner: Historian, Scholar, Teacher* (New York: Oxford University Press, 1973).

———. "Frederick Jackson Turner and the Closing of the Frontier," in Roger Daniels, ed., *Essays in Western History in Honor of Professor T. A. Larson* (Laramie: University of Wyoming Publications, 1971), 37: 45–56.

———. "Frederick Jackson Turner and Walter Prescott Webb: Frontier Historians," in Harold Hollingsworth, ed., *Essays on the American West* (Austin: University of Texas Press, 1969), 89–114.

———. "The Frontier and I," *Western Historical Quarterly* 1 (January 1970): 4–20.

———. "The Frontier Disappears," in Earl S. Miers, ed., *American Story* (New York: Channel Press, 1956), 253–58.

———. *The Frontier Thesis: Valid Interpretation of American History?* (New York: Holt, Rinehart and Winston, 1966).

———. "The Garden of the World: Fact and Fiction," in John J. Murray, ed., *The Heritage of the Middle West* (Norman: University of Oklahoma Press), 27–53.

———. *The Genesis of the Frontier Thesis: A Study in Historical Creativity* (San Marino, Calif.: Huntington Library, 1971).

———. "A Guide to American History Manuscripts Collections in the United States," *Mississippi Valley Historical Review* 38 (December 1951): 467–95.

———. *Land of Savagery, Land of Promise: The European Image of the American Frontier in the Nineteenth Century* (New York: W. W. Norton, 1981).

———. "Our Frontier Heritage of Waste," in John A. Garraty, ed., *Historical Viewpoints* (New York: Harper and Row, 1983), 378–87.

———. "Selling the West," in W. William Miller et al., eds. *The Power of Print in American History* (New York: St. Regis Paper, 1976), 74–88.

Billington, Ray A. with James Blaine Hedges. *Westward Expansion: A History of the American Frontier* (New York: Macmillan, 1974).

Billington, Ray A., and Wilbur R. Jacobs. "The Frederick Jackson Turner Papers in the Huntington Library," *Arizona and the West* 2 (Spring 1960): 73–77.

Blake, Casey Nelson. *Beloved Community: The Cultural Criticism of Randolph Bourne, Van Wyck Brooks, Waldo Frank, and Lewis Mumford* (Chapel Hill: University of North Carolina Press, 1990).

Blakely, George T. *Historians on the Homefront: American Propagandists for the Great War* (Lexington: University of Kentucky Press, 1971).

Bloch, Robert H. "Frederick Jackson Turner and American Geography," *Annals of the Association of American Geographers* 70 (March 1980): 31–42.

Bogard, William Judson. "The West as a Cultural Image at the End of the Nineteenth Century" (Ph.D. dissertation, Tulane University, 1971).

Bogue, Allan G. "Social Theory and the Pioneer," *Agricultural History* 34 (January 1960): 21–34.

Bogue, Allan G., Thomas D. Phillips, and James E. Wright, eds. *The West of the American People* (Itasca, Ill.: F. E. Peacock Publishers, 1970).

Bowers, William L. *The Country Life Movement in America, 1900–1920* (Port Washington, N.Y.: Kennikat Press, 1974).

Boynton, Percy H. *The Rediscovery of the Frontier* (New York: Greenwood Press, 1968).

Bragdon, Henry Wilkinson. *Woodrow Wilson: The Academic Years* (Cambridge, Mass.: Harvard University Press, Belknap Press, 1967).

Branch, Douglas. *The Cowboy and His Interpreters* (New York: Cooper Square Publishers, 1976).

Brooks, Van Wyck. *Days of the Phoenix: The Nineteen-Twenties I Remember* (New York: E. P. Dutton, 1957).

Burnette, Lawrence, Jr., ed. *Wisconsin Witness to Frederick Jackson Turner* (Madison: State Historical Society of Wisconsin, 1961).

Burns, Edward McNall. *The American Idea of Mission: Concepts of National Purpose and Destiny* (New Brunswick, N.J.: Rutgers University Press, 1957).

Burton, David H. "The Influence of the American West on the Imperialist Philosophy of Theodore Roosevelt," *Arizona and the West* 4 (January 1962): 5–26.

Cairns, Huntington, ed. *H. L. Mencken, the American Scene: A Reader* (New York: Alfred A. Knopf, 1965).

Campbell, A. E. *Expansion and Imperialism* (New York: Harper and Row, 1970).

Campbell, Charles C. *The Transformation of American Foreign Relations, 1865–1900* (New York: Harper and Row, 1976).

Carlson, Martin E. "William E. Smythe: Irrigation Crusader," *Journal of the West* 7 (January 1968): 41–47.

Carstensen, Vernon, ed. *The Public Lands: Studies in the History of the Public Domain* (Madison: University of Wisconsin Press, 1963).

Carpenter, Ronald H. *The Eloquence of Frederick Jackson Turner: Academic Addresses* (San Marino, Calif.: Huntington Library, 1983).

_____. "Wisconsin's Rhetorical Historian, Frederick Jackson Turner: A Review Essay," *Wisconsin Magazine of History* 68 (Spring 1985): 199–203.

Carter, Paul A. *Revolt against Destiny: An Intellectual History of the United States* (New York: Columbia University Press, 1989).

Carter, Paul J. *Waldo Frank* (New York: Twayne, 1967).

Cashman, Sean D. *America in the Gilded Age* (New York: New York University Press, 1984).

Cassity, Michael J. *Defending a Way of Life: An American Community in the Nineteenth Century* (Albany: State University of New York Press, 1989).

Cate, Wirt A. "Lamar and the Frontier Hypothesis," *Journal of Southern History* 1 (February 1935): 497–501.

_____. Preface to Lucius Q. C. Lamar, *Secession and Reunion* (Chapel Hill: University of North Carolina Press, reprinted 1969): vii–x.

Caughey, John W. "The Insignificance of the Frontier in American History, or 'Once upon a Time There Was an American West,' " *Western Historical Quarterly* 5 (January 1974): 5–16.

Chase, Allan. *The Legacy of Malthus: The Social Costs of the New Scientific Racism* (New York: Alfred A. Knopf, 1977).

Chinard, Gilbert. *Thomas Jefferson: The Apostle of Americanism* (Boston: Little, Brown, 1929).

Clark, Dan Elbert. *The West in American History* (New York: Thomas Y. Crowell, 1937).

Clepper, Henry. *Leaders of American Conservation* (New York: Ronald Press, 1971).

Commager, Henry Steele. *The American Mind: An Interpretation of American Character and Thought since the 1880's* (New Haven, Conn.: Yale University Press, 1967).

Conkin, Paul K. *The Southern Agrarians* (Knoxville: University of Tennessee Press, 1988).

————. *Tomorrow a New World: The New Deal Community Program* (Ithaca, N.Y.: Cornell University Press, 1959).

Cooke, Alistair, ed. *The Vintage Mencken* (New York: Vintage Books, 1955).

Crapol, Edward P. *America for Americans: Economic Nationalism and Anglophobia in the Late Nineteenth Century* (Westport, Conn.: Greenwood Press, 1973).

Craven, Avery. "F. J. T," in William T. Hutchinson, ed., *Marcus W. Jernigan Essays in American Historiography* (Chicago: University of Chicago Press, 1937), 252–70.

Cronon, William. *Nature's Metropolis: Chicago and the Great West* (New York: W. W. Norton, 1991).

————. "Revisiting the Vanishing Frontier: The Legacy of Frederick Jackson Turner," *Western Historical Quarterly* 18 (April 1987): 157–76.

Cunliffe, Marcus. "American Watersheds," *American Quarterly* 12 (Winter 1961): 480–94.

Curry, Larry. *The American West: Painters from Catlin to Russell* (New York: Viking Press, 1972).

Curti, Merle E. *The Growth of American Thought* (New York: Harper and Row, 1943).

————. "The Immigrant and the American Image in Europe, 1860–1914," *Mississippi Valley Historical Review* 37 (September 1950): 203–30.

————. "Literary Patriots of the Gilden Age," *Historical Outlook* 19 (April 1928): 153–56.

————. *Probing Our Past* (New York: Harper and Brothers, 1955).

————. "The Section and the Frontier in American History: The Methodological Concepts of Frederick Jackson Turner," in Stuart Rice, ed., *Methods in Social Sciences* (Chicago: University of Chicago Press, 1931), 353–67.

Curtis, Bruce. *William Graham Sumner* (Boston: Twayne Publishers, 1981).

Daly, David, and Joel Persky. "The West and the Western," *Journal of the West* 29 (April 1990): 3–64.

Darrah, William Culp. *Powell of the Colorado* (Princeton, N.J.: Princeton University Press, 1951).

Danborn, David B. "Rural Education Reform and the Country Life Movement, 1900–1920," *Agricultural History* 52 (April 1979): 462–74.

Davie, Maurice B. *William Graham Sumner* (New York: Thomas Y. Crowell, 1965).

Davis, David B. "Ten Gallon Hero," *American Quarterly* 6 (Summer 1954): 111–25.

Debo, Angie, ed. *The Cowman's Southwest* (Glendale, Calif.: Arthur H. Clark, 1953).

Degler, Carl N. *Out of Our Past: The Forces That Shaped Modern America* (New York: Harper and Row, 1984), especially 133–39.

Deverell, William F. "To Loosen the Safety Valve: Eastern Workers and Western Lands," *Western Historical Quarterly* 19 (August 1988): 269–85.

Dick, Everett. *The Lure of the Land: A Social History of the Public Lands from the Articles of Confederation to the New Deal* (Lincoln: University of Nebraska Press, 1970).

Dippie, Brian. "American Wests: Historiographical Perspectives," *American Studies International* 27 (October 1989): 3–25.

Dobson, John M. *America's Ascent: The United States Becomes a Great Power, 1880–1914* (Dekalb: Northern Illinois University Press, 1978).

Doughty, Howard. *Francis Parkman* (New York: Macmillan, 1962).

Drinnon, Richard. *Facing West: The Metaphysics of Indian-Hating and Empire-Building* (Minneapolis: University of Minnesota Press, 1980).

Dunham, H. H. *Government Handout: A Study in the Administration of the Public Lands, 1875–1891* (Ann Arbor, Mich.: Edwards Brothers, 1941).

Dyer, Thomas G. *Theodore Roosevelt and the Idea of Race* (Baton Rouge: Louisiana State University Press, 1980).

Edwards, Everett E. *References on the Significance of the Frontier in American History* (Washington D.C.: Department of Agriculture Library, 1939).

Ekirch, Arthur A., Jr. *Ideologies and Utopias: The Impact of the New Deal on American Thought* (Chicago: Quadrangle Books, 1969).

———. *Man and Nature in America* (New York: Columbia University Press, 1963).

Ellis, David M., ed. *The Frontier in American Development: Essays in Honor of Paul Wallace Gates* (Ithaca, N.Y.: Cornell University Press, 1969).

Emmons, David M. *Garden in the Grasslands: Boomer Literature of the Central Great Plains* (Lincoln: University of Nebraska Press, 1971).

Erisman, Fred, and Richard W. Etulain, eds. *Fifty Western Writers: A Bio-Bibliographical Sourcebook* (Westport, Conn.: Greenwood Press, 1982).

Etulain, Richard W. "Frontier, Region and Myth: Changing Interpretations of Western American Culture," *Journal of American Culture* 3 (Summer 1980): 268–84.

———. *Owen Wister* (Boise, Idaho: Boise State College, 1973).

———, ed. *Writing Western History: Essays on Major Western Historians* (Albuquerque: University of New Mexico Press, 1991).

Ewers, John C. *Artists of the Old West* (Garden City, N.Y.: Doubleday, 1965).

Fite, Gilbert C. *American Farmers: The New Minority* (Bloomington: Indiana University Press, 1981).

———. "The Farmer's Dilemma, 1919–1929," in John Braeman, Robert A. Bremner, and David Brody, eds., *Change and Continuity in Twentieth Century America: The 1920's* (Columbus: Ohio State University Press, 1968), 67–103.

———. *The Farmer's Frontier: 1865–1900* (New York: Holt, Rinehart and Winston, 1966).

Foner, Philip S., ed. *Jack London: American Rebel: A Collection of His Social Writings Together with an Extensive Study of the Man and His Times* (New York: Citadel Books, 1947).

Forcey, Charles B. *The Crossroads of Liberalism: Croly, Weyl, Lippman and the Progressive Era, 1900–1925* (New York: Oxford University Press, 1967).

Fox, Stephen. *John Muir and His Legacy: The American Conservation Movement* (Boston: Little, Brown, 1981).

Frantz, Joe B. and J. Ernest Choate, Jr. *The American Cowboy: The Myth and the Reality* (Norman: University of Oklahoma Press, 1955).

French, Warren. "Death of the Dream" (unpublished seminar paper for Walter Prescott Webb, University of Texas, Austin, c. 1953).

Freund, Rudolph. "Turner's Theory of Social Evolution," *Agricultural History* 19 (April 1945): 78–87.

Friedman, Lawrence M. *A History of American Law* (New York: Simon and Schuster, 1973).

Friesen, Gerald. *The Canadian Prairies: A History* (Lincoln: University of Nebraska Press, 1984).

Fusfeld, Daniel R. *The Economic Thought of Franklin D. Roosevelt and the Origins of the New Deal* (New York: Columbia University Press, 1956).

Fussell, Edwin. *Frontier: American Literature and the American West* (Princeton, N.J.: Princeton University Press, 1965).

Gabriel, Ralph Henry. *The Course of American Democratic Thought*, 3d ed. (New York: Greenwood Press, 1986).

Gardner, A. Dudley, and Verla R. Flores. *Forgotten Frontier: A History of Wyoming Coal Mining* (Boulder, Colo.: Westview Press, 1989).

Gardner, Lloyd C. *A Different Frontier: Selected Readings in the Foundations of American Economic Expansion* (Chicago: Quadrangle Books, 1966).

Garraty, John A. *Henry Cabot Lodge: A Biography* (New York: Alfred A. Knopf, 1965).

Gates, Paul Wallace. *A History of Public Land Law Development* (Washington, D.C.: Government Printing Office, 1968).

————. *Landlords and Tenants on the Prairie Frontier* (Ithaca, N.Y.: Cornell University Press, 1973).

Gilbert, James B. *Work without Salvation: America's Intellectuals and Industrial Alienation, 1880–1910* (Baltimore, Md.: Johns Hopkins University Press, 1977).

Ginger, Ray. *Age of Excess: The United States from 1877–1914* (New York: Macmillan, 1965).

Goetzmann, William. *Exploration and Empire* (New York: Alfred A. Knopf, 1966).

————. *New Lands, New Men: America and the Second Great Age of Discovery* (New York: Viking Press, 1986).

Goetzmann, William H. and William N. Goetzmann. *The West of the Imagination* (New York: W. W. Norton, 1986).

Goodwyn, Lawrence. *Democratic Promise: The Populist Moment in America* (New York: Oxford University Press, 1976).

Gordon, Milton M. *Assimilation in American Life: The Role of Race, Religion and National Origins* (New York: Oxford University Press, 1964).

Gottfried, Herbert W. "Spatiality and the Frontier: Spatial Themes in Western American Literature" (Ph.D. dissertation, Ohio University, 1974).

Graebner, Norman A. *America as a World Power* (Wilmington, Del.: Scholarly Resources, 1984).

————. *Empire on the Pacific: A Study in American Continental Expansion* (New York: Ronald Press, 1955).

Graham, Otis L., Jr. *Toward a Planned Society: From Roosevelt to Nixon* (New York: Oxford University Press, 1977).

Graybar, Lloyd J. *Albert Shaw of the Review of Reviews: An Intellectual Biography* (Lexington: University of Kentucky Press, 1974).

Gressley, Gene M. "The Turner Thesis: A Problem in Historiography," *Agricultural History* 32 (October 1958): 227–49.

————. *West by East: The American West in the Gilded Age* (Provo, Utah: Brigham Young University Press, 1972).

Gurian, Jay. *Western American Writing; Tradition and Promise* (Deland, Fla.: Everett Edwards, 1975).

Gutman, Herbert G. "Social and Economic Structure and Depression in American Labor in 1873 and 1874" (Ph.D. dissertation, University of Wisconsin, 1959).

Guttman, Allen. *The Wound in the Heart: America and the Spanish Civil War* (Glencoe, Ill.: Free Press, 1962).

Hagedorn, Herman. *Roosevelt in the Bad Lands* (Boston: Houghton Mifflin, 1921).

Hansen, Marcus Lee. *The Immigrant in American History* (Cambridge, Mass.: Harvard University Press, 1942).
_____. *The Mingling of the Canadian and American Peoples* (New Haven, Conn.: Yale University Press, 1940).
Hauptman, Laurence M. "Mythologizing Westward Expansion: Schoolbooks and the Image of the American Frontier before Turner," *Western Historical Quarterly* 8 (July 1977): 269–82.
Hawgood, John A. *America's Western Frontiers: The Exploration and Settlement of the Trans-Mississippi West* (New York: Alfred A. Knopf, 1967), 384–412.
_____. "British Interest in the History of Western America," in K. Ross Toole, ed., *Probing the American West; Papers from the Santa Fe Conference* (Santa Fe, N.Mex.: Museum of New Mexico Press), 175–84.
Hays, Samuel P. *Conservation and the Gospel of Efficiency: The Progressive Conservation Movement, 1890–1920* (Cambridge, Mass.: Harvard University Press, 1959).
Healy, David. *U. S. Expansionism: The Imperialist Urge in the 1890's* (Madison: University of Wisconsin Press, 1970).
Hearn, Charles R. *The American Dream in the Great Depression* (Westport, Conn.: Greenwood Press, 1977).
Heaton, Herbert. "Other Wests Than Ours," *Journal of Economic History* 6 (supplement, 1946): 50–62.
Hibbard, Benjamin H. *A History of the Public Land Policy* (New York: Peter Smith, 1939).
Hicks, John D. "The Western Middle West, 1900–1914," *Agricultural History* 20 (April 1946): 65–77.
Higham, John. *Strangers in the Land: Patterns of American Nativism, 1860–1925* (New Brunswick, N.J.: Rutgers University Press, 1955).
Hine, Robert V. *The American West: An Interpretive History* (Boston: Little, Brown, 1973).
_____. "The American West as Metaphysics: A Perspective on Josiah Royce," *Pacific Historical Review* 58 (August 1989): 267–91.
_____. *Community on the Frontier: Separate But Not Alone* (Norman: University of Oklahoma Press, 1980).
Hofstadter, Richard. "Manifest Destiny and the Philippines," in Daniel Aaron, ed., *America in Crisis* (New York: Alfred A. Knopf, 1952), 172–200.
_____. "The Myth of the Happy Yeoman," in Nicholas Cords and Patrick Gerster, eds., *Myth and the American Experience* (New York: Harper Collins Publishers, 1991), 2: 69–77.
_____. *The Progressive Historians: Turner, Beard, Parrington* (Chicago: University of Chicago Press, 1968).
_____. *Social Darwinism in American Thought*, 2d ed. (New York: George Braziller, 1959).
_____. "Turner and the Frontier Myth," *American Scholar* 18 (Autumn 1949): 433–43.
Hofstadter, Richard, and Seymour Martin Lipset, eds. *Turner and the Sociology of the Frontier* (New York: Basic Books, 1968).
Holly, Donald. *Uncle Sam's Farmers: The New Deal Communities in the Lower Mississippi Valley* (Urbana: University of Illinois Press, 1975).
Holt, W. Stull. "Hegel, the Turner Hypothesis, and the Safety-Valve Theory," *Agricultural History* 22 (July 1948): 175–76.
Holtgrieve, Donald G. "Frederick Jackson Turner as a Regionalist," *The Professional Geographer* 26 (May 1974): 159–65.
Horn, Miriam. "How the West Was Really Won," *U.S. News and World Report*, 21 May 1990, 56–62, 65.

House, Albert V., Jr. "Proposals of Government Aid to Agricultural Settlement during the Depression of 1873–1879," *Agricultural History* 12 (January 1938): 47–66.

Hoxie, Frederick E. *A Final Promise: The Campaign to Assimilate the Indians, 1880–1920* (Lincoln: University of Nebraska Press, 1984).

Hunt, David C. *Legacy of the West* (Lincoln: University of Nebraska Press, 1982).

Huth, Hans. *Nature and the American: Three Centuries of Changing Attitudes* (Berkeley: University of California Press, 1957).

Hutson, James H. "Benjamin Franklin and the West," *Western Historical Quarterly* 4 (October 1973): 425–34.

Israel, Jerry. *Progressivism and the Open Door* (Pittsburgh: University of Pittsburgh Press, 1971).

Issel, William H. "Ralph Borsodi and the Agrarian Response to Industrial America," *Agricultural History* 41 (April 1967): 155–66.

Jacobs, Wilbur R. "Frederick Jackson Turner's Views on International Politics, War and Peace," *Australian National University Historical Journal* 6 (November 1969): 10–15.

————. "The Indian and the Frontier in American History: A Need for Revision," *Western Historical Quarterly* 4 (January 1973): 43–56.

————. *The Historical World of Frederick Jackson Turner* (New Haven, Conn.: Yale University Press, 1968).

————. "*Wider Frontiers*—Questions of War and Conflict in American History: The Strange Solution by Frederick Jackson Turner," *California Historical Society Quarterly* 47 (September 1968): 219–36.

Jacobs, Wilbur R., John W. Caughey, and Joe B. Frantz. *Turner, Bolton and Webb: Three Historians of the American Frontier* (Seattle: University of Washington Press, 1965)

Jacobs, Wilbur R., ed. *America's Great Frontiers and Sections: Frederick Jackson Turner's Unpublished Essays* (Lincoln: University of Nebraska Press, 1965).

————, ed. *Frederick Jackson Turner's Legacy: Unpublished Writings in American History* (San Marino, Calif.: Huntington Library, 1965).

————, ed. "Frederick Jackson Turner's Notes on the Westward Movement, California, and the Far West," *Southern California Quarterly* 46 (June 1964): 161–68.

Jaher, Frederic Cople. *Doubters and Dissenters: Cataclysmic Thought in America 1885–1918* (London: Collier-Macmillan, 1969).

James, Stuart B. "Western American Space and the American Imagination," *Western Humanities Review* 24 (June 1970): 147–55.

Jensen, Richard. "On Modernizing Frederick Jackson Turner: The Historiography of Regionalism," *Western Historical Quarterly* 11 (July 1980): 307–22.

John, Arthur. *The Best Years of the Century: Richard Watson Gilder, Scribner's Monthly and Century Magazine, 1870–1909* (Chicago: University of Illinois Press, 1981).

Johnson, George W. "The Frontier behind Frank Norris' McTeague," *Huntington Library Quarterly* 26 (November 1962): 91–104.

Jones, Alfred Haworth. "The Search for a Useable American Past in the New Deal Era," *American Quarterly* 23 (December 1971): 710–24.

Jones, Maldwyn A. *The Limits of Liberty: American History, 1607–1980* (New York: Oxford University Press, 1983).

Juricek, John T. "American Usage of the Word 'Frontier' from Colonial Times to Frederick Jackson Turner," *American Philosophical Society Proceedings*, 60 (1966): 10–34.

Kaplan, Lawrence S. "Frederick Jackson Turner and Imperialism," *Social Science* 27 (January 1952): 12–16.

Kaufman, Burton I. *Efficiency and Expansion: Foreign Trade Organization in the Wilson Administration, 1913–1921* (Westport, Conn.: Greenwood Press, 1974).

Kazin, Alfred. *On Native Grounds: An Interpretation of Modern American Prose Literature* (New York: Harcourt Brace Jovanovich, 1970).

Keller, Morton. *Affairs of State: Public Life in Late Nineteenth Century America* (Cambridge, Mass.: Harvard University Press, Belknap Press, 1977).

Kelley, Robert L. *Gold Versus Grain: The Hydraulic Mining Controversy in California's Sacramento Valley: A Chapter in the Decline of the Concept of Laissez Faire* (Glendale, Calif.: Arthur H. Clark, 1959).

Kesselman, Steven. "The Frontier Thesis and the Great Depression," *Journal of the History of Ideas* 29 (April 1968): 253–68.

_____. *The Modernization of American Reform: Structures and Perceptions* (New York: Garland, 1979).

Knee, Stuart. "Awakening in the West," *Journal of the West* 17 (April 1978): 105–11.

Kolko, Gabriel. *Main Currents in Modern American History* (New York: Harper and Row, 1976).

Kolodny, Annette. *The Land before Her: Fantasy and Experience of the American Frontier, 1630–1860* (Chapel Hill: University of North Carolina Press, 1984).

Kramer, Frank. *Voices in the Valley: Mythology and Folk Belief in the Shaping of the Middle West* (Madison: University of Wisconsin Press, 1964).

Krog, Carl E. "Organizing the Production of Leisure: Herbert Hoover and the Conservation Movement in the 1920s," *Wisconsin Magazine of History* 67 (Spring 1984): 199–218.

La Feber, Walter. *The New Empire, An Interpretation of American Expansion, 1860–1898* (Ithaca, N.Y.: Cornell University Press, 1977).

Lamar, Howard R. *The Far Southwest, 1846–1912* (New Haven, Conn.: Yale University Press, 1966).

_____. "Frederick Jackson Turner," in Marcus Cunliffe and Robin Winks, eds., *Pastmasters: Some Essays on American Historians* (New York: Harper and Row, 1969), 74–109.

_____. *The Reader's Encyclopedia of the American West* (New York: Thomas Y. Crowell, 1977).

Lamar, Howard, and Leonard Thompson, eds. *The Frontier in History: North America and Southern Africa Compared* (New Haven, Conn.: Yale University Press, 1981).

Lambert, Neal. "Owen Wister's Virginian: The Genesis of a Cultural Hero," *Western American Literature* 6 (Summer 1971): 99–107.

Larsen, Lawrence H. *The Urban West at the End of the Frontier* (Lawrence: University Press of Kansas, 1978).

Lavender, David. *The Great West* (Boston: Houghton Mifflin, 1987).

Layton, Stanford J. *To No Privileged Class: The Rationalization of Homesteading and Rural Life in the Early Twentieth Century American West* (Salt Lake City, Utah: Brigham Young University, Charles Redd Center for Western Studies, 1988).

Lears, T. Jackson. *No Place of Grace: Antimodernism and the Transformation of American Culture, 1880–1920* (New York: Pantheon Books, 1981).

Leuchtenburg, William E. *The Needless War with Spain* (New York: American Heritage, 1957).

Leverette, William E., Jr. and David E. Shi. "Agrarianism for Commuters," *South Atlantic Quarterly* 79 (Spring 1980): 204–18.

_____. "Herbert Agar and *Free America*: A Jeffersonian Alternative to the New Deal," *Journal of American Studies* 16 (August 1982): 189–206.

Lewis, Frank D. "Farm Settlement on the Canadian Prairies, 1898–1911," *Journal of Economic History* 41 (September 1981): 517–33.

Lewis, Merrill E. "The American Frontier as Literature: The Historiography of George

Bancroft, Frederick Jackson Turner and Theodore Roosevelt" (Ph.D. dissertation, University of Utah, 1968).

Lewis, R. W. B. *The American Adam* (Chicago: University of Chicago Press, 1955).

Lillibridge, G. D. *Beacon of Freedom: The Impact of American Democracy upon Great Britain, 1830–1870* (Philadelphia: University of Pennsylvania Press, 1955).

Limerick, Patricia Nelson. *Desert Passages: Encounters with the American Deserts* (Albuquerque: University of New Mexico Press, 1985).

————. *The Legacy of Conquest: The Unbroken Past of the American West* (New York: W. W. Norton, 1987).

Limerick, Patricia Nelson, Clyde A. Milner II, and Charles E. Rankin, eds. *Trails: Toward a New Western History* (Lawrence: University Press of Kansas, 1991).

Lord, Clifford L., and Elizabeth H. Lord. *Historical Atlas of the United States* (New York: Henry Holt, 1972).

Lowitt, Richard. *The New Deal and the West* (Bloomington: Indiana University Press, 1984).

Lyon, William H. "The Third Generation and the Frontier Hypothesis," *Arizona and the West* 4 (Spring 1962): 45–50.

Lyon, Thomas, et al., eds. *A Literary History of the American West* (Fort Worth: Texas Christian University Press, 1987).

McCloskey, Maxine E., and James P. Gilligan, eds. *Wilderness and the Quality of Life* (San Francisco: Sierra Club, 1967).

McCloskey, Robert. *American Conservatism in the Age of Enterprise* (Cambridge, Mass.: Harvard University Press, 1951).

McCormick, Thomas J. *China Market* (Chicago: Quadrangle Books, 1967).

McCracken, Harold. *Frederick Remington: Artist of the Old West* (Philadelphia: J. B. Lippincott, 1947).

McCullough, Joseph B. *Hamlin Garland* (Boston: Twayne, 1978).

McDermott, John Francis, ed. *The Frontier Re-Examined* (Urbana: University of Illinois Press, 1967).

McGerr, Michael. "The Price of the New Transnational History," *American Historical Review* 96 (October 1991): 1056–67.

McHenry, Robert, and Charles Van Doren, eds. *A Documentary History of Conservation in America* (New York: Praeger, 1972).

McMurtry, Larry. "Westward Ho Hum: What the New Historians Have Done to the Old West," *New Republic*, 9 October 1990, 32–38.

McNeill, William H. *The Great Frontier: Freedom and Hierarchy in Modern Times* (Princeton, N.J.: Princeton University Press, 1983).

Malin, James C. *The Contriving Brain and the Skillful Hand in the United States* (Ann Arbor, Mich.: Edwards Brothers, 1954).

————. *Essays on Historiography* (Ann Arbor, Mich.: Edwards Brothers, 1946).

————. "Mobility and History: Reflections on the Agricultural Policies of the United States in Relation to the Mechanized World," *Agricultural History* 17 (October 1943): 379–95.

————. *On the Nature of History: Essays about History and Dissidence* (Ann Arbor: Mich.: Edwards Brothers, 1954).

————. "Space and History," *Agricultural History* 18 (April 1944): 65–74.

————. "Space and History, Part II," *Agricultural History* 18 (July 1944): 107–26.

Malone, Michael P. "Beyond the Last Frontier: Toward a New Approach to Western American History, *Western Historical Quarterly* 20 (November 1989): 409–27.

————, ed. *Historians and the American West* (Lincoln: University of Nebraska Press, 1983).

Malone, Michael P., and Richard W. Etulain. *The American West: A Twentieth-Century History* (Lincoln: University of Nebraska Press, 1989).

Martin, Jay. *Harvest of Change: American Literature, 1865–1914* (Englewood Cliffs, N.J.: Prentice Hall, 1967).

Marx, Leo. *The Machine in the Garden: Technology and the Pastoral Ideal in America* (New York: Oxford University Press, 1964).

Mattson, Vernon E., and Rick Tilman, "Thorstein Veblen, Frederick Jackson Turner, and the American Experience," *Journal of Economic Issues* 20 (December 1986): 219–235.

Mattson, Vernon E., and William E. Marion, comps. *Frederick Jackson Turner: A Reference Guide* (Boston: G. K. Hall, 1985).

Maude, George. "Drawing a Line in Water: America's Nordic Frontier," in Michael Berry, George Maude, and Jerry Schuchalter, *Frontiers of American Political Experience* (Turko University, Finland: Turun Yliopisto, 1990), 87–139.

May, Ernest R. *Imperial Democracy: The Emergence of America as a Great Power* (New York: Harcourt, Brace and World, 1961).

May, Henry F. *The End of American Innocence: A Study of the First Years of Our Own Times, 1912–1917* (New York: Alfred A. Knopf, 1959).

Merk, Frederick. *History of the Westward Movement* (New York: Alfred A. Knopf, 1978).

———. *Manifest Destiny and Mission in American History* (New York: Alfred A. Knopf, 1963).

Miller, Donald L. *Lewis Mumford: A Life* (New York: Weidenfeld and Nicolson, 1989).

Miller, Orlando W. *The Frontier in Alaska and the Matanuska Colony* (New Haven, Conn.: Yale University Press, 1975).

Miller, Richard N. *American Imperialism in 1898* (New York: John Wiley and Sons, 1970).

Milner, Clyde A., II, ed. *Major Problems in the History of the American West* (Lexington, Mass.: D. C. Heath, 1989).

Milton, John. *The Novel of the American West* (Lincoln: University of Nebraska Press, 1980).

Mitchell, Lee Clark. *Witnesses to a Vanishing America: The Nineteenth Century Response* (Princeton, N.J.: Princeton University Press, 1981).

Mood, Fulmer. "A British Statistician of 1854 Analyzes the Westward Movement in the United States," *Agricultural History* 19 (July 1945): 142–51.

———. "The Concept of the Frontier, 1871–1898: Comments on a Select List of Source Documents," *Agricultural History* 19 (January 1945): 24–31.

———. "The Development of Frederick Jackson Turner as a Historical Thinker," *Publications of the Colonial Society of Massachusetts* 34 (1937–1942): 283–352.

———. "Notes on the History of the Word Frontier," *Agricultural History* 22 (April 1948): 78–83.

Morgan, H. Wayne, ed. *The Gilded Age* (New York: Syracuse University Press, 1970).

Morison, Elting E., ed. *The Letters of Theodore Roosevelt*, 8 vols. (Cambridge, Mass.: Harvard University Press, 1951–1954).

Morris, Edmund. *The Rise of Theodore Roosevelt* (New York: Coward, McCann, Geoghegan, 1979).

Morris, John W., Charles R. Goins, and Edwin C. McReynolds. *Historical Atlas of Oklahoma* (Norman: University of Oklahoma Press, 1976).

Mott, Frank Luther. *A History of American Magazines*, 4 vols. (Cambridge, Mass.: Harvard University Press, Belknap Press, 1957).

Muller, Dorothea R. "Josiah Strong and American Nationalism: A Reevaluation," *Journal of American History* 53 (December 1966): 487–503.

Nagel, Paul C. *This Sacred Trust: American Nationality, 1798–1898* (New York: Oxford University Press, 1971).

Nardroff, Ellen von. "The American Frontier as a Safety Valve: The Life, Death, Reincarnation and Justification of a Theory," *Agricultural History* 36 (July 1962): 123–42.

Nash, Gerald D. "The Census of 1890 and the Closing of the Frontier," *Pacific Northwest Quarterly* 71 (July 1980): 98–100.

————. *Creating the West: Historical Interpretations, 1890–1990* (Albuquerque: University of New Mexico Press, 1991).

————. "Where's the West?" *Historian* 49 (November 1986): 1–9.

Nash, Gerald D., and Richard W. Etulain, eds. *The Twentieth-Century West: Historical Interpretations* (Albuquerque: University of New Mexico Press, 1989).

Nash, Roderick F. *American Environmentalism: Readings in Conservation History* (New York: McGraw Hill, 1990).

————. "The American Invention of National Parks," *American Quarterly* 22 (Fall 1970): 726–35.

————. *The Nervous Generation: American Thought, 1917–1930* (Chicago: Ivan R. Dee, 1970).

————. "The Roots of American Environmentalism," in *Indiana Historical Society Lectures, 1983: Perceptions of the Landscape and Its Preservation* (Indianapolis: Indiana Historical Society, 1984), 29–50.

————. *Wilderness and the American Mind*, 3d ed. (New Haven, Conn.: Yale University Press, 1982).

————, ed. *The Call of the Wild, 1900–1916* (New York: George Braziller, 1970).

Nichols, Roger L., ed. *American Frontier and Western Issues: An Historiographical Review* (Westport, Conn.: Greenwood Press, 1986).

Nixon, Herman C. "The Precursors of Turner in the Interpretation of the American Frontier," *South Atlantic Quarterly* 27 (January 1929): 83–89.

Noble, David W. "American Studies and the Burden of Frederick Jackson Turner," *Journal of American Culture* 4 (Winter 1981): 34–45.

————. *The End of American History: Democracy, Capitalism, and the Metaphor of Two Worlds in Anglo-American Historical Writing, 1880–1980* (Minneapolis: University of Minnesota Press, 1984).

————. *The Eternal Adam and the New World Garden* (New York: George Braziller, 1968).

————. *Historians against History: The Frontier Thesis and the National Covenant in American Historical Writing since 1830* (Minneapolis: University of Minnesota Press, 1965).

————. *The Progressive Mind, 1890–1917* (Minneapolis, Minn.: Burgess, 1981).

Nugent, Walter T. K. "Frontiers and Empires in the Late-Nineteenth Century," *Western Historical Quarterly* 20 (November 1989): 393–408.

————. *The Tolerant Populists: Kansas Populism and Nativism* (Chicago: University of Chicago Press, 1963).

Nye, Russel B. *This Almost Chosen People* (East Lansing: Michigan State University Press, 1966).

Olin, Spencer J., Jr. "Toward a Synthesis of the Social and Political History of the American West," *Pacific Historical Review* 55 (November 1986): 599–611.

Opie, John. "Frederick Jackson Turner, the Old West, and the Formation of a National Mythology," *Environmental Review* 5 (Fall 1981): 79–91.

Osborn, George C. *Woodrow Wilson: The Early Years* (Baton Rouge: Louisiana State University Press, 1968).

————. "Woodrow Wilson and Frederick Jackson Turner," *Proceedings of the New Jersey State Historical Society* 74 (July 1956): 208–29.

Ostrander, Gilman M. *American Civilization in the First Machine Age, 1890–1940* (New York: Harper and Row, 1970).

———. "Turner and the Germ Theory," *Agricultural History* 32 (October 1958): 258–61.

Otis, D. S. *The Dawes Act and the Allotment of Indian Lands* (Norman: University of Oklahoma Press, 1973).

Paolino, Ernest N. *The Foundations of the American Empire* (Ithaca, N.Y.: Cornell University Press, 1973).

Parish, John Carl. *The Persistence of the Westward Movement and Other Essays* (Berkeley: University of California Press, 1943).

Parker, Edith H. "William Graham Sumner and the Frontier," *Southwest Review* 41 (Autumn 1956): 357–65.

Paul, Rodman W. *The Far West and the Great Plains in Transition, 1859–1900* (New York: Harper and Row, 1988).

Paul, Rodman W., and Richard W. Etulain. *The Frontier and the American West* (Arlington Heights, Ill.: AHM Publication Corp., 1977).

Peffer, E. Louise. *The Closing of the Public Domain* (Palo Alto, Calif.: Stanford University Press, 1951).

Pells, Richard H. *Radical Visions and American Dreams: Culture and Social Thought in the Depression Years* (Middletown, Conn.: Wesleyan University Press, 1973).

Peterson, Clell. "Jack London and the American Frontier" (M.A. thesis, University of Minnesota, 1951).

Phillips, David, and Robert A. Weinstein. *The West: An American Experience* (Chicago: Henry Regnery, 1973).

Phillips, Ulrich B. "The Traits and Contributions of Frederick Jackson Turner," *Agricultural History* 19 (January 1945): 21–24.

Pickens, Donald K. "Westward Expansion and the End of American Exceptionalism: Sumner, Turner and Webb," *Western Historical Quarterly* 14 (October 1981): 409–18.

Pierson, George W. "American Historians and the Frontier Hypothesis in 1941," parts 1 and 2, *Western Magazine of History* 26 (September and December 1942): 36–60, 170–85.

———. "The Frontier and Frontiersmen of Turner's Essays: A Scrutiny of the Foundations of the Middle Western Tradition," *Pennsylvania Magazine of History and Biography* 64 (October 1940): 449–78.

Plesur, Milton. *America's Outward Thrust: Approaches to Foreign Affairs, 1865–1890* (De-Kalb: Northern Illinois University Press, 1971).

———, ed. *Creating an American Empire, 1865–1914* (New York: Pitman, 1971).

Pocock, J. G. A. *The Machiavellian Movement: Florentine Political Thought and the Atlantic Republican Tradition* (Princeton, N.J.: Princeton University Press, 1975).

Pole, J. R. *The Pursuit of Equality in American History* (Berkeley: University of California Press, 1978).

Pollock, Norman, ed. *The Populist Mind* (Indianapolis: Bobbs Merrill, 1967).

Pomeroy, Earl S. *In Search of the Golden West: The Tourist in Western America* (New York: Alfred A. Knopf, 1957).

———. *The Territories and the United States, 1861–1890* (Seattle: University of Washington Press, 1969).

———. "What Remains of the West," *Utah Historical Quarterly* 25 (Winter 1967): 37–55.

Popper, Frank J. "The Strange Case of the Contemporary American Frontier," *Yale Review* 76 (December 1986): 101–21.

Popper, Frank J., and Deborah E. Popper. "The Reinvention of the American Frontier," *Amicus Journal* 13 (Summer 1991): 4–7.

Potter, David M. *People of Plenty: Economic Abundance and the American Character* (Chicago: University of Chicago Press, 1968).
Powell, John Wesley. *Report on the Lands of the Arid Region of the United States* (Cambridge, Mass.: Harvard University Press, Belknap Press, 1962).
Pratt, Julius W. *Expansionists of 1898: The Acquisition of Hawaii and the Spanish Islands* (Baltimore, Md.: Johns Hopkins University Press, 1936).
————. "The Ideology of American Expansion," in Avery Craven, ed., *Essays in Honor of William E. Dodd* (Chicago: University of Chicago Press, 1935).
————. "The Large Policy of 1898," *Mississippi Valley Historical Review* 19 (September 1932): 219–42.
Price, A. Grenfell. *The Western Invasion of the Pacific and Its Continents: A Study of Moving Frontiers and Changing Landscapes* (New York: Oxford University Press, 1963).
Prucha, Francis Paul. *Americanizing the American Indians: Writings on the Friends of the Indian, 1880–1900* (Cambridge, Mass.: Harvard University Press, 1973).
Rader, Benjamin G. *The Academic Mind and Reform: The Influence of Richard T. Ely in American Life* (Lexington: University of Kentucky Press, 1966).
Radosh, Ronald. *Prophets on the Right: Profiles of Conservative Critics of American Globalism* (New York: Simon and Schuster, 1975).
Reiger, John F. *American Sportsmen and the Origins of Conservation* (Norman: University of Oklahoma Press, 1975).
Reisner, Marc. *Cadillac Desert: The American West and Its Disappearing Waters* (New York: Penguin Books, 1987).
Richardson, James D., ed. *A Compilation of the Messages and Papers of the Presidents,* 11 vols. (Washington, D.C.: Bureau of National Literature and Art, 1911).
Ridge, Martin. "The American West: From Frontier to Region," *New Mexico Historical Review* 64 (April 1989): 125–41.
————. "Frederick Jackson Turner, Ray Allen Billington and American Frontier History," *Western Historical Quarterly* 19 (January 1988): 4–20.
————. *Ignatius Donnelly: The Portrait of a Politician* (Chicago: University of Chicago Press, 1962).
————. "A More Jealous Mistress: Frederick Jackson Turner as a Book Reviewer," *Pacific Historical Review* 55 (February 1986): 49–63.
————. "Ray Allen Billington, Western History, and American Exceptionalism," *Pacific Historical Review* 56 (November 1987): 495–511.
Ridge, Martin, Elizabeth A. H. John, Alvin M. Josephy, Jr., Howard Lamar, Kevin Starr, and George Miles. *Writing the History of the American West* (Worcester, Mass.: American Antiquarian Society, 1991): 65–76.
Riegel, Robert E. *America Moves West* (New York: Henry Holt, 1945).
Robbins, Roy M. "Horace Greeley: Land Reform and Unemployment, 1837–1862," *Agricultural History* 7 (January 1933), 18–41.
————. *Our Landed Heritage: The Public Domain, 1776–1936* (Princeton, N.J.: Princeton University Press, 1942).
————. "The Public Domain in the Era of Exploitation, 1863–1901," *Agricultural History* 13 (April 1939): 97–108.
Robbins, William G. "Western History: A Dialectic on the Modern Condition," *Western Historical Quarterly* 20 (November 1989): 429–49.
Robertson, James Oliver. *American Myth and Reality* (New York: Hill and Wang, 1980).
Rohrer, Wayne C., and Louis H. Douglas. *The Agrarian Transition in America* (Indianapolis: Bobbs Merrill, 1969).
Rosenof, Theodore. *Dogma, Depression and the New Deal: The Debate of Political Leaders over Economic Recovery* (Port Washington, N.Y.: Kennikat Press, 1975).

_____. "The Economic Ideas of Henry A Wallace, 1933–1948," *Agricultural History* 41 (April 1967): 143–54.

_____. "Young Bob La Follette on American Capitalism," *Wisconsin Magazine of History* 55 (Winter 1971–1972): 130–39.

Rosenberg, Emily S. *Spreading the American Dream: American Economic and Cultural Expansion, 1890–1945* (New York: Hill and Wang, 1982).

Ross, Earl D. "Horace Greeley and the Beginnings of the New Agriculture," Agricultural History 7 (January 1933): 3–17.

Rundell, Walter, Jr. "Concepts of the Frontier and the West," *Arizona and the West* 1 (Spring, 1959): 13–41.

_____. "A Historian's Impact on Federal Policy: W. P. Webb as a Case Study,"*Prologue* 15 (Winter 1983): 215–28.

_____. "Interpretations of the American West: A Descriptive Bibliography," *Arizona and the West* 3 (Summer 1961): 69–88, 148–68.

_____. "Steinbeck's Image of the West," *American West* 1 (Spring 1964): 4–17, 79.

_____. "Walter Prescott Webb's *Divided We Stand*: A Publishing Crisis," *Western Historical Quarterly* 13 (October 1982): 391–407.

Russett, C. E. *Darwin in America: The Intellectual Response, 1865–1912* (San Francisco: W. H. Freeman, 1976).

Sanford, Charles L. *The Quest for Paradise: Europe and the American Moral Imagination* (Urbana: University of Illinois Press, 1961).

Saum, Lewis O. "Pat Donan's West and the End of the Age of Hate," *Pacific Northwest Quarterly* 60 (April 1969): 66–76.

_____. "The Western Volunteer and the New Empire," *Pacific North Western Quarterly* 57 (January 1966): 18–27.

Saveth, Edward N. *American Historians and European Immigrants, 1875–1925* (New York: Columbia University Press, 1948).

Schlesinger, Arthur M. *New Viewpoints in American History* (New York: Macmillan, 1922).

_____. *The Rise of the City, 1878–1898* (New York: Macmillan, 1933).

Schlesinger, Arthur, Jr. *The Age of Roosevelt*, 3 vols. (Boston: Houghton Mifflin, 1957–1960).

Schmitt, Peter J. *Back to Nature: The Arcadian Myth in Urban America* (New York: Oxford University Press, 1969).

_____. "Wilderness Novels in the Progressive Era," *Journal of Popular Culture* 3 (Summer 1960): 72–90.

Schriftgiesser, Karl. *The Gentleman from Massachusetts: Henry Cabot Lodge* (Boston: Little, Brown, 1944).

Schuchalter, Jerry. "Some Kindly Comet: Frederick Jackson Turner's Frontier Thesis and the Politics of Despair," in Michael Berry, George Maude, and Jerry Schuchalter, *Frontiers of American Political Experience* (Turko University, Finland: Turun Yliopisto, 1990), 1–29.

Schwantes, Carlos A. "The Concept of a Wageworkers' Frontier: A Framework for Future Research," *Western Historical Quarterly* 18 (January 1987): 269–85.

Scott, William B. *In Pursuit of Happiness: American Conceptions of Property from the Seventeenth to the Twentieth Century* (Bloomington: Indiana University Press, 1977).

Seager, Robert, II. *Alfred Thayer Mahan* (Annapolis, Md.: Naval Institute Press, 1977).

Sell, Henry Blackman, and Victor Weybright. *Buffalo Bill and the Wild West* (New York: Oxford University Press, 1955).

Shaler, Nathanial S. *Nature and Man in America*, (New York: Charles Scribner's Sons, 1900).

Shannon, David A. *Twentieth Century America: The United States since the 1890's* (Chicago: Rand McNally, 1964).

Shannon, Fred A. *The Farmer's Last Frontier: Agriculture, 1860–1897* (New York: Farrar and Rinehart, 1945).

Shapiro, Edward S. "American Conservative Intellectuals, the 1930's, and the Crisis of Ideology," *Modern Age* 23 (Fall 1979): 370–80.

———. "Catholic Agrarian Thought and the New Deal," *Catholic Historical Review* 65 (October 1979): 583–99.

———. "Decentralist Intellectuals and the New Deal," *Journal of American History* 58 (March 1972): 938–57.

Shapiro, Henry D. *Appalachia on Our Mind: The Southern Mountains and Mountaineers in the American Consciousness, 1870–1920* (Chapel Hill: University of North Carolina Press, 1978).

Sharp, Paul F. "The American Farmer and the 'Last Best West,'" *Agricultural History* 21 (April 1947): 65–75.

———. "When Our West Moved North," *American Historical Review* 55 (October 1949): 286–300.

Shi, David E. *The Simple Life: Plain Living and High Thinking in American Culture* (New York: Oxford University Press, 1985).

———. *In Search of the Simple Life: American Voices, Past and Present* (Salt Lake City, Utah: Peregrine Smith Books, 1986).

Silet, Charles L. P., Robert E. Welch, and Richard Bourdeau, eds. *The Critical Reception of Hamlin Garland, 1891–1978* (Troy, N.Y.: Whitston, 1985).

Simler, Norman J. "The Safety-Valve Doctrine Re-Evaluated," *Agricultural History* 32 (October 1958): 251–57.

Simonson, Harold P. *Beyond the Frontier: Writers, Western Regionalism and a Sense of Place* (Fort Worth: Texas Christian University Press, 1989).

———. *The Closed Frontier* (New York: Holt, Rinehart and Winston, 1970).

Sinclair, Andrew. *Jack: A Biography of Jack London* (New York: Harper and Row, 1977)

Singer, Aaron, ed. *Campaign Speeches of American Presidential Candidates, 1928–1972* (New York: Frederick Ungar, 1976).

Slotkin, Richard. *The Fatal Environment: The Myth of the Frontier in the Age of Industrialization, 1800–1890* (New York: Atheneum, 1985).

———. *Regeneration through Violence: The Mythology of the American Frontier, 1600–1860* (Middletown, Conn.: Wesleyan University Press, 1973).

Smith, Frank E. *The Politics of Conservation* (New York: Pantheon Books, 1966).

Smith, Henry N. *Virgin Land: The American West as Symbol and Myth* (Cambridge, Mass.: Harvard University Press, 1978).

———. "The West as an Image of the American Past," *University of Kansas City Review* 18 (Autumn 1951): 29–40.

Smythe, Albert K., ed. *The Writings of Benjamin Franklin*, 10 vols. (New York: Macmillan, 1907), vol. 10.

Snell, James G. "The Frontier Sweeps Northwest: American Perceptions of the British American Prairie West at the Point of Canadian Expansion," *Western Historical Quarterly* 11 (October 1980): 381–400.

Socolofsky, Homer. *Landlord William Scully* (Lawrence: Regents Press of Kansas, 1970).

Starr, Kevin. *Americans and the Californian Dream, 1850–1915* (New York: Oxford University Press, 1973).

———. *Inventing the Dream: California through the Progressive Era* (New York: Oxford University Press, 1985).

_____. *Material Dream: Southern California through the 1920's* (New York: Oxford University Press, 1990).

Steensma, Robert. "Rolvaag and Turner's Frontier Thesis," *North Dakota Quarterly* 27 (Autumn 1959): 100–104.

Steffen, Jerome O., ed. *The American West, New Perspectives, New Dimensions* (Norman: University of Oklahoma Press, 1979).

Stegner, Wallace. *The American West as Living Space* (Ann Arbor: University of Michigan Press, 1987).

_____. *Beyond the Hundredth Meridian: John Wesley Powell and the Second Opening of the West* (Boston: Houghton Mifflin, 1954).

Stephenson, Wendell H., ed. "The Influence of Woodrow Wilson on Frederick Jackson Turner," *Agricultural History* 19 (October 1945): 249–53.

Stewart, Edgar I. *Penny-an-Acre Empire in the West* (Norman: University of Oklahoma Press, 1968).

Susman, Warren I. "The Useless Past: American Intellectuals and the Frontier Thesis," *Bucknell Review* 11 (March 1963): 1–20.

Swierenga, Robert P. "Land Speculation and Its Impact on American Economic Growth and Welfare: A Historiographical Review," *Western Historical Quarterly* 8 (July 1977): 283–302.

Takaki, Ronald. *Strangers from a Different Shore: A History of Asian Americans* (New York: Penguin Books, 1990), 535–48.

Tatum, Stephen. "A Picture Gallery Unrivalled of Its Kind: *Blackwood's* American Frontier and the Idea of Democracy," *Western Historical Quarterly* 4 (January 1983): 29–48.

Taylor, Walter F. *The Economic Novel in America* (Chapel Hill: University of North Carolina Press, 1942).

Thelen, David. *Paths of Resistance: Tradition and Democracy in Industrializing Missouri* (New York: Oxford University Press, 1986).

Thomas, Norman. *Human Exploitation* (New York: Frederick A. Stokes, 1934).

Thompson, Gerald. "Frontier West: Process or Place," *Journal of the Southwest* 29 (Winter 1987): 364–75.

Thompson, John. *Closing the Frontier: Radical Response in Oklahoma, 1889–1923* (Norman: University of Oklahoma Press, 1986).

Trachtenberg, Alan. *The Incorporation of America: Culture and Society in the Gilded Age* (New York: Hill and Wang, 1982).

Trimble, William J. "Influence of the Passing of the Public Lands," *Atlantic Monthly* 113 (June 1914): 755–67.

Trooper, Harold Martin. *Only Farmers Need Apply: Official Canadian Government Encouragement of Immigration from the United States, 1896–1911* (Toronto: Griffin House, 1972).

Turner, Frederick A. *Beyond Geography: The Western Spirit against the Wilderness* (New Brunswick, N.J.: Rutgers University Press, 1983).

Tuttle, William M., Jr. "Forerunners of Frederick Jackson Turner: Nineteenth-Century British Conservatives and the Frontier Thesis," *Agricultural History* 41 (July 1967): 219–27.

Tyrrell, Ian. "American Exceptionalism in an Age of International History," *American Historical Review* 96 (October 1991): 1031–55

Udall, Stewart L. *The Quiet Crisis* (New York: Holt, Rinehart and Winston, 1963).

United States Bureau of the Census. *Historical Statistics of the United States: Colonial Times to 1970* (Washington, D.C.: Government Printing Office, 1975).

United States Census Office. *Statistics of the Population of the United States at the Tenth Census* (June 1, 1880) (Washington, D.C.: Government Printing Office, 1883).

United States Census Office. *Report on the Population of the United States at the Eleventh Census: 1890*, Part I: Progress of the Nation (Washington, D.C.: Government Printing Office, 1895).

Vevier, Charles. "American Continentalism: An Idea of Expansion, 1845–1910," *American Historical Review* 65 (January 1960): 323–35.

Veysey, Lawrence. "The Autonomy of American History Reconsidered," *American Quarterly* 31 (Fall 1979): 455–77.

Volwiler, Albert T., ed. *The Correspondence between Benjamin Harrison and James G. Blaine, 1882–1893* (Philadelphia: American Philosophical Society, 1940).

Vorphal, Ben Merchant, ed. *My Dear Wister: The Frederic Remington–Owen Wister Letters* (Palo Alto, Calif.: American West, 1972).

Walker, Dale L., ed. *In a Far Country: Jack London's Tales of the West* (Ottawa, Ill.: Jameson Books, 1987).

Walker, Don D. "Freedom and Destiny in the Myth of the American West," *New Mexico Quarterly* 33 (Winter 1963–1964): 381–87.

Walsh, Margaret. *The American Frontier Revisited* (Atlantic Highlands, N.J.: Humanities Press, 1981).

Ward, John William. "The Age of the Common Man," in John Higham, ed., *The Reconstruction of American History* (New York: Harper and Row, 1962): 82–97.

———. *Andrew Jackson: Symbol for an Age* (New York: Oxford University Press, 1981).

———. "The Meaning of Lindbergh's Flight," *American Quarterly* 10 (Spring 1958): 3–16.

Warner, Donald F. *The Idea of Continental Union: Agitation for the Annexation of Canada to the United States, 1849–1893* (Lexington: University of Kentucky Press, 1960).

Washburn, Wilcomb E. *The Indian in America* (New York: Harper and Row, 1975).

Watkins, T. H., and Charles S. Watson, Jr. *The Land No One Knows: America and the Public Domain* (San Francisco: Sierra Club, 1975).

Welch, Richard E., Jr. *Imperialists Vs. Anti-Imperialists: The Debate over Expansionism in the 1890's* (Itasca, Ill.: F. E. Peacock, 1972).

Welter, Rush. "The Frontier West as Image of American Society," *Pacific Northwest Quarterly* 52 (January 1961): 1–6.

———. "The Frontier West as Image of American Society: Conservative Attitudes before the Civil War," *Mississippi Valley Historical Society*, 46 (March 1960): 593–614.

Weston, Jack. *The Real American Cowboy* (New York: Schocken Books, 1985).

Weston, Rubin F. *Racism in U. S. Imperialism: The Influence of Racial Assumptions on American Foreign Policy, 1893–1946* (Columbia: University of South Carolina Press, 1972).

Whipple, T. K. *Study Out the Land* (Berkeley: University of California Press, 1943).

White, Richard. *"It's Your Misfortune and None of My Own": A New History of the American West* (Norman: University of Oklahoma Press, 1991).

———. *Land Use, Environment and Social Change: The Shaping of Island County, Washington* (Seattle: University of Washington Press, 1980).

Widenor, William C. *Henry Cabot Lodge and the Search for an American Foreign Policy* (Berkeley: University of California Press, 1980).

Willett, Ralph. "The American Western Myth and Anti-Myth," *Journal of Popular Culture* 4 (Fall 1970): 455–63.

Williams, W. H. *A. H. L. Mencken* (Boston: Twayne, 1977).

Williams, William Appleman. *The Contours of American History* (Chicago: Quadrangle Books, 1966).

———. *Empire as a Way of Life; An Essay on the Causes and Character of America's Present Predicament Along with a Few Thoughts about an Alternative* (New York: Oxford University Press, 1980).

_____. "The Frontier Thesis and American Foreign Policy," *Pacific Historical Review* 24 (August 1955): 379–95.

_____. *The Roots of the Modern American Empire* (New York: Random House, 1969).

_____. *The Tragedy of American Diplomacy* (New York: Dell, 1962).

_____, ed. *The Shaping of American Diplomacy.* (Chicago: Rand McNally, 1970), vol. 1.

Willis, Jack, with Howard Smith. *Roosevelt in the Rough* (New York: Washburn, 1931).

Wilson, R. Jackson. *In Quest of Community: Social Philosophy in the United States, 1860–1920* (New York: John Wiley and Sons, 1968).

Winks, Robin W. *The Myth of the Frontier: Its Relevance to America, Canada, and Australia* (Leicester, Eng.: Leicester University Press, 1971).

Winther, Oscar O. *Classified Bibliography of the Periodical Literature of the Trans-Mississippi West, 1811–1957* (Bloomington: Indiana University Press, 1961).

_____. "Promoting the American West in England, 1865–1890," *Journal of Economic History* 16 (December 1856): 506–13.

_____. *The Trans-Mississippi West: A Guide to Its Periodical Literature* (Bloomington: Indiana University Press, 1942).

Winther, Oscar O., and Richard A. Van Orman. *A Classified Bibliography of the Periodical Literature of the Trans-Mississippi West: A Supplement, 1957–1967* (Bloomington: Indiana University Press, 1970).

Wisan, Joseph E. *The Cuban Crisis As Reflected in the New York Press, 1895–1898* (New York: Octagon Books, 1965).

Wise, Gene. *American Historical Explanations: A Strategy for Grounded Inquiry* (Minneapolis: University of Minnesota Press, 1973).

Wish, Harvey. *American Historians: A Selection* (New York: Oxford University Press, 1962).

Wish, Harvey, ed. *Antebellum: Writings of George Fitzhugh and Hinton Rowan Helper* (New York: Capricorn Books, 1960).

Woods, Lawrence M. *British Gentlemen in the Wild West: The Era of the Intensely English Cowboy* (New York: Free Press, 1989).

Worster, Donald. *Dust Bowl: The Southern Plains in the 1930s* (New York: Oxford University Press, 1979).

_____. *Nature's Economy: A History of Ecological Ideas* (New York: Cambridge University Press, 1985).

_____. "New West, True West: Interpreting the Region's History," *Western Historical Quarterly* 18 (April 1987): 141–56.

_____. *Rivers of Empire: Water, Aridity, and the Growth of the American West* (New York: Pantheon Books, 1985).

Wunder, John R., ed. *Historians of the American Frontier: A Bio-Bibliographical Sourcebook* (Westport, Conn.: Greenwood Press, 1988).

Wyant, William K. *Westward in Eden: The Public Lands and the Conservation Movement* (Berkeley: University of California Press, 1982).

Wyman, Walker D., and Clifton B. Kroeber. *The Frontier in Perspective* (Madison: University of Wisconsin Press, 1957).

Young, Mary. "The West and American Cultural Identity: Old Themes and New Variations," *Western Historical Quarterly* 1 (April 1970): 137–60.

Zaslow, Morris. *The Opening of the Canadian North: 1870–1914* (Toronto: McClelland and Steward, 1971).

Zeigler, Benjamin Munn, ed. *Immigration: An American Dilemma* (Boston: D. C. Heath, 1966).

Ziff, Larzer. *The American 1890's: The Life and Times of a Lost Generation* (New York: Viking Press, 1966).

Zinn, Howard. *The Twentieth Century: A People's History* (New York: Harper and Row, 1984).

INDEX

Abbott, Lyman, 61
Adams, Andy, 92
Adams, Brooks, 65–66, 68
Adams, James Truslow, 128–29, 132
Adventures of Huckleberry Finn (Twain), 24
Agrarian heritage, 4–6, 85. See also Myths: of the garden
Agrarian radicalism, 29, 39
Agricultural Adjustment Administration (AAA), 131, 138
Agriculture, 86, 113–14
"Agriculture and Population Increase" (forum), 120
Aikman, Duncan, 103–4
Alaska, 87, 89–90, 91, 141, 143
Algeria, 117–18
Alien landholding, 5, 17, 18
Alone in the Wilderness (Knowles), 90
America at the Crossroads (Landon), 138
America Moves West (Riegel), 127
American Communist party, 139
American Exodus, An (Lange and Taylor), 126
American Farmer, The (Simons), 75
American Geographic Society of New York, 119
American Historical Association, 36, 78, 114
American Individualism (Hoover), 101–2
American Mercury, 106
American Monthly Magazine, 94
American Park and Outdoor Society, 47
American Review, 117
American Statistical Association, 120
America's Coming of Age (Brooks), 109
"America's Coming of Age" (Howland), 111
Anglo Saxons, 50, 64, 75, 110; purity of, threatened, 76, 116; traits of, 56, 60, 65, 108
Appalachia, 122
Arena, 72, 74

Arizona, 30, 72
Asians, in America, 75, 108, 120–21
Athearn, Robert, 148n5
Atlantic Monthly, 14, 46, 47, 49, 58, 75, 78, 85, 94, 114
Aurousseau, Marcel, 114–15
Ayers, Roy E., 138

Back to the Future III, 144
Back-to-the-land movements, 47, 85, 140–42
Baker, Oliver E., 120
Baker, Ray Stannard, 93–94, 95, 96
Battle for Democracy, The (Tugwell), 136
Beard, Charles A., 127, 134
Bender, Prosper, 21, 22
Benson, Lee, 156n6, 157nn22, 25, 162n39
Beveridge, Albert J., 64–65, 67
Big Sky, The (Guthrie, Jr.), 144
"Biology of the Immigration Question" (East), 120
Birth control, 116, 120
Birth rates, decline in, 121
Black, Hugo L., 139
Black Americans, 108
Blackwood's Edinburgh Magazine, 7–8
Boone, Daniel, 41
Boone and Crockett Club, 37, 106
Borsodi, Ralph, 142
Boston Post, 90
Bowman, Isaiah, 119, 122–23
Boyeson, Hjalmar Hjorth, 19–20
Boy Scouts, 89, 141
Brazilian rain forest, 144
Britain, 7–8, 15
Brooks, Van Wyck, 107, 109–10, 128
Bryan, William Jennings, 108
Bryce, James, 24–25, 56, 61
Buffalo, 95
Buffalo Bill, 23, 41, 103

225